This study was undertaken as part of the Development Centre's programme on the theme of the Financing of Development. The study was carried out by Dr. Jacques J. Polak, Senior Adviser to that component of the programme.

Also available

DEVELOPING COUNTRIES DEBT: THE BUDGETARY AND TRANSFER PROBLEM by Helmut Reisen and Axel Van Trotsenburg (1988)
(41 88 01 1) ISBN 92-64-13053-5   196 pages   £14.00   US$26.40   F120.00   DM52.00

DEVELOPMENT POLICIES AND THE CRISIS OF THE 1980s by Louis Emmerij (1987)
(41 87 03 1) ISBN 92-64-12992-8   178 pages   £11.00   US$23.00   F110.00   DM47.00

BANKS AND SPECIALISED FINANCIAL INTERMEDIARIES IN DEVELOPMENT, by Phillips Wellons, Dimitri Germidis and Bianca Glavanis (1986)
(41 86 06 1) ISBN 92-64-12867-0   150 pages   £10.00   US$20.00   F100.00   DM44.00

INTERNATIONAL BANKS AND FINANCIAL MARKETS IN DEVELOPING COUNTRIES, by Dimitri Germidis and Charles-Albert Michalet (1984)
(41 84 04 1) ISBN 92-64-12635-X   94 pages   £6.50   US$13.00   F65.00   DM29.00

RECLYCLING JAPAN'S SURPLUSES FOR DEVELOPING by T. Ozawa (1989)
(41 88 02 1)   ISBN 92-64-13177-9   108 pages   £11.00   US$19.00   F90.00   DM37.00

FINANCING AND EXTERNAL DEBT OF DEVELOPING COUNTRIES. 1987 **SURVEY (1988)**
(43 88 04 1) ISBN 92-64-13095-0   224 pages   £13.00   US$24.50   F110.00   DM48.00

EVALUATION IN DEVELOPING COUNTRIES: A Step in a Dialogue (1988)
(43 88 03 1) ISBN 92-64-13071-3   56 pages   £7.00   US$13.50   F60.00   DM26.00

* * *

DEVELOPMENT CO-OPERATION. Efforts and Policies of the Members of the Development Assistance Committee. 1988 REPORT
(43 88 06 1) ISBN 92-64-13174-4   254 pages   £20.10   US$37.50   F170.00   DM74.00

Prices charged at the OECD Bookshop.

*THE OECD CATALOGUE OF PUBLICATIONS and supplements will be sent free of charge on request addressed either to OECD Publications Service,
2, rue André-Pascal, 75775 PARIS CEDEX 16, or to the OECD Distributor in your country.*

DEVELOPMENT CENTRE S...

FINANCIAL POLICIES AND DEVELOPMENT

OF THE

...VELOPMENT

Pursuant to article 1 of the Convention signed in Paris on 14th December, 1960, and which came into force on 30th September, 1961, the Organisation for Economic Co-operation and Development (OECD) shall promote policies designed:

- to achieve the highest sustainable economic growth and employment and a rising standard of living in Member countries, while maintaining financial stability, and thus to contribute to the development of the world economy;
- to contribute to sound economic expansion in Member as well as non-member countries in the process of economic development; and
- to contribute to the expansion of world trade on a multilateral, non-discriminatory basis in accordance with international obligations.

The original Member countries of the OECD are Austria, Belgium, Canada, Denmark, France, the Federal Republic of Germany, Greece, Iceland, Ireland, Italy, Luxembourg, the Netherlands, Norway, Portugal, Spain, Sweden, Switzerland, Turkey, the United Kingdom and the United States. The following countries became Members subsequently through accession at the dates hereafter: Japan (28th April, 1964), Finland (28th January, 1969), Australia (7th June, 1971) and New Zealand (29th May, 1973).

The Socialist Federal Republic of Yugoslavia takes part in some of the work of the OECD (agreement of 28th October, 1961).

The Development Centre of the Organisation for Economic Co-operation and Development was established by decision of the OECD Council on 23rd October, 1962.

The purpose of the Centre is to bring together the knowledge and experience available in Member countries of both economic development and the formulation and execution of general economic policies; to adapt such knowledge and experience to the actual needs of countries or regions in the process of development and to put the results at the disposal of the countries by appropriate means.

The Centre has a special and autonomous position within the OECD which enables it to enjoy scientific independence in the execution of its task. Nevertheless, the Centre can draw upon the experience and knowledge available in the OECD in the development field.

Publié en français sous le titre :

POLITIQUES FINANCIÈRES
ET DÉVELOPPEMENT

 THE OPINIONS EXPRESSED AND ARGUMENTS EMPLOYED IN THIS PUBLICATION ARE THE RESPONSIBILITY OF THE AUTHOR AND DO NOT NECESSARILY REPRESENT THOSE OF THE OECD

TABLE OF CONTENTS

Chapter 1

INTRODUCTION AND PLAN OF THE STUDY

Chapter 2

PHASES OF DEVELOPMENT SINCE WORLD WAR II

Chapter 3

SAVING AND THE USE OF SAVINGS

6

ACKNOWLEDGEMENTS

In the preparation of this monograph, I have received help from many friends and old and new colleagues — in the International Monetary Fund, both its staff and its Executive Board, in the World Bank, the OECD (in particular the Development Centre), the Inter-American Development Bank, the Brookings Institution, the Institute for International Economics and the Institute of International Finance.

To all those helping hands, I want to express here my gratitude both for their suggestions which have enriched the text, and for making me aware of some errors, half-truths and infelicities of expression that had found their way into early drafts of various chapters and that have now, I hope, all been expunged. For any weaknesses remaining, no one but the author is, of course, responsible.

A special word of thanks is due to the World Bank which provided me with an office and secretarial assistance.

PREFACE

This is an important book written by an extraordinary person. Jacques Polak's creative career started more than fifty years ago when Jan Tinbergen asked him to become his assistant at the League of Nations in Geneva. It was there that Professor Tinbergen, a theoretical physicist by training, experimented with early econometric techniques for which he was later awarded the Nobel Prize for Economics in 1969. Whilst Tinbergen returned to the Netherlands, Jacques Polak continued his career abroad, joining the International Monetary Fund in January 1947. From 1958 he became Director of the Research Department and, from 1966, concurrently Economic Counsellor. His main contributions have been to the development of the Fund's policies. After he became Director of the Research Department in 1958, he continued to follow the tradition whereby economic research was undertaken essentially to serve the Fund's policy and operational needs. He was thus one of the founders of the monetary approach to balance-of-payments analyses, and hence of the Fund's conditionality. He was also responsible for much of the Fund's work on exchange rates and international liquidity. In this context, Dr. Polak's most significant contribution is the SDR. He was largely responsible for developing most of the economic features of the SDR that gradually emerged in the 1960s and were specified in the Outline that was agreed in Rio de Janeiro in 1967.

In addition, Dr. Polak was Principal Adviser to the Managing Director on all economic policy topics. For some years he also led the staff team in consultations with the United States. In 1968 he played a role in persuading the officials of the United Kingdom to take stricter monetary and fiscal measures in order to make the devaluation of the pound sterling of November 1967 more effective. After his retirement from the staff at the end of 1979, Dr. Polak

9

served briefly as Adviser to the Managing Director, and in January 1981 he was elected Executive Director of the IMF for the constituency of Cyprus, Israel, the Netherlands, Romania and Yugoslavia. He retired for the second time in 1985, still full of energy and ideas.

As someone who has always taken a dim view of the waste of human capital represented by the retirement of people who are still creative and who have a goldmine of experience, I asked Dr. Polak to become the OECD Development Centre's Senior Adviser for its work on the Financing of Development. To act in this capacity, I wanted someone who could look at the policies of development from the perspective of long experience at the International Monetary Fund and whose behind-the-scenes impact on world financial policy has been substantial. The present book on *Financial Policies and Development* is one result of Jacques Polak's association with the Development Centre. It is an important book and, to an extent, constitutes the intellectual testament of an expert who has been writing about these and related issues for the past fifty years.

The author has himself neatly summarised the major policy conclusions in the Executive Summary that follows. It would perhaps be fair to point out, as the author does in Chapter 1, that not all financial aspects of development receive adequate treatment, nor do all types of capital flows. However, the intent was not to write a textbook, but to deal with those subjects on which the author had valuable insights to share. The fact that the author has not only brought to bear half a century of creative thinking and writing on the issues he deals with in the present book, but has also shown consistency, is evident in the following quotation which I have taken from an article by J.J. Polak on "Balance-of-Payments Problems of Countries Reconstructing with the Help of Foreign Loans", published for the first time in the *Quarterly Journal of Economics* of February 1943 and reprinted many times since:

> In general the correct attitude for creditor countries financing reconstruction would seem to be that of the investment banker who sees his client through a long period of possible trouble, rather than that of the investor who buys a share and tries to sell it when the enterprise seems to be less successful than he expected. The uncertainties of a country — not to mention a continent — embarking upon a great investment programme are far greater than those of an individual starting a new enterprise. The latter can take the economic milieu in which he intends to work as given; he can exactly calculate his costs and make reliable estimates of his selling possibilities. A reconstruction plan of a large scope, however, changes the

whole economic milieu in a way which it is impossible to forecast with any great degree of precision; and these very dangers will seriously affect the outcome of the plan. These great and unpreventable uncertainties call for *a most interested banker's attitude on the part of the creditor countries.* (Emphasis added.)

Louis Emmerij
President, OECD Development Centre
November 1988

EXECUTIVE SUMMARY

1. Scope of the study

This monograph focuses on the role that financial policies play in the process of economic development. The term "financial policies" relates not only to the domestic financial structure of the economy but also to: the external financial structure, such as the exchange rate and the institutions and rules that guide the flow of capital into and out of the country; the financial structure of the outside world, such as the international banking system, the World Bank and the International Monetary Fund (IMF), aid giving agencies, multinational companies, etc. "Development" is defined narrowly as growth in GNP.

Financial flows and financial policies are presented as two interrelated dimensions of the development task. This integration should help to avoid a one-sided approach that puts undue emphasis on the supply of capital, in particular of foreign capital, and that pays insufficient attention to financial policies. Thus, attention is directed not only to raising the supply of capital but equally to coaxing the maximum possible growth out of all available factors of production.

2. Phases of development since World War II

In the period 1950-75, the rate of growth in the industrial and the developing countries was without precedent; in the latter countries, the average GNP per capita increased by 3.4 per cent per annum. But the smooth expansion of the world economy was sharply changed by the first oil shock, which occurred in late 1973. The resulting income transfer from the many oil

13

consumers to the far fewer oil producers brought about a noticeable increase in world saving, as well as a decline in investment demand in the industrial countries. Banks in the industrial countries were instrumental in recycling OPEC savings, mostly to the developing countries. The financial resources that became available permitted the oil-importing LDC's to raise their investment ratios to GNP while lowering their savings ratios and maintaining a reasonable growth rate.

The second oil shock in 1979 put an end to this — at least on the surface — favourable economic climate. The non-oil LDC's were hit not only by a doubling of the oil price, but by three interrelated adverse changes as well: the rise in interest rates that resulted from the anti-inflationary monetary policies adopted by the industrial countries, a recession-induced major decline in the terms of trade, and an abrupt cessation of foreign credit as the earlier adverse developments undermined the debtors' creditworthiness. The resulting debt crisis hit many, but by no means all, oil-importing developing countries; some, including some heavy bank borrowers, managed to maintain respectable growth rates.

Why did some countries fall victim to the debt problem and others not? Comparative statistics on the "problem" and "non-problem" countries show striking differences between the two groups both before and after 1981. Thus, for example, the former countries mostly used their sudden large access to foreign resources to raise consumption, the latter to raise investment. A detailed comparison of the experience of Brazil, Mexico and South Korea brings out some additional characteristic differences that proved relevant to these countries' experience in the 1980s, including differences in fiscal policies and the far greater outward orientation of the South Korean economy.

One inference drawn at this stage is that countries wanting to avoid future debt problems must constrain foreign borrowing even when interest rates abroad are below the marginal productivity of capital at home, because the supply of foreign capital to any one country is limited (at some point, the supply curve of foreign capital turns steeply upward). Colombia's moderation of foreign borrowing in the 1970s along this line paid off in the next decade.

3. Saving and the use of savings

While no-one would deny that the quality of investment is as important to growth as the quantity, this proposition tends to receive insufficient attention in development modeling. In Chapter 3, a systematic attempt is made to give this proposition as much quantitative content as possible. Attention is focused in this connection on the distortion of capital markets in many developing countries, attributable in part to government policies to keep bank interest rates far below equilibrium levels. In fact, in the 1970s, almost all developing countries kept bank deposit rates below the rate of inflation, thus producing negative real interest rates. As a result, credit intermediation through the banking system is economically inefficient, and the available supply of capital tends to be allocated among potential investment projects in a manner that is far from optimal. Some theoretical exercises show that, depending on the degree of inefficiency in their method of allocating capital, countries may get growth rates one-third, or even two-thirds, below the rates potentially available on the basis of the savings (domestic plus foreign) at their disposal. Cross-country correlations to explain differences in growth rates over a twenty-year period in terms of real interest rates and a number of other variables confirm these theoretical findings. Keeping the real interest rate 5 per cent too low might cost a country about 1 per cent in its annual growth rate, and it might require a rise in the investment ratio by 5 percentage points (e.g. from 20 to 25 per cent of GNP) to compensate for this. It would follow that international organisations that supply additional resources to developing countries should insist on these countries pursuing interest rate policies that economise on the use of capital; in the past, neither the World Bank nor the Fund have put sufficient emphasis on this matter.

4. Determinants of the domestic savings rate

With few exceptions, domestic saving is the dominant determinant of domestic investment. A wide range of factors influence the domestic savings rate. Simple development models tend to assume that the savings rate is a positive function of per capita income, but China and India have among the highest savings rates and in Latin America, some countries with the highest incomes have the lowest savings rates. A review of the savings literature suggests a weak positive influence of interest rates, and no noticeable influence of social security variables, on household saving. The effect of social security systems on total national saving and investment depends on the financing structure and the investment policy of the systems. Not all private domestic savings are available for domestic investment if the government becomes a net dissaver, as has been the case in many of the heavily indebted countries, or if resources move abroad as capital flight.

5. Government finance and the debt problem

Government deficits (whether on current or capital account) have played a major causative role in the balance-of-payments deficits of many heavily indebted countries in recent years. With the easy availability of foreign credits in the late 1970s, many Latin American countries allowed a deterioration of public sector finance in the order of 8 to 10 per cent of GDP to take place. These had to be reversed a few years later, under the pressure of the payments problems to which they gave rise, but the fiscal improvements frequently did not stick, e.g. as essential capital spending, maintenance, social services, or real government salaries were reduced below economically or socially acceptable levels. In other cases, the process of adjustment itself had a negative impact on the fiscal situation. Thus, a very necessary real depreciation of the currency could raise the real interest cost of the foreign debt, and the inability of the government to contain inflation reduced the real yield of existing taxes. It is increasingly realised that control over the fiscal situation is a precondition for control over the international payments situation.

In this context, the definition of the fiscal deficit has become an important issue. It is suggested that the correct starting point for this purpose is the "operational deficit", which excludes that component of interest payments in a highly inflationary situation that serves to compensate creditors for the decline in the real value of their claims. In recent years, the difference of this deficit from the conventional deficit has been of the order of 10 to 15 per cent of GDP for Mexico or Brazil.

6. Domestic and foreign savings

Extensive statistical attempts have been made in the past to demonstrate that as a general rule the inflow of capital from abroad (including aid) reduces domestic savings; however, these attempts are essentially worthless, for both statistical and economic reasons. This is not to say that there have not been important instances in the past where precisely such negative impacts occurred, e.g. in some countries in the late 1970s. While the "natural" direction of the international flow of capital is towards the developing countries, there are two main exceptions. One, the accumulation by these countries of official reserves, is necessary (although part of it could be financed by allocations of SDRs by the IMF). The other exception is capital flight. There may be many structural reasons, such as taxation or the diversity of investment choices, why residents of low-income countries prefer to hold part of their assets abroad; but experience shows that countries can in general prevent important outflows of domestic capital by remaining sufficiently competitive in terms of two crucial financial variables: the rate of interest and the exchange rate.

7. The search for foreign savings

The debt problem has left many countries short of inflows of foreign capital; hence the search for new, or the revival of old, techniques for the transfer of capital to developing countries. This search is proceeding against the background of a radical change in the system, where the United States has become a massive absorber of the savings of the rest of the world. The resumption of a broad flow of capital to the developing world will require that the United States payments situation is brought under control. There is no corresponding world interest in a simultaneous reduction of the current account surpluses of the surplus countries; it would be better if the corresponding savings were maintained, but redirected towards the developing countries.

It is not useful to look for a single number measuring the supply of capital from abroad available to, or needed by, the developing countries. The creditworthy countries, mostly in Asia, are on the whole not suffering from a lack of foreign capital. Any new initiatives would provide them, but not the other LDCs, with more, or less costly, capital. The low-income countries depend almost entirely on the supply of aid money; developments with respect to other foreign sources of capital are almost entirely irrelevant to them. In between, the middle-income highly indebted countries are likely to be subject to a long period of capital scarcity even if the world supply of capital is plentiful. Against this general background, three categories of capital flows deserve particular attention.

a) Direct investment flows have shown no increase in real terms in the last two decades. During this period, major companies in the industrial countries have increasingly developed techniques to control their involvement in production in other countries through "new forms of international investment" not necessarily involving important movements of capital. For a time,

17

this approach of "unbundling" direct investment also suited the investee countries as they could attract capital through bank loans. It is questionable whether this process can now be reversed. Like other flows of capital, the resumption of direct investment flows is likely to require the prior re-establishment of creditworthiness.

b)   In principle, there are wide opportunities for capital flows to developing countries through other forms of equity investment, e.g. in emerging stock markets, through venture capital, or leasing. In practice, the growth of these various forms of investment has been slow, in spite of efforts by the OECD and IFC.

c)   Official export credit agencies had played a major role in financing the export of capital goods until the early 1980s. In the next few years, as arrears developed, the agencies typically ceased to provide cover. More recently, they have been willing to resume cover as borrowing countries agreed stabilization programmes with the Fund; but this has not led to a strong resumption of export credits as debtor countries cut back on large public sector investment projects.

8.   Financial flows and financial policies: the IMF and the World Bank

Since the mid-1970s, the financial activities of the International Monetary Fund have been concentrated entirely on the developing countries. Through its conditions for lending, as well as by means of its consultations, the Fund has attempted to influence the financial policies of these countries in directions conducive to economic growth. Over the years, supply policies have acquired an established place in Fund programmes, side by side with policies to contain demand within the limits of available resources (with the latter enlarged by the supply of Fund resources on a temporary basis). For the lowest-income countries the Fund now actively collaborates with the World Bank in drawing up joint policy papers to guide the financing activities of both institutions.

Allocations of SDRs, introduced into the system in 1970, have fallen out of favour with most of the major industrial countries. Their resumption would lighten the burden for developing countries of maintaining adequate reserves and would at the same time make the international monetary system less dependent on borrowed reserves. The contentious question whether SDR allocations should be used to provide development finance appears to have been buried; the potential benefits of this approach had in any event been greatly reduced by the introduction of a market interest rate for the SDR.

In its early years, the World Bank's loans were overwhelmingly for individual projects, mostly for infrastructure. In recognition of the crucial importance to the development process of correct macro- and microeconomic policies, the Bank since about 1980, has moved increasingly towards "policy loans"; such loans are now about one-fourth of its total annual lending. Their attraction to borrowers is that they provide quick finance for general imports, thus relieving the foreign exchange constraint on growth. These policy-based loans, which are normally granted in the context of an arrangement of the borrower with the Fund, have enhanced the policy dialogue between the Bank and many of its members.

In recent years, both the Fund and the Bank have greatly enlarged their lending to the highly indebted countries. In so doing the institutions responded to the risks to the system and in the light of the unique contribution that they could make. As these risks have receded, however, the time has come to loosen the linkage between the lending activities of the Fund and the commercial banks. Both institutions will also have to observe caution in the further commitment of resources in connection with the continuing effects of the debt crisis.

9.   The debt crisis and the resumption of growth

For the heavily indebted countries, there is a two-way connection between the resumption of a satisfactory growth rate and the resolution of the debt problem; the burden of the debt continues to stifle growth, but as growth is achieved, a given amount of debt will become less burdensome. But the possibilities for growth are also importantly affected by external factors, such as the growth rate in the industrial countries, the containment of protectionism, and the world interest rate. Yet within the setting of these world variables, the policy choices made by each country can still make a large difference to its growth outcome.

In the recent attention to "policies for growth", three distinct causal strands can be observed: growth can be raised by greater efficiency, by additions from abroad to the supply of saving, and by reducing the constraint on imports.

The growth rate in exports is seen as a crucial variable for the attainable growth rate for the economy as a whole, with allowance for changes in the terms of trade, world interest rates and available flows of capital imports. If the resulting growth rate is not considered acceptable, further adjustment will be required, including probably depreciation of the real exchange rate to enhance the export growth rate.

10.   The debt crisis and beyond

It is suggested that many of the middle-income highly indebted countries may be able to work themselves out of their debt problems while maintaining or resuming a satisfactory growth rate, provided three conditions are fulfilled: *(i)* the country perseveres in the necessary adjustment policies, *(ii)* world economic conditions remain reasonably satisfactory, *(iii)* the creditor banks play their part in the process. If the banks were prepared to offer, for a period of some years, annual "new money" loans (or to capitalise) up to say half the interest due provided the debtor country stuck to a satisfactory adjustment programme, the debt crisis could be on the way out for those highly indebted countries that met that condition. A different approach is needed to resolve the debt crisis of the low-income countries with high debts, most of which are in Sub-Saharan Africa. For these countries a bold generalised approach will be required (such as that proposed by the African Development Bank) under which a sharply curtailed debt service replaces the current annual Paris Club rescheduling rounds.

Chapter 1

INTRODUCTION AND PLAN OF THE STUDY

This monograph focuses on the role financial policies play in the process of economic development. These are two broad concepts, and the reader is entitled to an indication as to how they are used in this work.

Financial policies range over the domestic and external financial structures of an economy. Domestically, they include its fiscal and monetary systems, banks of various types, and its capital market. Externally, they include the exchange rate, the institutions and rules that guide the flow of capital into and out of the country. These policies are, of course, influenced by the financial structures of the outside world, which to a large extent control the in- and outflow of capital. Major external players include trade partners, the international banking system as a provider of credit and a solicitor of "flight capital," international institutions such as the World Bank and International Monetary Fund, aid donors, and multinational companies. Our concern here, of course, is not with these structures and institutions in themselves, but with their impacts on the development process.

Our study will not treat all of these issues in depth. One major area that is slighted is public finance; while Chapter 5 deals with various aspects of government finance that relate to the problem of international debt, questions of tax policy and reform, improving the allocation of public spending, and reforming budgetary policies are not touched upon. These omissions seem justified because of the full treatment of these subjects in other recent works such as the World Bank's *World Development Report 1988 (WDR),* which devoted eight chapters to public finance issues in development.

Other broad sub-areas of financial policy are well covered in textbooks. Experts are fully familiar with these issues, and they have little interest for the non-expert. Rules for the execution of monetary policy through open-market operations, reserve requirements and the like will, thus, not be found in this study.

For a definition of development I essentially follow Ian Little, who, after discussing alternative concepts of the term, opts for "the growth of national income per head" (Little 1982, Chapter 1). I am inclined, however, to omit from this definition its last two words: "per head", whose main function seems to be to introduce a subliminal welfare function. While it can readily be admitted that output growth without adjustment for population increases fails to measure welfare changes, growth in per capita output is not necessarily a good welfare yardstick either because it says nothing about distribution.

In any event, the distinction loses much of its meaning if the focus is on the effects of financial policies, as it is in this study. For the periods over which such policies are usually expected to yield results, population growth can be taken as given or, at least, not significantly influenced by the policies under discussion. The proportional impact of policies on national income — or on related variables such as GNP or GDP — will be the same whether these are measured in absolute or per capita terms; if a policy measure is expected to add 1 per cent to GNP growth it will add an equal percentage to GNP per capita. In the presentation of data over the long run, however, population growth cannot be ignored; this is the reason per capita figures are cited in Chapter 2.

The choice of this narrow, perhaps even materialistic, definition of development is not inspired by a belief that growth in output is the only aspect of development that matters. It is aimed, instead, to set a manageable scope for this study, and reflects a judgment that whatever financial policies may contribute to development in the broader welfare sense they contribute primarily through the enlargement of output.

Some financial policies may well have effects on other dimensions of development, such as income distribution. Examples, such as the setting of tax, interest, or exchange rates, spring readily to mind. These effects present a double challenge that cannot be met within the limits of this study. For the economic analyst of productivity trends, they raise issues concerning the supply of factors of production in the long run, including such little-researched questions as how to mitigate or reverse the "brain drain" from developing to developed countries, or how to attract and hold internationally mobile entrepreneurial talent. For the policy maker, they pose the unenviable task of assigning appropriate relative weights to the growth and non-growth dimensions of welfare, of balancing short-term welfare losses against longer-term gains, and of discerning and allowing for interactions between these dimensions.

Correct financial policy is important either because it adds to the supply of financial resources or because it encourages more efficient use of capital and other factors of production. The concepts of finance and financial policy can, thus, be seen as complementary. "Finance" is quantitative: it measures the supply of capital, expressed in units of currency, and can be translated, using the marginal productivity of that capital, into expected additions to output.

The effects of some forms of financial policy can also be expressed in terms of their impacts on the availability of capital. For example, if a given increase in interest rates is expected to raise domestic savings by x billion or reduce capital flight by y billion there is a direct translation from financial policy to finance. In other cases the link is less direct, as when higher interest rates or a more efficient stock exchange serve to channel the available supply of capital to more effective uses. But the yield of such policy actions can still be expressed, at least in principle, directly in terms of increased output.

While it may be difficult to associate an increase in output with a single factor of production, it is of great interest in some circumstances — as we shall see — to know what increase in the amount of capital would have been needed to produce the same increase in output. Finding that out amounts, essentially, to applying the marginal productivity of capital backwards. An example of this transformation will be worked out in Chapter 3, which discusses the benefits to development of efficient financial policies. In this context, much attention is paid to the role of interest rates as an allocator of capital, and an attempt is made to gain quantitative knowledge of the contribution efficient capital policies can make to economic growth.

Economic growth — development — is the yardstick by which financial flows and financial policies can be made commensurate. In this study, these parameters are seen as interrelated dimensions of the development process. Their integration into a two-dimensional approach should help avoid a one-sided development policy framework that puts undue emphasis on the supply of capital, particularly foreign capital, and pays insufficient attention to financial policies. This somewhat myopic viewpoint, which will be touched on in Chapter 9, was common to the development theory of the 1950s and 1960s, and still afflicts many analysts. A one-dimensional approach also has a natural appeal to many developing countries, as it can be used to focus attention on a single external cause for disappointing growth.

Yet, theory and rhetoric aside, policy will have to focus not only on raising the supply of capital, but equally on coaxing the maximum possible growth out of all factors of production.

Chapter 4 explores the determinants of the domestic savings rate, including the influence of such factors as income levels, interest rates, and social security. Not all domestic savings are available for domestic investment if the government becomes a net dissaver, as has been the case in many of the heavily indebted countries — partly as a cause of the indebtedness and partly as a consequence of it. Several aspects of this problem are discussed in Chapter 5. Chapter 6 examines the links between the supply of savings from domestic sources and the net availability of savings from abroad, with particular attention to the factors that may turn the latter flow negative and generate capital flight.

Chapter 7 explores aspects of the supply of foreign savings in world capital markets and the options open to developing countries to attract a share of it. This subject cannot be divorced from the disequilibrium in payments positions that has prevailed in recent years among the industrial countries, with the United States — the richest and until recently the largest creditor country — now absorbing more of the world supply of capital than all the developing countries combined ever managed to attract. The scale on which developing countries could rely on foreign capital in the 1970s and early 1980s cannot be expected to return after the debacle brought about by excessive commercial bank lending, but a possible (and relatively modest) resumed role for alternative financing methods such as direct investment and official export credits is analysed in this chapter.

The International Monetary Fund and the World Bank have played important roles in the post-war period in supplying credit to developing countries: the Fund providing short- and medium-term credit on an expanding scale, and the Bank and its affiliated International Development Association on a longer-term basis. The IMF and the Bank have also actively concerned themselves with the financial policies of their members, and both have adapted their activities to the overwhelming problems that some of these countries have faced as a result of the debt crisis. The evolution of Bank and Fund policies relevant to our study are examined in Chapter 8.

The international debt crisis has loomed over the economic growth efforts of a large part of the developing world for six years, and no let-up is in sight. This crisis affects virtually all of Latin America and the African countries, including some above the Sahara. To put it differently, with a few exceptions on both sides, the developing countries in Asia are the only ones still proceeding — often with considerable success — on the development path laid out in the first three post-war decades. On the other continents, the debt crisis and its after-effects dominate and continue to frustrate the development effort.

Accordingly, an understanding of development issues in the 1980s must be based on a thorough analysis of the nature and consequences of the debt crisis. One part of this analysis is presented in Chapter 2: Why were so many countries swept away in the maelstrom set off by the radical adjustment policies the industrial countries adopted at the start of the 1980s? What differentiates these countries from those that managed to keep their heads above water and, soon thereafter, to continue more or less on course? What lessons can be learned from this experience as to the true costs of development undertaken with heavy reliance on foreign capital?

The chapter, after describing in broad strokes the halcyon period of development finance during the first two or three decades after World War II, attempts to answer these questions. It also introduces a dichotomy among developing countries — those *with* and those *without* current debt servicing problems — that is taken up again in later chapters.

I return to the debt crisis in the final chapters, which address two central related issues posed by the debt problem: How can an adequate rate of growth be resumed in the heavily indebted countries (Chapter 9), and how can these countries emerge from the strangle-hold of past debt (Chapter 10)? Chapter 9 emphasizes the importance to developing country growth of a number of external factors that are determined by the degree of success the *developed* countries have in steering their economies on a healthy path of non-inflationary growth with open markets. It is against this background that the policy factors that determine the opportunities for growth in developing countries are discussed.

That discussion proceeds first on the assumption that service on foreign debt will be maintained. In Chapter 10, however, this assumption is relaxed and alternative suggestions with respect to debt relief are examined, first for the middle-income countries whose debt is largely to commercial banks and then, separately, for the poorest countries, most of them in Africa, whose creditors are mostly the governments of the industrial countries.

The conclusion is drawn in that chapter that many of the highly-indebted middle-income countries can work their way out of the debt problem while resuming satisfactory growth provided that: *(i)* they persevere in the necessary adjustment policies; *(ii)* world economic conditions remain reasonably satisfactory, and — and this is essential — *(iii)* the creditor banks play their part in the process. It is suggested that if the banks offered to make annual "new money" loans — or capitalise interest — up to, say, half the interest due each year on the condition that debtor countries continued to pursue satisfactory adjustment programmes, the debt crisis could be on the way out for the countries willing and able to meet that condition. If the banks cannot bring themselves to make this contribution to solving the debt problem, they are likely in the end to incur a much heavier cost as debtors become unable or unwilling to perform the full interest service out of their own resources.

A different approach is needed to resolve the debt crisis of the low-income highly indebted countries, most of which are found in Sub-Saharan Africa. These countries need a bold general approach — such as that proposed by the African Development Bank and described in Chapter 10 — that recognises the impossibility for them to resume satisfactory growth rates unless sharply curtailed debt service replaces the current annual rescheduling rounds of the Paris Club.

Chapter 2

PHASES OF DEVELOPMENT SINCE WORLD WAR II

2.1   The First Twenty Five Years

During the twenty five years 1950-75, economic development took great strides in the non-industrial countries. After a century that had witnessed virtually no growth in per capita income (OECD 1985, p. 12), the average GNP per capita of the developing countries in that quarter century increased by 3.4 per cent per annum. This was far in excess of the highest sustained historic growth rate of per capita income in the industrial countries, which was about 2 per cent, and well above the official goals for growth entertained around the beginning of that quarter century (Morawetz 1977, p. 12). These material achievements were accompanied by sharp improvements in such indicators of human progress as the lengthening of average life expectancy, the reduction in infant mortality and the rise in literacy.

This economic growth in the developing world can best be understood in the context of the world economy at large. In the industrial countries too, the rate of economic growth was "substantially stronger than in any earlier period of similar duration in recorded economic history" (OECD 1970, pp. 13-14), as per capita output increased by 3.2 per cent a year between 1950 and 1975. Trade among industrial countries, gradually liberated from the shackles of the early post-war years, grew in volume about $1\frac{1}{2}$ times as fast as output, or more than 7 per cent a year (OECD 1970, p. 50).

The growth of the industrial countries' imports from the developing countries was less spectacular, but still very strong. Between 1950 and 1975, these imports increased seven-fold in value and perhaps $2\frac{3}{4}$ times (roughly 4 per cent a year) in purchasing power over the exports from the industrial countries.

Actual exports from the industrial to the non-oil developing countries increased even faster: more than eleven-fold in value terms and 4 times (6 per cent a year) in volume terms, as capital flows that had not been available in 1950 permitted developing countries to finance large import surpluses by 1975 (IMF 1982, p. xi).

At the same time, the international economic system appeared to be clearly moving toward the ideals that had inspired the drafters of the Bretton Woods design. The economies of the industrial countries expanded at close to full employment, with only minor cyclical dips. After a short surge related to the Korean War, inflation did not seem to be a major problem. Following a major correction in 1949 of the overvaluation that had been considered acceptable for many currencies during the initial post-war years, exchange rates for the main currencies remained stable — with minor exceptions — until 1967. Rapid economic recovery permitted the European industrial countries to make their currencies convertible by the end of the 1950s: *de facto* in 1958 and *de jure* in 1961. These countries also proceeded to dismantle their restrictions on trade and, going beyond the expectations inherent in the Bretton Woods system, their restrictions on capital movements as well.

The IBRD finished the immediate post-war task indicated by the R for Reconstruction in its name before 1950 and turned its full attention to Development, assisted by the creation in 1960 of the IDA as a source of highly concessional finance for low-income countries. All these achievements were accompanied by a remarkable blossoming of international co-operation in economic policies. With no fundamental differences in economic philosophy among the industrial countries, constructive exchanges of views on appropriate policies took place within the framework of the IMF — especially the annual consultations — in the OECD, in particular within its "Working Party No. 3" of the Economic Policy Committee, and in the Bank for International Settlements.

The steady rise of incomes in the OECD countries provided the basis for an expanding flow of financial resources to the developing countries. Foreign aid, initially almost exclusively the domain of the United States and the colonial or ex-colonial powers (OECD 1985, pp. 40-41) became the recognised responsibility of all industrial countries. The Development Assistance Group (DAC) was established in the OECD in 1960 with the three goals of increasing aid, adapting its terms and forms to the needs of recipient countries, and improving the effectiveness of development co-operation. Direct investment, although heavily concentrated in the industrial countries, also began to channel financial resources to the developing countries. Commercial banks resumed the practice, abandoned since the Great Depression, of channeling capital abroad in response to encouraging economic developments in a wide range of countries, including the more advanced developing countries.

In these circumstances the prevalent feeling was that the supply of external finance for the developing countries, while somewhat below the optimum, was not grossly insufficient. In their authoritative book *International Aid,* I.M.D. Little and J-M. Clifford devote a long chapter to "The Need for Capital" (Little, Clifford 1965, pp. 213-236). In it they appraise the need for development capital, whether provided as aid or as loans, for each continent and with considerable country detail within each continent. Their conclusion is as follows: "In quantitative terms, and relative to 1962, we would suggest that probably India can use another net $1 billion per annum, and Latin American maybe $½ billion. ... If, as seems likely, most of the capital flight from Africa dies away, it should be possible to reduce aid by $½ billion, without making any difference to economic development. In total, therefore, we suggest that the underdeveloped world might usefully absorb for development about another $1-1½ billion per annum, an increase of around 20 per cent" (pp. 234-235).

Thus, in the course of the 1960s, the view could be held that the flow of foreign finance towards the developing countries was broadly adequate in magnitude and tended to increase over time, if not dramatically, at least in a manner that inspired confidence that the rising needs of the developing countries for a supplement to their domestic savings would continue to be met. A major concern of DAC at that time was to put development aid on an "assured and convincing basis" (OECD 1985, p. 42). The degree of satisfaction felt at the time reflected perhaps not so much the modest rise in the aid effort (note) as the evidence of rapid growth in the developing world. This rate of growth was of course attributable to many factors other than the stream of foreign capital. A quantitatively more important factor was the rising supply of domestic savings: in most developing countries outside Sub-Saharan Africa, domestic savings accounted for some 90 per cent of total investment, as against about 10 per cent provided by foreign saving (note). And, as mentioned, the broadly favourable conditions of the world economy and the entire package of relevant domestic policies in developing countries were equally responsible for the total outcome in terms of growth.

An important accompanying element in the course of the quarter century from about 1950 was the broadening view taken by development economists on the factors that made for a successful development effort. The initial "almost

29

exclusive emphasis on increasing capital as a way to raise incomes" was replaced by an appreciation of the importance of other factors in the production function, of relative prices, and of economic policies (Krueger 1986, pp. 58-60). Next to the Harrod-Domar model that saw development determined by the interaction of the marginal savings rate and the incremental capital output ratio, early development economics had, under the guidance of Prebisch (1950), taken a pessimistic attitude toward the possibility of developing countries earning additional foreign exchange from exports, and had put a corresponding emphasis on import substitution as the natural road to growth. In the 1960s the validity of that approach began to be questioned on the basis of intensive and extensive empirical research. In a project sponsored by the OECD Development Centre that was initiated in late 1965, Ian Little, Tibor Scitovsky and Maurice Scott commissioned country studies on the industrial development of seven relatively advanced developing countries: Argentina, Brazil, Mexico, India, Pakistan, the Philippines and Taiwan. The results of these studies were combined in a detailed report by the three authors, published by Oxford University Press for the OECD in 1970 under a title that rather hides the broad scope of its coverage: *Industry and Trade in Some Developing Countries* (Little, Scitovsky and Scott 1970). For the seven countries analysed it finds "plenty of scope for increasing exports, especially of manufactures, despite the restrictions imposed by developed countries" (p. 17).

These views have gained widespread acceptance among development economists since that time; the World Bank, for example, has presented extensive evidence demonstrating the advantages of an open-economy, export-oriented approach to development (WDR 1985).

The smooth expansion of the world economy was sharply changed by the first oil shock, which arose from the steep increase in the price of oil announced by OPEC in December 1973. The price increase acted as a tax levied on the consumption of oil, collected by the oil exporting countries and by oil producers in other countries as well. The tax fell overwhelmingly on the incomes of the developed countries, since they accounted for the bulk of world oil consumption. Initially, only a relatively small proportion of the purchasing power transferred to the oil exporters was used by them for additional imports of goods and services. Some was channeled into much enlarged aid programmes; the rest was saved, mostly in the form of liquid claims on banks in the industrial countries.

The income transfer from the many oil consumers to the far fewer oil producers thus produced a noticeable increase in world saving. At the same time, the unsettled economic conditions that resulted from the sharp increase in oil prices were not favourable to investment activity, which fell as a proportion of GNP in the industrial countries by about two percentage points from the first to the second half of the 1970s, and then by a further 1.5 percentage point in the next half decade (Figure 2.1). The first decline took place in spite of a decline in real interest rates — a development that could be attributed to the rise in savings and the decline in the demand for investment, or to the effects of inflation; for more than a century, high inflation rates have been associated with low real interest rates, at least in the United States (Summers 1982).

Given the subdued economic climate in large parts of the industrial world, the banks recycled the resources they received in the form of OPEC deposits mostly to developing countries. The latter were anxious to absorb an additional

Figure 2.1. INVESTMENT AS A PERCENTAGE OF GDP:
INDUSTRIAL VERSUS NON-OIL DEVELOPING COUNTRIES, 1970-86

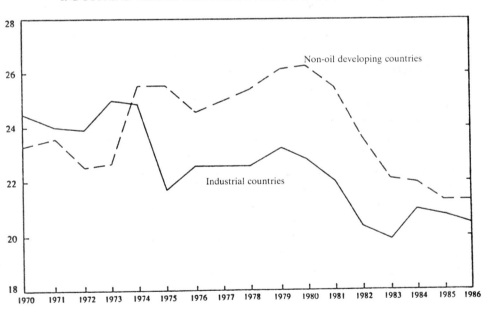

Sources: International Monetary Fund, *Annual Report,* Washington, 1987, and *World Economic Outlook,* Washington, 1987.

stream of credit, partly for investment and partly to maintain or increase consumption in the face of rising prices of imported oil. Indeed, many observers saw the sudden upsurge of the availability of foreign savings to the developing countries as the one beneficial effect of OPEC's increases in the price of petroleum. The availability of finance on an unexpectedly large scale permitted the oil-importing LDCs to run large current account deficits and raise their investment ratios to GNP by some 3 percentage points, while lowering their savings ratios by the same extent, from 1971-75 to 1978-82 (Table 2.2, Section A). At the same time, these countries kept up a growth rate in excess of 5 per cent per annum (Goldsbrough and Zaidi 1986, p. 151).

2.2   The Debt Crisis: Its Origins and the Experiences of Different Groups of Countries

This — at least on the surface — favourable economic climate for the non-oil developing countries came to an abrupt end at the end of the 1970s. Within a short period these countries were hit by four successive sharply adverse changes in the world economy: first, the second oil shock, which raised the world petroleum price by more than 100 per cent from 1978 to 1980, and a total of 150 per cent from 1978 to 1981; second, a contractionary monetary policy adopted by the industrial countries to contain the inflationary impact of the rise in petroleum prices that raised London Interbank Offered Rate (Libor) for dollar-denominated credits from just over 10 per cent in 1979 to 19 per cent in 1981; third, a recession-induced major decline in the terms of trade of the developing countries on merchandise other than oil, mainly in 1981-82, and finally, as the combined unfavourable effects of these developments undermined the credit standing of many of the countries affected, an abrupt cessation of the supply of foreign bank credit. The deterioration of the current account of the non-oil developing countries between 1978 and 1982 caused by the first three factors has been estimated at $78 billion, of which $10 billion was accounted for by the higher cost of oil imports, even at a reduced volume; $41 billion by higher net interest payments, and $27 billion by worsened non-oil terms of trade [IMF World Economic Outlook (WEO) 1984, p. 49]. The increase between 1978 and 1982 in these countries' combined actual current account deficit was kept to $40 billion, mainly as a result of reductions in non-oil imports.

It is not particularly surprising that these developments presented major difficulties to many of the developing countries affected by them. What is perhaps surprising is that the outcome was not a generalised debt crisis, but that many oil-importing developing countries, including some that borrowed heavily from the commercial banks, managed to avoid a debt crisis and maintain respectable growth rates.

Table 2.1.   BEFORE AND AFTER THE DEBT CRISIS:
A COMPARISON OF CAPITAL IMPORTING DEVELOPING COUNTRIES [a]
WITHOUT AND *WITH* DEBT SERVICING PROBLEMS

| | Period | Developing countries | |
| | | Without | With |
		Recent debt servicing problems	
A. Developments up to 1981			
1. Current account deficit (% of exports of goods and services)	1969-78	8	18
2. External debt (% of exports of goods and services)	1981	81	186
3. Growth rate of real GDP (% p.a.)	1968-81	5.5	5.1
4. Gross capital formation (% p.a.)	1978-81	28	26
B. Developments after 1981			
5. Growth rate of real GDP (% p.a.)	1982-86	4.1	1.2
6. Gross capital formation	1983-86[b]	24	18

a)   Developing countries except Iran, Iraq, Kuwait, Libya, Oman, Qatar, Saudi Arabia and the United Arab Emirates; China has also been excluded for reasons of continuity of the series.
b)   The period selected starts in 1983, because although the gross capital formation ratio in the problem countries started to decline in 1982, it did not reach its new level of around 18 per cent until 1983.
Source: IMF (WEO) 1986 and 1987, Tables A-5, A-7, A-35 and A-50; IMF calculations.

The question thus arises why some countries fell victim to the debt problem and others did not. One way to approach this question is by means of a careful dissection of the experience of a number of individual countries. We shall follow that approach in the next section, where the developments from about 1975 to 1985 are analysed for three countries that were major heavy borrowers but differed in other policy aspects: Mexico, Brazil and South Korea. Mexico, which borrowed heavily on top of an oil bonanza to finance large government deficits, was the country that initiated the debt crisis in August 1982. Brazil, which had taken important corrective measures in 1980 and 1981, had hopes in the summer of 1982 to stave off the debt crisis. In spite of these measures it still fell victim to it a few months after Mexico. South Korea went through months of great uncertainty concerning its ability to maintain its position in international credit markets; it did in the end manage to do so.

Another approach, which will be followed in the balance of this section, lies in a comparative consideration of statistics for groups of countries. For this purpose we use a dichotomy introduced some years ago by the International Monetary Fund, which distinguishes among capital importing developing countries according to whether they did or did not get into debt servicing problems in the 1980s. Using this distinction one finds a striking difference, both before and after 1981, between the group of countries that got into debt servicing difficulties (hereafter sometimes referred to as "problem countries") and those countries that did not ("non-problem countries") (see Tables 2.1 and 2.2).

By 1981 the "problem countries" had incurred an external debt in relation to exports of goods and services twice as large as the non-problem group (Table 2.1, line 2). This difference in indebtedness reflected a combined current account deficit, from 1968 to 1981, that was more than twice as large for the problem countries as the non-problem countries. Up to 1981 growth rates (line 3) and gross capital formation (line 4) were not greatly different in

Table 2.2. DIFFERENCES IN SAVINGS AND INVESTMENT BEHAVIOUR BEFORE THE DEBT CRISIS AMONG CAPITAL IMPORTING DEVELOPING COUNTRIES

			1971-75	1978-82	Change
A.	All countries	Savings rate	18	15	−3
		Investment rate	22.5	25.5	+3
		Current balance	− 4.5	−10.5	−6
B.	Countries *with* debt-servicing problems	Savings rate	19	13.5	−5.5
		Investment rate	22	23	+1
		Current balance	− 3	− 9.5	−6.5
C.	Countries *without* debt-servicing problems	Savings rate	16	16.5	0.5
		Investment rate	22.5	26.5	4
		Current balance	− 6.5	−10	−3.5

Note: The original figures for the medians were given with two decimal places; I have rounded them to the nearest one-half percentage point, although even that conveys more precision than the data deserve.

Source: IMF data underlying Tables 65, 67 and 68 in Goldsbrough and Zaidi, 1986. The figures (which are expressed in per cent of GDP) represent medians for the three groups of countries shown. Figures for comparable periods to those used in Table 2.1 suggest that these medians are consistent with the averages used in that table.

the two groups; they were in any event not better for the prospective problem countries. Apparently, these countries received no comparative benefit in terms of growth from the larger debt they had incurred.

As is evident from a comparison of sections B and C of Table 2.2, the problem countries turned their higher use of foreign savings only marginally into a higher rate of investment, but mostly used them to offset a sharp fall in their savings rate; the non-problem countries used the additional foreign resources, plus a marginal increase in their own savings, to achieve a substantial increase in investment.

Moreover, there is much ground to question the efficiency of the investments made in some countries in the latter part of the 1970s. A recent Fund study (WEO April 1987, pp. 79-80) comments on this question by presenting data showing that, for the 15 heavily indebted countries, investment rates in 1978-80 similar to those in 1973-77 were associated with growth rates that were one quarter smaller in the later than the earlier period[1].

These rather indirect statistical findings[2] are supported by a more direct analysis of the sequence of events in the main area where the debt crisis struck: Latin America. As pointed out by the Inter-American Development Bank, large external borrowings led in 1974 and 1975 to increased investment (IDB 1982, p. 35); thereafter, investment declined while borrowing increased; by the end of the 1970s, "Latin America had shifted somewhat to a strategy of sustaining growth by using foreign credits to maintain domestic consumption" (Enders and Mattione 1984, p. 7). The sharp increase in the supply of credit from abroad permitted governments to avoid hard domestic choices. Appreciation of the real exchange rate (on average for the continent by 31 per cent from 1970 to 1980) mitigated the impact on the population of rising oil costs and kept imported consumer goods and capital goods relatively cheap. "Investment in the public sector, and in the protected private sector, often did not meet efficiency criteria, with incremental capital-output ratios averaging 8 in 1978-82 in Latin America"[3] (Balassa et al. 1987, p. 67). Moreover, the fact that large budget deficits could easily be financed abroad opened the door to permissive financial policies while mitigating the inflationary impact of such policies.

The figures in Part B of Table 2.1 confirm these impressions. In the years after 1981 the problem countries did much worse than the non-problem countries. While growth and capital formation declined only modestly in the latter countries and average growth for this group was sustained in the 3 to 5 per cent range, the problem countries had two years of negative average growth (1982 and 1983) and did not exceed 3 per cent growth in any of the four following years. At the same time, they experienced a reduction in their investment ratio by 9 percentage points as against a mere 4 percentage point reduction for the non-problem countries.

While these low net investment figures can hardly be considered the cause of the low growth rates in recent years, which brought output in the countries involved only a little beyond their end-1981 levels, they raise nevertheless some issues for future growth. The IMF *1987 World Economic Outlook* rightly called recent investment trends "disturbing" (p. 78). It noted that large capital inflows during the period of heavy borrowing did not lead to increases in investment ratios in the heavily indebted countries, but that, when external financing dried up, these ratios fell sharply while consumption tended to be safeguarded. Thus, by 1986, average per capita consumption in these countries was at the same level as in 1980, while investment was down by one-third (chart on p. 80). The sustained cuts in public sector investment since 1982 weakened its contribution to future rises in living standards both directly, and indirectly because of the complementarity of public and private investment. In this manner, both the policies that led up to the debt crisis and those that were pursued in response to it, while designed to benefit consumption in the short run, may well have set it back grievously over the longer run.

2.3   The Experience of Three Countries: Brazil, Mexico, and South Korea[4]

How did it happen that Brazil and Mexico became deeply mired in the debt crisis in 1982 and proved unable to extricate themselves from it over the next six years, while South Korea escaped that crisis and by 1986 could afford to start reducing its foreign debt while continuing to enjoy rapid economic growth?

Much effort has already been spent in comparing the impressive record over the last decade and before of developing countries in East Asia (minus the Philippines) with the depressing record of Latin America (minus Colombia) (Sachs 1985, and sources there cited). It would be too much to expect that a thorough comparison of three of the main countries involved would provide definitive answers, especially since two of them, Brazil and South Korea, represent clear-cut cases of failure and success only when seen in retrospect. In 1981 and 1982, the chances that Brazil might pull through or that South Korea would succumb were by no means negligible. One also has to acknowledge that there may not be a fully rational explanation; "regional contagion" may have entered as a psychological factor explaining creditors' behaviour (Williamson

36

1985, p. 659). This observation is particularly relevant because the difference in the forces that pushed one country over the edge of the debt abyss and allowed another country to just hang on may not have been large, and was certainly much smaller than could be inferred from a comparison of the subsequent fate of the two countries.

However, insofar as an answer can be found from analysis, it would appear that it lies to a limited extent only in differences in external circumstances, and predominantly in differences in policies.

As regards circumstances:

— All three countries suffered from the rise in world interest rates on their floating rate debt, from the 1980-82 slowdown in the industrial countries, and from increasing protectionism in these countries;
— Brazil and South Korea were sharply affected by the increase in world petroleum prices (the "second oil shock"), which in its direct effects greatly assisted Mexico's balance of payments;
— With respect to a variety of structural aspects, the Korean economy could not be considered as more *laissez-faire* oriented or supply-side friendly than those of Mexico and Brazil. All three countries heavily regulated business and imports; in all three, public enterprises accounted for a large proportion of output (and made losses financed from the budget); marginal income tax rates were far higher in South Korea than in the two other countries.

The conditions that pre-existed in the three countries in the 1970s and 1980s presented an interesting mixture of similarities and dissimilarities:

— The foreign trade of the three countries was of the same order of magnitude. Exports in 1980 were $16 billion in Mexico; $18 billion in South Korea, and $20 billion in Brazil; in 1983, the figures were even closer: $22 billion each for Mexico and Brazil, and $24 billion for South Korea;
— Growth in the 1970s had been rapid in South Korea (9.5 per cent per annum) and Brazil (8.4 per cent), more moderate in Mexico (5.2 per cent);
— Per capita incomes were little different in 1980, especially if some allowance is made for currency overvaluation in Brazil and Mexico;
— All three countries had incurred large foreign debts, which in terms of GNP were in 1982 about 55 per cent in Mexico and South Korea and 34 per cent in Brazil. By 1985 the ratios the all three countries were

between 50 and 60 per cent[5]. In all three countries, too, part of the borrowed money — which came at low initial real interest rates — was invested in ways that were far from optimal. The evidence for Mexico and Brazil is abundant and has already been cited. In South Korea, too, part of foreign finance was misdirected, at least as far as the medium term was concerned, into inefficient import institution.

Hiding below these mostly similar numbers, was one characteristic with respect to which the two Latin American countries were very different from South Korea: the ratio of external trade to GNP. In 1980, this ratio (measured as exports of goods and services over GNP) stood at 37 per cent for South Korea, at 13 per cent for Mexico, and at 10 per cent for Brazil. In part, this striking difference reflected natural factors, such as differences in population and even greater differences in land area. The population of Mexico is nearly twice, and that of Brazil, more than three times that of South Korea; in terms of area, Mexico is 20 times, and Brazil 85 times, as large as South Korea[6]. But it was also to an important extent the consequence of long-standing policy differences: a high degree of export orientation in South Korea, as against a far more inward-looking and protectionist stance in Latin America.

Moreover, the composition of exports was radically different: about 10 per cent in the form of manufactures in Mexico, 30 per cent in Brazil, and well over 80 per cent in South Korea. Both the policy orientation and the composition of exports played a role in the differences in export growth in the decade of the 1970s: an average of 23 per cent per year for South Korea, 13.4 per cent for Mexico and 7.5 per cent for Brazil (World Bank WDR 1982, p. 125).

The differences in the relative importance of trade to GDP lie behind the fact that in comparison to external earnings, the debt burden and the interest burden of South Korea were only about one-third of the corresponding burden for Brazil and Mexico. They also explain why a somewhat similar build-up of debt *as a percentage of GDP* produced much wider swings in the current account position in the two Latin American countries than in South Korea, both when the debt was incurred and when the necessary adjustment took place. This is shown in Figure 2.2, which plots current account deficits for the three countries. In spite of about equal trade (as mentioned above), South Korea's current account deficit peaked at $5.3 billion in 1980, as against Mexico's peak deficit of $14 billion (1981) and Brazil's of more than $16 billion (1982). The reversal in the latter two countries was also far more radical. South Korea could afford to return, in 1983-85, to current account deficits in the range of $1 to $2 billion, not far from the 1975-78 figures. Thanks also to

Figure 2.2. CURRENT ACCOUNT BALANCES, BRAZIL, SOUTH KOREA AND MEXICO,
1971-86
($ billions)

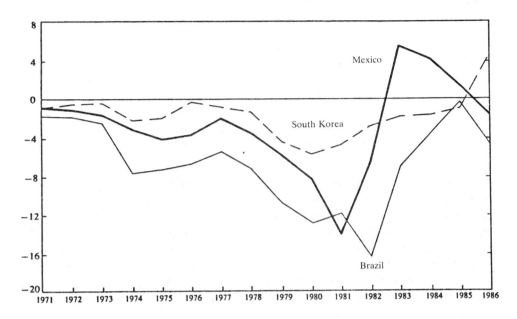

Source: International Monetary Fund, *International Financial Statistics.*

continued access to capital markets, it could afford similar-sized deficits on the trade account. Mexico, on the other hand, was forced by its adjustment process and the effects of large capital flight into three years (1983-85) of large current account surpluses, and of course even much larger trade surpluses, and Brazil (where capital flight was not a major factor) needed, and achieved, approximate current account balance in both 1984 and 1985.

A further important difference can be noted in the quality of the fiscal situation. Good data are not available for Brazil[7], but those for Mexico and South Korea show a notable contrast in level, in spite of a similarity in movement over the period 1979-84 (Table 2.3). Both countries show a sharp increase in the overall public sector deficit from 1979 to 1981-82, and both reversed this increase in the next year. But at the start and the end of the period, South Korea's deficit was a modest 1.4 per cent of GDP, while Mexico's was some six times as large. This large Mexican deficit began to play a dangerous role of its own as foreign loans became scarce, inflation worsened and, as described in Chapter 5, public finance became a major causative factor in the deepening of the debt crisis.

Table 2.3.   OVERALL PUBLIC SECTOR DEFICITS AS PER CENT OF GDP/GNP, MEXICO AND SOUTH KOREA

	1979	1980	1981	1982	1983	1984
Mexico (% GDP)	7.4	7.9	14.7	17.5	8.9	9.0
South Korea (% GNP)	1.4	3.2	4.6	4.3	1.6	1.4

Source: Mexico, Table 5.3; South Korea, Aghevli and Marquez-Ruarte 1985, p. 26.

Historic differences in economic structures, reflecting decades of differences in policy orientation and the differences in the quality of fiscal policies, constituted probably the most important systemic differences between the three countries analysed in their susceptibility to the risks of serious debt problems. But there were also notable differences in the degree of responsiveness of policy to the outside shocks that hit all three countries, which will be briefly commented upon to conclude this chapter. South Korea responded rather speedily to shocks that also — and this may have been a blessing in disguise — hit the country well before the onslaught of the debt crisis. Brazil took some steps toward adjustment at a relatively early stage — in 1980 — but its actions remained insufficient; and Mexico, which as an oil exporter on balance benefited from the changes in external circumstances, responded with an expansionary policy that would have been of questionable wisdom even it could have been assumed that the positive external factors would be lasting.

The difference in timing is reflected in the years in which these countries first saw important declines in GDP after decades of growth: South Korea in 1980 (-3.0 per cent), Brazil in 1981 (-1.6 per cent) and again in 1983 (-3.2 per cent); and Mexico in 1982 and 1983 (-0.6 per cent and -5.3 per cent).

The difficulties that *South Korea* experienced as a result of the oil-recycling boom began to manifest themselves in 1977-78, i.e. before the second oil shock and the rise in world interest rates (Aghevli and Marquez-Ruarte 1985; Kim 1987). They were, primarily, domestic imbalances: too much investment in heavy industries, a housing boom, a tight labour market due to the departure of many construction workers to the Middle East, excessive wage increases, accelerated inflation and a consequent loss of competitiveness. To meet these pressures, the government initiated a stabilization programme in mid-1978. The external shocks of 1979 and 1980 made it necessary to strengthen these measures, but led nevertheless to deteriorating conditions: in 1980, real GNP fell by 5 per cent, inflation reached 35 per cent, the overvaluation of the won worsened, and the current account deficit rose to almost 9 per cent of GNP. But the early start made in South Korea with a broad range of fundamental adjustment policies allowed the country to overcome the effects of the internal and the external crises, starting in 1981 when GNP growth returned to 6 per cent. The policies included fiscal and monetary tightening, allowing the pass-through of the second oil shock in domestic prices — together with strict energy conservation measures — a freeze on government salaries, pressure to reduce private sector wage increases and moderation in grain procurement prices.

Starting in early 1980, South Korea began a gradual correction in the real exchange rate for the won by unhooking it from the rising US dollar. By the beginning of 1981 the stage had been set by the drastic measures taken in the preceding $2\frac{1}{2}$ years for a resumption of growth, supported then in part by some relaxation of financial policies.

In *Brazil,* some adjustment measures were taken relatively early, but not as early as in South Korea. In late 1979 and early 1980, in response to the second oil shock, the government adopted a comprehensive package of measures. This included a major devaluation of the currency to restore competitiveness, together with fiscal and monetary restraint and trade liberalisation. But much of the external effect of this package was undone almost at once by a decision to base the further downward crawl of the cruzeiro during 1980 on a forecast rate of inflation of 50 per cent, against an actual rate closer to 100 per cent. As a consequence, the real effective rate appreciated sharply during 1980; it was allowed to appreciate further until well into 1982. The same reliance on an unrealistic inflation forecast produced sharply negative real interest rates, which increased the demand for credit and contributed to reserve losses. Strict adherence to wage indexation also was not helpful in improving the trade picture. When the interest rate policy was reversed to discourage borrowing abroad, there was a sharp effect on investment demand and on imports. But Brazil's ability to roll over credits falling due and to negotiate new credits to meet its huge current account deficits became increasingly shaky in the course of 1981 and 1982. As a result its net reserves moved into large negative figures, which then became an independent cause for credit to dry up.

Mexico, up to 1982, presented a case of excessive adjustment in the wrong direction (Ortiz 1985). The explosion of crude oil exports, from $1 billion in 1977 to $13 billion in 1981, seemed to make everything possible. Outlays by the public sector increased, in the same span of years, by 11 percentage points of GDP (from 29.5 to 40.6 per cent), while GDP itself increased by some 8 to 9 per cent in real terms every year. Revenues increased much less, so that the total financial deficit increased by 8 percentage points of GDP (from 6.7 to 14.7 per cent). Increased government outlays went to the oil and non-oil sectors, for investment and consumption expenditures. The government embarked on massive industrial projects of dubious profitability in areas where it considered private investment insufficient. The easy availability of oil money and foreign loans was exploited to allow the real exchange rate to appreciate and to finance large losses of public sector enterprises. At the same time, private enterprises could also freely — and cheaply — tap foreign capital markets to the extent that they were crowded out of the domestic capital market by the government.

Little was done about the situation until pressure on the peso, due in large part to capital flight by residents who read the writing on the wall better than foreign bankers, forced a devaluation of the currency in the first quarter of 1982. By that time, however, Mexico was in the last stretch of its presidential succession process, and little constructive action was taken until that process came to its end in December 1982. Indeed, some of the last-minute actions taken by the outgoing government, such as the institution of general exchange control and the nationalisation of the banks, were far from constructive.

As noted, the root cause of the payments problems of Mexico, whose position as an oil exporter gave it even by 1982 a positive balance of external factors compared to 1977, was its domestic fiscal policies, and the 1983 correction of these policies was, indeed, drastic: the deficit was cut by 9 percentage points of GDP in one year (from 17.6 per cent in 1982 to 8.7 per cent in 1983)[8]. As in South Korea, these measures brought about a recession; they also produced a sharp fall in real wages and pushed the current account into an (unexpected) large surplus.

2.4   Inferences With Respect to the Cost of Foreign Capital

According to traditional theory, the cost of financing development by means of loans taken up abroad equals the interest rate on these loans. If the expected yield of the investment financed with the loans is higher than the interest to be paid, the combined transaction — investment financed by the foreign loan — should be expected to be profitable. By the same line of reasoning, investment financed by foreign capital should proceed until its marginal product equals the interest rate prevailing on the international capital market. Only then will the capital stock in the country have reached its optimum level (Gutowski and Holthus 1986, p. 102).

If this theoretical proposition is analysed against the background of the huge flow of commercial bank loans to the developing countries in the decade leading up to the debt crisis, a number of major unanswered questions present themselves.

1. A large part of the foreign loans contracted during that period were taken up by governments or government enterprises. Many of these loans had no direct link to specific investment projects. Indeed for some of the loans, the immediate reason for borrowing was a general government deficit. In these circumstances the yield of a loan to the national economy would be hard to define, and even harder to measure. It would, presumably, be the social yield of the expenditure the government would have forgone if in the absence of that loan it had curtailed expenditure — or the private yield of the expenditure reductions that taxpayers would have had to make if the alternative to the loan would have been an increase in taxation. Even when the loan proceeds went to an identifiable project, its hard-to-measure social yield would have been the proper comparator with the interest rate, not its often much lower financial yield.

2. There is no overwhelming evidence — to put it mildly — that governments engaged in optimising calculations before contracting additional foreign loans that banking syndicates were anxious to place. Even if these sorts of calculations had been made, they would presumably have been based on a *rebus sic stantibus* assumption, i.e. a continuation of the prevailing tendencies in the world economy with respect to inflation, growth, export markets, etc. Few borrowers in developing countries, like few borrowers in industrial countries, would have come up with the actual yields of the 1980s as the expected yields estimated in the 1970s.

3. Any attempt on the part of a borrower to make a rational cost-benefit comparison was further undermined by uncertainty concerning the cost, namely the rate of interest. In the course of the 1970s, the commercial banks had moved from fixed-rate to floating-rate lending as a device to protect themselves against fluctuations in the interest costs they had to pay as credit intermediators. Borrowers might console themselves with the construction that

interest rates were likely to fluctuate with world inflation and that high inflation could be expected to raise the profitability of investment projects in developing countries. The vagaries of a floating rate might, thus, be offset, in a very approximate way, by fluctuations in the yield of the country's investment projects. But for this to work out as a reasonable hedge for the debtor borrowing at a floating rate would require the fulfilment of at least two heroic assumptions: that interest rates would move *pari passu* with inflation, i.e. that real interest rates would remain unchanged, and that inflation itself would proceed at a uniform rate, in particular that the terms of trade of the borrower would remain unaffected by an abatement of inflation. Neither of these conditions materialised: real interest rates swung from their abnormally low levels in the 1970s to exceptionally high rates in the early 1980s and are still at historically high levels and the terms of trade of primary products against industrial products worsened.

The three issues raised would have made it extraordinarily difficult for borrowing countries in the 1970s to follow the precepts of traditional theory in their decisions on the optimum amount of foreign borrowing. There is every reason to believe that these precepts were not followed and that more prudent calculations would have produced less borrowing. It is in any event clear after the event that the economic and social cost of the actual passage through the debt crisis by some of the heaviest borrowers was far in excess of what any country would have been prepared to accept *ex ante* as a means of plugging a budget deficit and avoiding the much less costly adjustment that was the alternative at the time when the foreign loans were contracted.

But the lesson to be learned from the debt crisis is not only that some borrowing countries — and almost all commercial banks — were overoptimistic and lacked caution. A further inference to be drawn is that the traditional precepts themselves — even if a country managed to observe them — would lead to overborrowing, unless the country observed two qualifications.

The first of these has to do with the yield that is expected to be derived from the use of borrowed money. A business firm that habitually borrowed for investments with expected yields just above the going interest rate would be courting bankruptcy, because at one time or another a number of these investments would fail to reach their expected yield. The same applies to governments borrowing in world capital markets. The government might "expect" a yield expressed by a single number, like 12 per cent, which would be in excess of an interest rate in international markets of, say, 10 per cent. But the 12 per cent figure obviously has a considerable margin of uncertainly.

Unless the country is confident that it can borrow additional funds to meet the debt service even if the actual yield is well below 10 per cent, the effects of uncertainty on its ability to service the debt are not symmetrical. Thus the first amendment to the guideline will have to be that foreign borrowing is only justified if the plausible lower estimate of the yield expected from the proceeds is in excess of the interest rate of the loan. In other words, in connection with borrowing abroad[9] governments would do well to adopt the practice of business that any investment project must meet some conventional conservative "pay-back rule".

These risks increase as a country raises the extent to which it relies on foreign capital to finance its investment. Assume that a country, beyond the use of available domestic savings, each year still has a large number of unfinanced investment projects on which the return would be at least 15 per cent, while the world market interest rate is 10 per cent. Why should it not borrow for all these projects, raise its level of output accordingly, and be left with an increase in GNP (after interest payments) of 5 per cent of the total amount borrowed abroad? If the country followed this practice year after year, it could end up with very high debt/GDP and debt service/exports ratios, much higher than we observe for actual countries; but why not, as long as substantial additional income could be earned this way[10].

One of the reasons restraining countries from pursuing the textbook benefits of foreign borrowing to the logical (and absurd) end is that since the service on the debt will have to be paid in foreign exchange, the country will have to change its structure of production toward an ever higher proportion of total output consisting of tradeables and hence to an ever higher risk of being unable to service the debt.

The second qualification[11] relates to the fact that borrowing countries will always have to be aware of the fact that the supply of capital to any one country at the prevailing international interest rate is limited. In technical economic terms, borrowing countries are faced with an upward-sloping supply curve, or at least with a supply curve that, at some point, turns steeply upward[12]. This shape of the curve for the supply of capital is related to the character of sovereign debt. For a while, that character may be conveniently ignored in the enthusiasm of lending abroad; one remembers the confident saying by Walter Wriston, then the Chairman of Citibank, that "sovereign nations don't go bankrupt". But nothing can change the fact that a sovereign nation can repudiate its debt and that its creditors have only a limited ability to force reimbursement. Thus, continued debt service by the debtor and, equally, willingness of creditors to lend are predicated on the knowledge by both parties that the costs of default are sufficiently high to deter the debtor from taking recourse to this "solution". These costs go beyond the seizure of the debtor's assets abroad; they would include the sudden interruption of trade credit and the unavailability of financing for at least some time. Every one of the elements in this calculation is subject to extreme uncertainty, but one rule seems obvious: the larger the country's sovereign debt, the greater the risk that at some time, in some circumstances, the debtor will conclude that the benefits of default exceed its costs. Hence, if creditors act rationally, they will ration credit or raise its price, so as to prevent the indebtedness of any country exceeding this critical limit, however imprecisely that limit may be defined (Krugman 1985).

The upward sloping character of the supply curve for capital should enter into the calculations of the borrowers even if the creditor is willing to throw caution to the winds. In calculating the cost of borrowing a given amount abroad, the sovereign debtor should make allowance for the fact that this borrowing transaction will make all future borrowing transactions more expensive. If countries want to achieve a relatively smooth inflow of capital over time (Harberger 1985, p. 236) and if they want to preserve some leeway in their access to foreign capital to handle future contingencies at a reasonable cost, they should constrain borrowing abroad well below the level that might be indicated by a comparison of domestic and foreign interest rates.

The maintenance, as a matter of policy, of a spread between domestic and foreign exchange rates has a number of implications for national policy on borrowing abroad. It implies, in the first place, that governments do not themselves automatically borrow in the cheapest market, if that means borrowing abroad. It implies further that the government controls borrowing abroad by its sub-divisions and state enterprises according to the same principle. Lastly, it implies that the government if necessary constrains private use of foreign credit so as to keep the overall rate of increase of foreign indebtedness within prudent limits[13]. One possible instrument of constraint, suggested by Harberger, would be a tax on foreign borrowing. (Harberger 1985, p. 236). In 1987, Israel introduced such a tax, at 3 per cent, on any short-term borrowing abroad, the rate being adjustable in the light of variations in the spread between foreign and domestic interest rates, and supplemented by a limit on short-term borrowing by commercial banks. Iceland has a similar tax.

Colombia avoided being drawn into the debt crisis by a very careful policy on its use of foreign credit, including strict control on capital imports, through the 1970s and 1980s. Operating on the announced principle that "policies are more important than resources", access to foreign loans was authorised in Colombia exclusively on the merits of projects, not on the basis of the availability of foreign loans (Wiesner, pp. 9, 81). Chile, too, held down the rate of capital inflow in the 1970s in spite of the attractiveness to foreign lenders of real interest rates in the range of 3 to 4 per cent per month. But when the controls were relaxed in early 1980, foreign money rushed in for about two years, followed by a sharp reversal in 1982 (Harberger 1985, pp. 241-249).

It should be observed that controls on the inflow of capital, whose effect will be to maintain a favourable spread between internal and external interest rates, will for this very reason discourage capital exports, and thus make it easier to control capital flight without the need to rely heavily for this purpose on controls on the export of capital. The observations made in Chapter 6 on the success of Colombia and Chile in avoiding serious problems of capital flight fit into the general picture of the analysis given in this section.

A more general conclusion is that one cannot be dogmatic on the benefits that developing countries could expect to gain by liberalising the international movement of capital. Much depends on the degree of liberalisation of other markets and the sequence in which different markets are liberalised (Michalopoulos 1987, p. 30); but each country will in any event want to ensure that the availability of foreign resources does not lead to a weakening of its domestic policies.

NOTES AND REFERENCES

1. Apparently more impressive evidence is provided in the same table for the period 1981-82, but its value is questionable. The measure of the efficiency of capital used, namely the inverse of the incremental capital output ratio, falls to near zero for that period; but for those years, the measure (which is admittedly crude at best) becomes meaningless, since it reflects essentially the disappearance of GDP growth for these two years of severe adjustment.

2. In an earlier comparison of changes in savings and investment ratios in developing countries

between the late 1960s and the early 1980s, the Fund had reached a much more optimistic interpretation (IMF *World Economic Outlook 1983*, pp. 142-44), which had attracted considerable attention (Cassen 1986, p. 28). At that time, the Fund had concluded "that saving performances were strong even among countries that incurred increased current account deficits", and that "the increases in external deficits can in most cases be accounted for by expansion of investment (relative to total output) rather than by growth of consumption".

3. The comment on ICOR figures presented in Note 1 is also applicable to this figure.

4. This section is to a large extent based on a paper prepared by Helmut Reisen of the OECD Development Centre, and published as "Export Orientation, Public Debt and Fiscal Rigidities: The Different Performance in Brazil, Korea and Mexico", *Journal of International Economic Integration* (Seoul), 1988. That paper is also the source for some of the statistics used in this section.

5. Brazil: 51 per cent, Mexico and Korea: 58 per cent. Data from World Bank, *World Debt Tables, 1986-87*. The figures change sharply from year to year, partly from changes in the debt, but even more from changes in the degree of over- or undervaluation of currencies. The ratio for South Korea changed little from 1980 (49 per cent) to 1985 (58 per cent), but for the two other countries the changes were much larger (Brazil 29 per cent to 51 per cent over the same period); Mexico (32 per cent in 1980, 70 per cent in 1983, 58 per cent in 1985). Moreover, debt figures from different sources also show notable differences.

6. The importance of size, as distinct from policy, in the export ratio is evident from a comparison of the figures for South Korea with those of Japan — population about three times that of South Korea, area nearly four times. Japan's export ratio was 14 per cent in 1980. It had been 11 per cent in 1960, when the ratio for South Korea, before it embraced an export-oriented policy, was 3 per cent!

7. It is revealing that an authoritative study by the Inter-American Development Bank published in 1987 gave "consolidated accounts" for Brazil's federal public sector for 1979 and 1980, with "estimates" for 1981 and 1982, and no data at all for later years (Dinsmoor 1987, Appendix Table 7). A different set of figures, compiled in the World Bank and starting in 1981, will be found in Table 5.1. That set approximates the public sector deficit from the financing side, as the public sector borrowing requirement of the non-financial public sector.

8. One of the measures taken, the conversion into pesos of Mexdollars at a highly unfavourable exchange rate, amounted to a partial default on Mexico's domestic dollar creditors (Ize and Ortiz 1987, p. 326).

9. The qualification is restricted to loans taken up abroad. Since the government can always borrow at home if the yield turns out to be a disappointment, it would be justified in borrowing at home up to the point where its best estimate (not its low estimate) of the yield equalled the rate of interest.

10. Numerical examples making this point are presented in Cooper and Sachs, 1985.

11. A third reason, which is not further elaborated here, is related to limitations on the government's ability to raise taxes to cover the service on its debt.

12. The point seems to have been made first by Harberger at a December 1981 conference in

Chile, hence shortly before the outbreak of the debt crisis made many borrowers painfully aware of it (Harberger 1981).

13. Such constraint may not be necessary. "Private firms can be expected to be careful in assessing the net return to be derived from borrowed funds as compared with the net cost since their survival as enterprises is at stake. Such an assessment cannot be taken for granted in the case of public sector entities" (Robichek 1981, p. 171).

Chapter 3

SAVING AND THE USE OF SAVINGS

3.1 Saving and Investment

Economists may have learned too well Keynes' lesson that saving and investment in a closed economy are not only equal in amount — they are the same thing looked at from different angles. Saving is income not devoted to consumption and investment is output not absorbed in consumption. With income defined as the value of current output, saving must be identical to investment (Keynes 1936, p. 63). True enough. But this can too easily lead to the erroneous inference that the amount of saving sets the contribution of investment to the economy. The essential point is that saving is different from investment in substance; or, perhaps more accurately, the point is that savings do not yet have substance: they are undifferentiated purchasing power, while investment has a substance that determines its contribution to the process of production.

A country that saved $100 million in one year must also have invested $100 million too; but while $100 million saved/invested *can* make a large contribution to the growth of output, its contribution may also be small, zero, or negative, depending on the specific components of investment that together account for the $100 million. The translation of savings into investment is crucial to the question of the contribution the identical twins, saving and investment, make to development.

The proposition in the preceding paragraph hardly qualifies as revolutionary or indeed original. Everyone knows that it is important for a country to devote the resources at its disposal to the best investment, where "best" means the investment with the highest discounted marginal contribution to output.

Yet, as stressed by McKinnon — the economist who perhaps more than anyone has castigated the view of a homogeneous stock of capital — that simplistic view "has been held explicitly by economic growth theorists and econometricians who incorporate homogeneous capital of uniform productivity into production functions" and it "has been abetted by calculations of the 'need' for foreign aid on the assumption that output-capital ratios in recipient countries are fixed" (McKinnon 1973, p. 9).

But even McKinnon does not carry the point beyond that of a qualitative observation. In view of its importance for the strategy of development, it seems worthwhile to attempt to give the proposition as much quantitative content as is possible. There are limits to what can be done toward this end, because the data necessary for a satisfactory treatment of the subject do not — to the author's knowledge — exist. But this may be one of those areas where baking what may not even qualify as half a loaf may still be worth the effort.

The exercise is conducted by means of a few figures. In the construction of these figures certain simplifying assumptions are made; these, however, are not particularly restrictive. The figures then permit the derivation of numerical conclusions with the help of some simple geometry.

3.2   The Allocation of Available Savings Over Potential Investment Projects

Figure 3.1 brings together the results of an imaginary complete inventory of potential investment projects by the authorities of a given country. The chart presents the queue of all such projects in that country. The width of each bar indicates the cost of the project, along the horizontal axis. Its height represents the marginal productivity of the project, measured as the ratio of the project's addition to national annual output to its cost. The vertical axis thus also indicates the highest rate of interest that the project could bear. The chart bears no numbers, because these would detract from the generality of the exposition. But suppose that project 1 (the most profitable project) had a marginal productivity of 50 per cent and a cost of $10 million. The area of the bar (.50 × $10 million = $5 million) would then indicate the addition to GNP from this project. Project 2, with a marginal productivity of 48 per cent and a cost of $5 million, would add $2.4 million to GNP, and so on. Once one specifies which projects are to receive finance for their execution, one can determine the aggregate additional output by summing the areas of the bars corresponding to the projects selected.

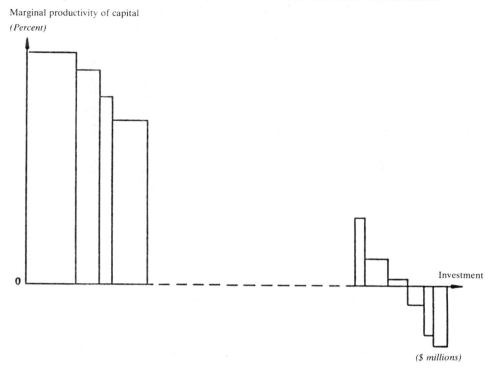

Figure 3.1. MARGINAL PRODUCTIVITY OF CAPITAL AND INVESTMENT

Marginal productivity of capital

(Percent)

0

Investment

($ millions)

As we move along the queue we find projects that are less and less profitable; and at the far right of the chart we encounter projects with negative marginal productivity — those which, if executed, would reduce GNP by operating at a loss. If some of these projects are included among those chosen for execution, the negative values of the corresponding bars will enter into the figure for the addition to GNP.

Figure 3.2 is derived from Figure 3.1 by fitting a straight line to the tops of the successive bars. The straight line is needed to facilitate the exposition that follows; it is believed that it does not significantly distort the exposition. Note that the slope shown in the chart for the line AB — which might be called the demand curve for capital — is immaterial. The variables measured along the two axes — percentages and millions of dollars — are not commensurate and the line can therefore be drawn with any slope.

As a first approximation it could be said that:

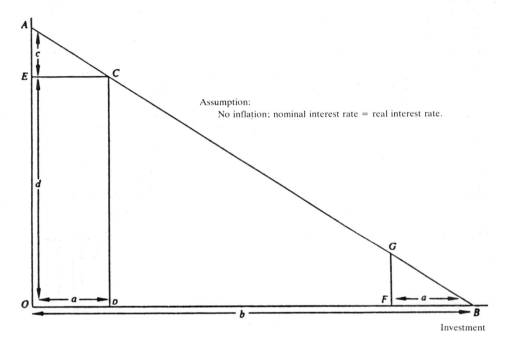

Figure 3.2. MARGINAL PRODUCTIVITY OF CAPITAL
INTEREST RATE, AND INVESTMENT

Marginal productivity
of capital
Real Interest rate

Assumption:
No inflation; nominal interest rate = real interest rate.

Investment

a)   *How much* of the investment potential represented on the two figures
     will be executed will depend on the total savings, with allowance
     (positive or negative) for net foreign savings, available to the country;
     and

b)   *Which* projects will be executed will depend on the mechanism in the
     country by which savings and projects are brought together.

    This is only a first approximation, because the supply of savings is
obviously not independent of the demand for it. If the matching mechanism
under *(b)* is a poor one, savings will not only move into sub-optimal
investments; they will also not be made, i.e. consumption will be encouraged,
or savings will be exported to take advantage of better matching mechanisms
abroad, so that net savings will be reduced. But we shall, nevertheless, proceed
on the basis of this first approximation. Even under that approximation the

results we shall find on the "waste of savings" will be distressing enough; it will be recalled at that stage that reality must be worse if account is taken of savings lost as well as savings wasted.

Subject to some pretty severe statistical qualifications, we know from the national account statistics how large a country's savings are. But since we do not have actual Figures 3.1 or 3.2 for any country, we have no factual way of comparing savings with the investment demand curve. We shall have to proceed on the basis of alternative assumptions, without much guidance — it would seem — on their plausibility.

Assume first that the supply of domestic savings equals exactly the demand for investment from projects with non-negative marginal productivity, i.e. it equals OB in Figure 3.2. Assume further that, perhaps thanks to exchange controls, the question of foreign savings is irrelevant and also that the country's selection mechanism is good enough to block off projects with a negative marginal productivity. All projects from O to B will then be executed and the resulting addition to GNP will be measured by the triangle AOB.

So ample a supply of saving in relation to investment demand would probably not normally be the case in developing countries, not even if allowance is made for a positive addition of savings from abroad.

In the second case we consider the available supply of savings, marked along the axis OB, as much smaller than OB, *viz.* OD. This amount of saving is determined by a great number of institutional domestic and foreign factors — income level, income distribution, banking facilities, foreign aid availability, etc. The interest rate in the country may also play a role (see Chapter 4 below), but we resist the economist's natural temptation to complete Figure 3.2 by means of an upward sloping supply curve of capital. For the time being, we proceed on the assumption of a given supply of saving OD (named "a") which is well below OB ("b").

The second question — which projects will be selected for execution — then becomes a crucial one.

What mechanisms are available to bring about the allocation of a country's supply of savings among alternative investment projects? The problem may appear solved when savers and investors are the same — e.g. when a government levies taxes in excess of its current expenditure and devotes the resulting savings to official investment projects — or foreign investors bring in foreign capital to start a direct investment project or domestic firms expand on the basis of retained earnings. But in none of these cases does the saver-investor identity ensure that the projects undertaken rank high among the list of all economically profitable projects. The government may be undertaking projects with political appeal rather than direct or indirect economic benefits; the foreign investor may be climbing a tariff wall to start an industry that would not be viable without protection. Domestic firms may be plowing profits back into low-yielding projects because they lack an opportunity to invest the money in other, highly profitable, enterprises in the absence of an efficient banking system or capital market. In all these instances, self-investment is inefficient investment.

To the extent that savings are not self-invested but have to be assembled from individual household or business savers and channeled towards economically deserving investment projects, the question of an efficient allocation mechanism presents itself even more explicitly.

In theory, we could think of two, totally opposite, mechanisms to bring together a country's savings and direct them toward the best investments. One would be a highly centralised government operation. All private savings would be garnered through, say, postal savings banks and the social security system, and business profits would be creamed off by high tax rates. Foreign savings too would flow into the central government. All investment projects would be submitted to the government and the government would decide, on the basis of cost-benefit analysis, and without political influence or preference for government corporations as against private businesses, where the available investment funds would flow.

The second system would be a fully decentralised market system. The system would consist of multiple banks, both general and specialised, security markets, investment bankers, etc., all of which would compete for the available funds through interest rates, dividends, etc. This market would establish a general cost of capital, with premia for each enterprise set on the basis of the market's best judgment of relative risk. Since no lender would want to make losses, projects that could not pay the market cost of capital would be screened out of the market. Self-investment projects that promised less than the prevailing market yield would not be undertaken, since the saver would have the alternative opportunity of earning the market yield by using any one of the available channels for intermediation.

Of these two theoretical models, there is no evidence that the first one operates anywhere, even as a remote form of approximation, as an efficient mechanism for the selection of investment projects. The centrally-planned economies may succeed in centralising a very large proportion of all savings;

but, if nothing else, their lack of proper costing of capital goods and of recognition for the proper function of the interest rate would prevent them from using these savings in an efficient manner. By contrast, the second model functions, in an approximate manner, in the advanced industrial countries, thanks to many types of banks, capital markets, and other intermediary instruments. Financial deregulation in recent years has moved the system closer to the model. The availability of a great deal of information on individual firms makes it possible for savers and those to whom savers have entrusted their savings to come to reasonable judgments as to the risk-adjusted yield of alternative assets. These judgments are inevitably subject to some degree of error; even very good markets do not avoid mistakes. But these mistakes, which can be corrected over time, are probably not the most important flaw in the system of allocation. Systematic weaknesses in the system are, rather, related to various aspects of the taxation system, such as its almost universal discrimination in favour of debt financing over equity financing.

Whatever the shortcomings of the system of financial intermediation in the industrial countries, it is clear that the same intermediation function is performed with far less efficiency in the great majority of developing countries. Fragmented capital markets — often linked to equally fragmented labour and goods markets — are one frequent cause of this inefficiency (McKinnon 1973, p. 8). In many developing countries that fragmentation is geographic, based historically on poor communications systems between regional and cultural groups. In others, it is vertical, as various unofficial markets of money lenders exist in parallel with a more formal official market structure. In many countries, both forms of fragmentation exist. As a result, the national pool of capital is broken into smaller markets too insular to clear regional surpluses and channel them efficiently to areas of capital shortage — much less link them into world markets.

U Tun Wai found that, in the early 1950s, the interest rates charged by money lenders in different regions of Sri Lanka varied from 10 to 36 per cent, and in Thailand from 18 to 44 per cent. Pani reported a similar range among 75 districts in India (Wai 1957, pp. 99-100; Pani 1966, pp. 201-202). These figures are indicative of a wide regional dispersion of marginal rates of return in these two countries. Businesses in developing countries depend on self-finance to a much greater extent than in the industrial countries; security issues by non-financial sectors as per cent of GNP in developing countries were one-half or less of those in developed countries (Goldsmith 1969, p. 120). Finally, the banking system plays a much more modest role as an intermediary of saving, as is evident from low monetisation ratios (M2/GNP). McKinnon found this ratio to lie in the range of 20 to 30 per cent in eleven semi-industrial countries in the late 1960s as against 60 to 70 per cent in most industrial countries (and close to 100 per cent in Japan, whose tradition of a highly monetised economy goes back to before World War I) (McKinnon 1973, pp. 92-95; Goldsmith 1983, p. 68).

Table 3.1.   INFLATION AS A DETERMINANT OF FINANCIAL INTERMEDIATION

		Average annual inflation rate 1980-85 %	M2/GDP 1985 %
A.	Four very high-inflation countries		
	Argentina	342	13
	Brazil	148	10
	Peru	99	16
	Turkey	37	24
B.	Four high-inflation countries		
	Colombia	22	20
	Chile	19	19
	Philippines	19	19
	Sri Lanka	15	36
C.	Three low-inflation countries		
	Venezuela	9	47
	Pakistan	8	38
	India	8	44
D.	Seven very low-inflation countries[a]		
	China	2	47
	Burma	2	32
	Ethiopia	3	38
	Thailand	3	59
	Malaysia	3	66
	Singapore	3	88
	Jordan	4	115

a)   All developing countries in WDR (1987) Table 25 with average annual inflation rates, 1980-85, below 5 per cent; Singapore figures in column (2) refer to 1984.

Note: The figures in the last column are not fully comparable with McKinnon's (1973) in that the M2 figures in this table are the averages for end-1984 and end-1985 (McKinnon used end-of-year data), while the divisor is GDP rather than GNP. There also appear to be breaks in the series for Chile and Pakistan. Comparable data on M2/GDP are also found in WDR 1987, Table 25; however, for a few countries, the ratios are higher than those calculated from IFS, as quasi-monetary liabilities of non-monetary financial institutions are included.

Sources: Inflation rate: World Bank WDR 1987, Table 25. M2/GDP: Calculated from IFS.

But the fragmentation of the capital market in developing countries is by no means entirely a natural phenomenon that only time, improved communications, and growth itself will cure. The low ratios of M2 to GNP cited above did not necessarily improve over time, nor were they universal. In both Argentina and Brazil, these ratios had been more than 50 per cent in 1950 before the onset of inflationary policies (McKinnon 1973, pp. 103-104).

The limited — or, indeed, the shrinking — role of the banking system in intermediation between savers and investors in many developing countries is due to two causes for which the responsibility clearly rests with governments: inflation and the imposition of artificially low interest rates (a subject discussed in the next section). Often both causes act side by side.

Inflation — a persistent rise in the price of commodities — makes holding financial assets unattractive, because such assets have typically negative real rates of interest at high levels of inflation. The normal development is therefore for the real money supply to decline in countries that experience high rates of inflation.

Recent data for the countries selected by McKinnon are shown in Sections A, B and C of Table 3.1. The countries in Section D have been added to complete the picture. The table brings out rather clearly the dominant role of inflation as a cause of a low degree of financial intermediation. At the same time, the role of per capita income is much less pronounced, with India and China, among others, showing relatively high intermediation ratios.

The very high-inflation countries still show very low ratios of money to GDP in 1985, as they did twenty years ago. In the countries with high inflation rates, the M2/GDP ratios are a little higher, but it is only in the countries with low rates of inflation, even if their income levels are low, that the degree of monetisation begins to approach that of the industrial countries. In the great majority of the latter, these ratios have changed little over the last twenty years. In some of the countries shown in Section D, those with inflation below 5 per cent, monetisation rates even exceeded those in all industrial countries except Switzerland (about 125 per cent).

3.3   The Effect of Below-equilibrium Interest Rates

Whether they had moderate, high, or explosive rates of inflation, developing countries have with few exceptions exercised controls on interest rates that banks were allowed to pay depositors and charge to borrowers, thus keeping these rates artificially low and indeed often below inflation rates. Governments have advanced a wide range of arguments in favour of their low interest rate policies, stretching from the religious to the protection of the poor (Benoit 1985, pp. 54-59; Adams 1984, pp. 65-77). Probably the most plausible economic reason given for such policies was — and continues to be — that low interest rates promote investment and thus the adoption of new technology. It is surprising that so obvious a fallacy could prove so persistent. True, at lower interest rates more investment projects meet the test of economic feasibility. But the total amount of investment demand that can be met is in any event constrained by the supply of domestic plus foreign savings. That total supply is certainly not increased by bringing interest rates down. On the contrary, though there may be some doubt on the effect of the level of interest rates on domestic saving (cf. Chapter 4), there can be absolutely no question that lower interest rates reduce the *total* supply of savings, and must therefore reduce investment. But their effect is worse than that. By making room in the queue for savings for projects that would automatically be disqualified on the basis of an equilibrium interest rate, controls on interest rates cause the use of part of the available scarce savings for the execution of sub-optimal investment projects — and the concomitant exclusion of a larger amount of more deserving projects. (A *larger*, not an *equal*, amount, because the reduction in interest rates also reduces the total supply of saving.)

The argument that cheap credit to small farmers — or to small-scale industry — improves the distribution of income and wealth by providing these classes with low-cost capital also sounds attractive — and has proven to be equally illusory in practice. A policy of forcing financial institutions to charge the lowest rates on loans to the least creditworthy borrowers tends to curtail the amount available to these borrowers as bankers give preference to large, which typically means rich, borrowers (Gonzalez-Vega 1984, pp. 78-93). This tendency has been described as "the iron law of interest rate restrictions": as government-regulated interest rate ceilings become more restrictive, the share of credit granted to large borrowers increases (World Bank WDR 1987, p. 118, Box 7.3).

The most powerful reasons for many governments to keep interest rates artificially low may well be political in nature — which may also imply that these interest rate policies may not easily be dislodged. Two aspects deserve mention in particular. First, "subsidised credit programmes...keep...governments in power through political patronage and in maintaining, and even enhancing, the position of rural elites" (Blair 1984, p. 187). Second, all governments are concerned with their ability to borrow, and the cost of borrowing. If the rate of interest on bank deposits is kept low, investors lack an attractive alternative to investing in government paper, so that interest rate control reduces the cost of the domestic debt service. Control over interest rates will then, of course, require exchange control as a companion measure in order to put more attractive interest rates abroad beyond the reach of domestic savers.

The extent to which interest rates that savers in developing countries can earn were kept below equilibrium levels in the 1970s is shown in a tabulation by Agarwala (1983, p. 23; as noted below, real interest rates during the 1970s were lower than in the 1960s or most of the 1980s). Of the 31 countries for which interest rates are presented for the period 1970-80, only two had positive real rates: Ethiopia, by about 2 per cent for the one-year time deposit rate and Thailand, by 0.5 per cent, for its central bank discount rate. The other 29 countries had negative real figures for one or both of these two rates, ranging from minus a fraction of 1 per cent to below -30 per cent in Argentina and Chile.

It should be stressed that the distortion of investment caused by uneconomically low interest rates paid by the banks is not limited to the amount of investment that the banks intermediate. It also applies to the savings that the banks do not receive, either because would-be savers are turned off by the low yields and consume rather than save, or because savers decide to invest in their own households or enterprises. Faced with highly negative real interest rates in the banks or on government paper, and in the absence of attractive other financial forms of investment, savers may opt to put their money into any available inflation hedge. The social and private yield of such investments may be zero or negative, but the saver might still select them as long as the yields were less negative than those available on monetary assets.

On the other hand, to the extent that artificially low interest rates in the banking system encourage intermediation through informal circuits, such as a curb market, saving will be encouraged and — to the extent that the curb market is efficient — the allocation of investment will be improved. Where there is a reasonably efficient curb market, raising bank interest rates to bring a larger proportion of the intermediation function into the banking circuit will then be less important in raising saving or enhancing its allocation[1].

Whenever interest rates paid by the banks are controlled, the maximum rates that the banks are allowed to charge are also set by the government. Unfortunately, statistics about bank lending rates are not generally available before the late 1970s. For ten developing countries, however, detailed rates are available for the period 1970-82, in a recent World Bank publication (Hanson and Neal 1986, p. 7). The rates were somewhat higher than deposit rates in banks in each country to cover the cost of intermediation. But in six of the ten countries, real lending rates were still negative, in three they were low-positive (between 2 and 3 per cent) and only in Uruguay did the real lending rate (for the shorter period 1976-82) work out at 14.7 per cent. In this sample of lending rates, therefore, the banks in all countries but one were lending to their non-preferred customers at rates that fell short — somewhat or a great deal — of the equilibrium interest rate in the country; their preferential lending rates for exports, agriculture, etc., depending on the country, were even lower.

At lending rates so low in real terms, it is obvious that the demand for credit far exceeds the available supply, and that the banks have to ration credit. A specified part of the credit often has to go to preferential borrowers at especially low rates; for the remainder, the banks are free in their choice of customers. The obvious interest of the banks is to lend "to completely safe borrowers whose reputation is known or whose collateral is relatively riskless" (McKinnon 1973, p. 73), or to borrowers with which the bank has special connections. There is no mechanism to ensure that this process will channel savings to the economically most deserving projects. Indeed, if the banks regularly concentrate their lending on a few chosen customers and lend to them all the credit that they can justify, the marginal productivity of the projects of these borrowers may be almost as low as the interest rate charged by the banks. In terms of Figure 3.2, the banks would be concentrating their loans towards the right hand corner of [triangle sign] AOB.

Thus, in the typical developing country, the selection process for investment projects is likely to produce results that are far removed from the optimal result. That optimum would be the selection of all projects from O to D, in Figure 3.2, leaving all those beyond D for possible execution in the future, when the supply of savings may be more generous or the competition from very good projects less intense. If the available savings "a" are used this way, the addition to GNP will be ODCA. If we name "c" the distance AE and "d" the distance EO, we can write:

(1) $ODCA = a(d + \tfrac{1}{2} c)$

The results, as said, will certainly be smaller than this. This leads to the calculation of two alternatives — one more or less intermediate and one approaching a worst case result. Under the first of these alternatives, the available supply of saving would be rationed among the projects from O to B on a random basis, without any guiding principle other than, perhaps, "first come first served". We would represent this in our graphic approach by the assumption that from each successive group of projects from O to B, a proportion a/b would be financed. The addition to GNP of that approach would be $\frac{a}{b} \times$ OAB, or

(2) $\qquad \frac{1}{2} \cdot \frac{a(d+c)b}{b} = \frac{a(d+c)}{2}$

Disregarding for the moment the possibility that some projects beyond B would be financed, the worst possible outcome would be the selection of the lowest-yielding projects moving from B to the left. These would be those between F and B (FB having been measured to equal OD=a). Their contribution to GNP would amount to only GFB, or

(3) $\qquad \frac{1}{2}$ ac

How do the alternative methods of allocation compare with optimal allocation? To answer this question, we derive the yield of (2) and (3) as a proportion of the optimal yield, by dividing them by (1). In the process of simplification we use (from similar triangles):

(4) $\qquad \dfrac{c}{d} = \dfrac{a}{b-a}$

In this way we find, by simple transformation,

(5) $\qquad \dfrac{(2)}{(1)} = \dfrac{\frac{1}{2}(d+c)}{d+\frac{1}{2}c} = \dfrac{1}{2-a/b}$

(6) $\qquad \dfrac{(3)}{(1)} = \dfrac{\frac{1}{2}c}{d+\frac{1}{2}c} = \dfrac{a/b}{2-a/b}$

It will be noted from (5) and (6) that the yield ratios depend on a/b only.

Table 3.2. PROPORTIONATE YIELD OF CAPITAL AS A FUNCTION OF THE
RATIO OF AVAILABLE TO USABLE SAVING (a/b)

a/b	=	.25	.50	.75
(2)/(1)		.57	.67	.80
(3)/(1)		.14	.33	.60

Table 3.2 applies formulae (5) and (6), i.e. it provides numbers on the proportionate yield of capital, for a number of hypothetical values for the ratio a/b, which stands for the ratio of savings available for domestic investment to the total amount of savings that could be used for this purpose with non-negative marginal productivity. Dividing both of these quantities by GDP, the ratio a/b can be seen as the ratio between investment/GDP and (maximum economic investment)/GDP. The former ratio is a known figure. There is no statistical basis to estimate the latter ratio, but one can have an approximate notion of it. It should lie some distance beyond the highest investment ratios on record, which are in the order of .4; yet it cannot be very much higher without leading to an unreasonably large sacrifice of current consumption. Hence a figure of b (expressed as a ratio to GDP) in the order of .5 might not be an unreasonable choice. This would mean that in countries with a rather high investment ratio of .25, financing would be available for one-half of the potential investment projects that had a positive yield; for such countries, a/b would be in the order of .5 (as indicated in the middle column of Table 3.2). The country would get the full value of its saving/investment if it managed the extreme feat of channeling these savings to projects strictly "from the top down", not allowing any investment to take place if it crowded out another one that had a higher marginal productivity. If the selection of projects in that country amounted in practice to a random choice, yield in terms of additional output would be two-thirds of the optimum, and selection "from the bottom up" (but still excluding projects with negative yields), would produce a proportionate yield of one-third, or a waste of two-thirds, of the available capital. Transposing these ratios in terms of alternative savings rates, the same 25 per cent of GNP would under random choice produce an increase in GNP equivalent to what could have been achieved with one-third less saving optimally allocated, i.e. at a savings rate of 16.7 per cent. And the very poor selection system (3) would place this country in the same growth class as one that saved only 8.3 per cent but used it to best advantage by economically efficient allocation.

The figures would be somewhat less startling, but still quite significant, if a/b were as high as .75 and even more upsetting if a/b for some countries were as low as .25. In other words, if the potential for economic investment, as measured by b, does not vary widely among countries, the risk of wasting what savings are available (as measured by a) would become the greater, the lower the value of a.

It should further be recalled that these numbers make no allowance for four other avenues of sub-optimal use of a country's savings potential:

i)   Savings not made because the reward provided the saver is too low, which could be due to the fact that the allocation mechanism failed to bring about a profitable matching between saving and investment.

ii) Savings made, but invested abroad for reasons of yield, safety, etc.

iii) Investment in projects with negative yields.

iv) Investment in projects with a positive yield, but one that is sub-optimal because of a poor choice of technology. This choice itself may be attributable to the selection mechanism: an unduly low interest rate may have encouraged an excessively capital-intensive technique of production.

The range of the figures derived in Table 3.2, from .80 to .14, is of a similar order of magnitude as that of incremental capital/output ratios, which have been recorded as low as 2 and as high as 8, with some observations falling even outside this range. The causes underlying a low yield from the available supply of saving and a high (average or marginal) capital/output ratio are to a large extent overlapping. Both measures record the effects of distorted investment due to fragmentation of the market for capital. Neither captures the loss due to potential savings not made, or not invested at home. But our yield figure is relative (to the optimum possible on the basis of given technology), while capital/output ratios are absolute and thus reflect also inefficiencies that are not attributable to investment distortion. Thus, if all capital in country A is used in two shifts, and in country B in one shift, A's capital/output ratio will be half as high as B's. But if the degree of capital market fragmentation in A and B is the same, i.e. if the distortion in the allocation of savings is the same, the coefficients of proportionate yield found in Table 3.2 will also be the same for both countries.

3.4 Empirical Evidence on the Relation Between Real Interest Rates and Growth

There is no way in which we can measure directly the extent of the fragmentation of capital markets, but we do have an indicator of that fragmentation, which is at the same time one of the causes of it: the level of interest rates. The greater the distance between an equilibrium market-clearing rate and the actual level at which controlled interest rates are set, the stronger the forces toward a distorted capital market. If a distorted capital market is an important factor making for slow growth — because less is saved, because the net inflow of savings is discouraged, and because available savings are poorly matched up with investment opportunities — then low real interest rates should be statistically associated with low growth rates. A full answer to this question would require specifying a growth model and measuring the impact of interest rate policies as one of many contributors to development. Given the difficulty of this task, simple cross-section comparisons of interest rates and growth are instructive as first evidence of the relationship.

A number of studies have followed this approach. Agarwala (1983) shows a negative correlation between a measure of interest rate distortions and growth. A group of developing countries with strongly negative *ex-post* real interest rates were found to average 4 per cent GDP growth in the 1970s, while countries with less distorted interest rate policies averaged GDP growth of 6.1 per cent. The *1987 World Development Report* (World Bank 1987 p. 118) presents data showing that countries with severely negative real interest rates achieved lower rates of growth over the 1971-85 period than countries with less distorted real interest rates. No mention is made of the statistical significance of the findings in these two studies. Lanyi and Saracoglu (1985) provide some evidence that positive real interest rates are related to relatively higher rates of growth. In a sample of 21 countries, an indicator of the degree of interest rate distortion is significantly related to output growth ($R^2 = .41$). Khatkhate (1986), on the other hand, finds no statistically significant relationship between real interest rates and GDP growth.

Given the inconclusiveness of these findings, it appeared useful to attempt a further and more systematic cross-sectional comparison of real interest rates and GDP growth. The study, the results of which are here reported, was done by William Shaw in the World Bank. It is based on a relatively lengthy time series (about twenty years) of real interest rates, developed in the World Bank, which for most countries goes back to the middle 1960s. The inclusion of data from the 1960s yields somewhat more countries with positive real interest rates than in earlier studies. Also, the four studies cited earlier used the average of annual figures for real interest rates; this measure may give too much weight to isolated instances of high inflation. In this study, therefore, rather than the average, the median real interest rate for each country is used. The real interest rate in any one year is defined as one plus the annual nominal interest rate (in almost all cases, the rate paid by banks on six months or twelve months deposits) divided by one plus the rate of increase of consumer prices in the same year. The actual rate of inflation is thus used as a proxy for the expected rate of inflation.

Table 3.3 divides the sample of 40 countries into three groups, ranked by the level of real interest rates:

Table 3.3.   REAL INTEREST RATES AND GDP GROWTH RATES, 1965-84

Per cent

Real interest rate

Group	n	Range of group[a]	Median of group	Average annual GDP growth rate
I.	10	Less than −5	−8.2	3.0
II.	17	Between −5 and 0	−2.6	4.0
III.	13	Greater than 0	2.1	6.1

a) Countries included in each group according to their median real interest rate over the period. Number of countries in each group: n.

The difference in average growth rates between the first and second group is significant at the 10 per cent level, and the difference between the second and third group is significant at the 1 per cent level. Further evidence is provided by an ordinary least squares regression between growth (y) and real interest rate (RRI), which indicates that, among the countries in the sample and for the period studied, a 10 per cent higher real interest rate was associated with a 2.7 per cent higher growth rate[2].

$$y = 5.21 + .27 \text{ RRI}$$
$$(.34) \quad (.06) \qquad \bar{R}^2 = .32 \qquad\qquad (1)$$

(The numbers in parentheses are the standard errors of the coefficients.)

One qualification to these results, and to those reported on below, is in order. The level of real interest rates is highly correlated with other financial sector policies, in the sense that countries with positive real interest rates tend to have less distorted financial systems in general. Thus, the statistical results may reflect the impact on growth of a series of financial sector policies rather than of interest rate policy alone.

Since inflation rates are likely to vary more than nominal interest rates across countries, one might wonder whether the relationship shown merely reflects the negative impact of high rates of inflation on GDP growth. A statistical test sub-dividing the sample further between high and low inflation countries (above and below 10 per cent) confirmed the findings within each of these two groups but found no significant differences in growth rates between the two groups.

It seemed desirable to test these findings further by introducing into the correlation two additional variables, both of which could be expected to contribute in an important way to the explanation of the difference in growth rates among developing countries[3]. The first of these is essentially a supply factor, namely the ratio of investment to GDP (INV). This ratio provides an indication of the magnitude of additions to the stock of fixed capital compared to current output. Unlike the ratio of domestic savings to GDP, it incorporates the results of savings drawn from abroad as well as those saved in the country[4]. The second variable reflects predominantly, but not exclusively, demand factors, namely the growth rate of the purchasing power of rate of exports (X), measured as the growth rate of the value of exports deflated by country-specific import price indices calculated by the World Bank[5]. This variable is indicative of the demand pressure exercised on growth through the channel of export income and changes in the terms of trade. It also measures the ability of the country to shake off the resource constraint on imports that may hold back the rate of activity and may further retard growth by distortions on the import side. Each of these two variables should be expected to reduce somewhat the coefficient for the real interest rate, because its effects via a more generous supply of saving will now be caught by INV, and its effects via a better availability of imports, by X.

The following tabulation, from which the constant terms have been omitted, compares the results of including alternatively INV and X, and then both, with RRI as variables explaining cross-country differences in growth rates. The period is approximately 1965-85; the same 40 countries are included and figures in brackets are standard errors.

Table 3.4.   EXPLANATION OF DIFFERENCES IN NATIONAL GROWTH RATES

Explanatory variable

Equation	RRI	INV	X	$\bar{R}^2$
(1)	.27 (.06)	—	—	.32
(2)	.23 (.06)	.092 (.045)	—	.37
(3)	.19 (.06)	—	.19 (.05)	.49
(4)	.18 (.06)	.044 (.043)	.17 (.05)	.49

The new calculations confirm the robustness of the earlier finding on the effect of interest rates on growth. The coefficients for RRI are somewhat reduced, as was to be expected; but the higher figure of equation (1) would still stand as the measure of the full impact of interest rates (representing at the same time other dimensions of the efficiency of the use of savings) on growth, acting through a variety of channels.

The tabulation also shows that the export factor makes a far larger, more certain, and more significant contribution to the explanation of growth than the investment ratio. Indeed, once X is used [equation (3)], there is no further improvement in $\bar{R}$ from the addition of INV, and the coefficient of the latter in equation (4) is only barely significant. (It should be acknowledged, however, that since the effect on growth of investment runs in part through exports, the coefficient for INV in equation (4), like that for RRI, understates the full effect of higher investment on growth.)

The uncertainty of the coefficient for INV makes it difficult to use this coefficient for a direct comparison between the impact on growth of alternative investment ratios as against that of alternative interest rate policies. So it is perhaps better, or in any event less likely to lead to overestimation of the relative importance of interest rates, to compare the relatively robust coefficient for RRI with an average of other available estimates for the capital coefficient assembled by Khan and Knight (1985, p. 4). They conclude, on the basis of the findings of five earlier papers, that a 1 per cent increase in the ratio of investment to income might, other things being equal, raise the overall growth rate by about 0.2 percentage points (or about twice as much as implied by the higher of the two coefficients for INV in Table 3.4). Taking the coefficient for RRI as also being in the order of 0.2, this would imply a one-for-one rate of substitution between the interest rate and the investment ratio. Thus, for example, it would take a 5 per cent rise in the investment ratio — say from 20 to 25 per cent — to offset the negative effects of setting the real interest rate 5 percentage points too low — say at zero instead of +5 per cent per annum. These numbers would confirm the impression created by the figures presented above that a correct interest rate policy can be of major importance to a country's growth rate.

3.5 Implications for Interest Rate Policy

It is clear from the preceding analysis that the cost to a country of distorted capital markets can be very high. The — admittedly very tentative — figures derived in the preceding section suggest that for many a developing country that cost, measured in terms of that part of the investment ratio necessary to compensate for it, might well be of the same order of magnitude as the amount of foreign capital that the country receives from abroad in the form of loans, grants and direct investment. These findings call for a maximum effort in developing countries to rationalise their capital markets.

In part, efforts to reduce fragmentation of capital markets will have to address deep-seated problems in the economy. Regional fragmentation, of which a few instances were cited earlier, can only be overcome by the expansion of national credit mechanisms, either governmental or by country-wide branch banking, so that they can channel surplus savings in some regions to others with large demands for credit. Where a large part of total credit is handled in the informal sector, e.g. by moneylenders, the evening out of interest rates across regions would also require, if not the replacement of the moneylenders by branches of nationwide banking network, at least — and probably more efficiently — the linkage of the moneylenders to such a network.

Interesting experiments are being carried out in a number of developing countries to improve the efficiency of their financial systems as a whole by linking the formal and informal financial sectors. Under this approach, financial institutions in the formal sector use informal lenders, such as traders or village heads, to channel credit to, for example, small farmers to which these institutions have no direct access. The supply of funds passed on to the final borrowers may be subject to conditions, e.g. as to interest rates, with a view to reducing regional differences in the cost of credit (Germidis and Meghir, forthcoming).

Two specific schemes that are operated in the Philippines may be mentioned. Under one, traders and millers have access to the banking system on the basis of grain stocks in warehouses, with a government guarantee for 80 per cent of the value of these stocks. They then extend production credit to grain farmers with a provision that the borrowers sell a portion of their harvests to specified warehouse operators. Through this mechanism, small farmers who have little collateral to offer are given access to government-guaranteed funds at relatively low rates. The scheme operates without subsidies and has expanded rapidly, largely on account of a 99 per cent repayment record. Under the other scheme, processors of agricultural commodities may borrow at a government-subsidised 6 per cent annual interest rate on condition that they extend production loans to farmers at 15 per cent per annum. The processors are responsible for the repayment of the loans. This scheme has achieved a respectable 92 per cent recovery rate as the credit middlemen select farmer-borrowers whose creditworthiness they are able to appraise (Yotopoulos and Floro 1988).

Improvements in matching the supply of savings with the demand for investment across regions is only one aspect of the general objective of overcoming the fragmentation of capital markets. In the industrial countries, where the integration of national capital markets has progressed very far, this objective has been achieved in a variety of ways. In some countries the solution has been found by the emergence of a wide variety of financial intermediaries, each specialising in meeting the demands of particular segments of the market for credit, and all related among themselves through linkages with the central credit mechanism of the commercial banks. In other countries the commercial banks themselves perform a very large part of credit intermediation, leaving less room (or need) for specialised financial intermediary institutions. Even in those countries, of which Germany is a typical example, the intermediating roles of stock exchanges, mutual savings banks and insurance companies are of paramount importance.

It should be understood, of course, that issues of financial policy in developing countries extend well beyond the level of interest rates. Some other important issues that deserve mention here although they cannot be pursued within the framework of the present study include the proper relative role of corporate equity and long-term debt, as against undue reliance on short-term credit; the benefits and drawbacks of government programmes that channel credit preferentially to "high-priority" borrowers, such as agriculture, exports, or small-scale industry and guidelines for the conduct of central bank monetary policy (Long 1983, p. 2).

Insofar as the creation of a single national market for credit, carefully differentiated according to the needs of different classes of savers and investors, requires processes of education and institution-building, it is obviously a demanding and time-consuming task. That task should be pursued with force, but may take decades to bear its full fruits.

But another cause of the distortion of the capital markets in many developing countries can be cured much more promptly. That is the imposition on existing institutions such as commercial banks or savings banks of ceilings on interest to be paid to depositors or charged to borrowers — or large classes of borrowers — that lie far below what would be an equilibrium rate in the market. These disequilibrium rates divert the savings flow from the banks, the very institutions that are among the most efficient intermediaries in the industrial world and which could play a similar role in the developing world. Those savings that still flow into the banks, because the savers' other options are limited, are allocated in a sub-optimal way, thus depriving the country of part of the growth dividend these savings could produce.

Here the policy change needed is simple and it can be implemented without delay: bring interest rates charged to borrowers to a level that is roughly in line with a market equilibrium rate, and rates paid to depositors to a level compatible with the lending rate *minus* the operating cost of the bank *minus* a prudent provision for loan losses. The attainment of approximate equilibrium lending and deposit rates may be achieved by means of a complete decontrol of interest rates if there is a sufficient degree of competition among the banks *and* bank supervision is sufficiently effective to prevent banks from offering deposit rates they cannot, in fact, afford to pay. If these conditions are not fulfilled, it may be better to continue interest rate regulation but to make sure that the prescribed rates are justified in economic terms[6].

Note that the objective should be to move interest rates to a reasonable approximation of the equilibrium level, not just to a less negative real level. To clarify this point, I return to the method of exposition used in the figures introduced earlier in this chapter. The top part of Figure 3.3 reproduces Figure 3.2, under the simplifying assumption that $a = \frac{1}{2}b$. The equilibrium real interest rate is measured by DC, and the maximum benefit from the available saving is the quadrangle AOBC, which equals $1\frac{1}{2}$ ac. The worst result, at a zero real rate of interest, would be the triangle CDB, equal to $\frac{1}{2}$ ac, one-third of the maximum. This agrees with the result found on page 63. To make the transition from real to nominal interest rates, the inflation rate is shown on the vertical axis from O down (OO'). Again for reasons of simplicity, it is assumed that OO'=OA, i.e. that the inflation rate is as high as the marginal productivity of the "first project". Since $a/b = \frac{1}{2}$, this would also imply that the inflation rate is twice the equilibrium interest rate CD. There is no suggestion that these assumptions are more plausible than any other ones that could be made; they have been chosen for the mere purpose of facilitating a graphic presentation of the cost of negative real interest rates.

Banks, of course, do not charge real interest rates; they charge nominal

Figure 3.3. MARGINAL PRODUCTIVITY OF CAPITAL, INTEREST RATE,
INFLATION RATE, AND INVESTMENT

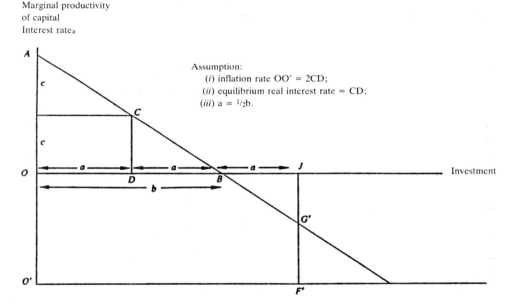

a   Real from O, nominal from O'.

interest rates that borrowers may find more or less attractive in the light of many relevant considerations, including their expectation of the rate of inflation. Assume that the banks, under government regulation, charge a nominal interest rate of G'F', which would equal the real equilibrium interest rate CD if there were no inflation, and that (duly operating under a money illusion) they accept all projects offered to them that can pay that nominal interest, proceeding from F' to the left. They will then use the resources available to them to finance projects from J to B, all of which will have a negative marginal productivity, lying to the right of B. All the capital will be wasted, producing an aggregate negative yield of BJG', or $-\frac{1}{2}$ ac.

If we return to the intermediate method of credit allocation discussed above, we would assume that the banks rationed the resources available over all projects that could pay the going nominal interest rate (by picking every third project moving from O to J). The yield to the economy of that investment portfolio would be:

$$\tfrac{1}{3} (\text{AOB} - \text{BJG'}) = \tfrac{1}{3} (2\text{ac} - \tfrac{1}{2}\text{ac}) = \tfrac{1}{2}\text{ac}$$

In other words, the net result of this intermediate method of selection based on a not-wildly negative real interest rate[7] would be as bad as the worst method applied at a zero real interest rate, shown in equation (3).

The calculations presented here and earlier in this chapter are, it should be repeated, purely illustrative exercises. The numbers that result from them cannot be pinned on particular countries and periods. There is, nevertheless every reason to take the general message that these numbers convey extremely seriously. It is perfectly possible that banking systems whose interest rates are kept at negative real levels waste all or a large part of the savings confided to them and that banking systems that charge interest rates that range from slightly negative to slightly positive in real terms waste a large part of these savings. In this connection it is not much of a consolation to observe that (as we have seen) banks that pay negative real interest rates to their depositors will not be able to attract large savings as a per cent of GDP: it is highly likely that the amount not captured by the banks — to the extent that these amounts are actually saved *and* kept at home — are similarly applied to sub-optimal investments.

These considerations, set against the still wide prevalence of negative real interest rates in developing countries, suggest that there is no reason at all to disparage "the narrow concern for raising real interest rates to positive levels, so often voiced in development policy dialogues" and to replace it by "broader concerns for improvements in the financial system as a whole and for greater consistency between financial and macroeconomic policies" (Hanson and Neal 1986, page v). The first argument put forward by the authors to justify the change in emphasis they recommend is that: "unless real rates are considerably out of line, i.e., highly negative and well below those prevailing in international capital markets, the scope for, and thus the impact of, raising real rates would be fairly limited". Reference to the immediately preceding numerical exercises should, on the contrary, make it clear that the call for positive real interest rates is too *weak* a recommendation. Rates that are positive but significantly below equilibrium levels will also lead to the important losses because they lead to the uneconomic allocation of resources[8].

Countries that are short of capital should make every effort to minimise this waste of capital, which is to an important extent attributable to the pursuit of a mistaken policy. International organisations that supply additional resources should also take a clear stand on this policy issue. There is a good deal of evidence that in the past neither the World Bank nor the Fund has pursued this issue with the emphasis it deserves.

In 1976 it was observed in the Bank (Long 1983, p. 28) that "Bank economists tend to write of the need for higher interest rates without being specific about the precise levels which are being proposed. As a result, governments tend to regard this advice as part of the Bank's general philosophy rather than as a practical response to real weaknesses in their economic policy framework".

After reviewing a large number of the Bank's financial sector reports in 1983, Millard Long observed that the Bank had attempted to be more specific in recommending rate increases but expressed uncertainty whether this had led to greater success in changing countries' practices. He summed up his findings on the Bank's position on interest rate policy as follows:

> The stated approach of the Bank is that deposit rates should be positive in real terms and that lending rates should approach the opportunity cost of capital. There are considerable differences, however, between the stated policy and its implementation. In practice, in the past the recommended increases in interest rates have been kept to "reasonable" levels by focusing attention on the lending rather than the deposit rate, by underestimating the expected future rate of inflation, and by setting a level for the onlending rate that is higher than the rate of inflation but not so high as the opportunity cost of capital. In addition, in many DFC and most agro-credit projects the beneficiaries were not required to carry the foreign exchange risk.

A similar divergence between theory and practice can be observed in the Fund. Like the Bank, the Fund strongly favours countries having positive real interest rates and this has become an objective of many Fund-supported adjustment programmes in recent years. The point was emphasized in the Fund's *1984 Annual Report* (p. 32), which stated that "artificially low interest rates, particularly when they are negative in real terms, reduce savings incentives and give rise to capital flight, thus limiting domestic investment".

Until 1984, however, interest rate policy had received little attention as part of the Fund's conditionality. Of the 18 countries that concluded standby arrangements with the Fund in 1979 or 1980, none had positive real interest rates in the two years following the start of the adjustment programme supported by the Fund. Taking all 18 countries together, real interest rates were if anything lower during that period than they had been in the two-year period before the programme. In the course of the 1980s, more countries became aware of the cost of negative real interest rates and positive real rates became more prevalent. But it is not clear that the Fund was, on balance, successful in raising rates for countries with which it had arrangements. Of the 36 countries that concluded arrangements with the Fund in 1983, half had positive real interest rates in 1982 and again half (partly the same, partly different ones) had such rates in 1984, with the median rate for all 36 countries in both years close to zero.

A further point to be stressed in this connection is that in countries suffering from the after-effects of the debt crisis, interest rates must be considerably higher than in the United States. With official dollar debt of these countries quoted well below par in secondary markets, internal interest rates in local currency must reflect not only the inflation differential (or the expected rate of depreciation of the local currency against the US dollar) but also the risk premium inherent in the discount registered in foreign markets for sovereign debt (Dooley 1987, pp. 6-9). Interest rates that do not reflect this risk premium will not suffice to pull in capital from abroad, nor to prevent local capital from fleeing abroad if it finds an opportunity to do so. The cessation (if not the reversal) of capital inflow that is characteristic of the debt crisis has sharply reduced the supply of capital in many debt-ridden countries. The natural consequence of such a development must be a rise in (real) interest rates as compared with rates abroad.

It is true, as Hanson and Neal (1986, page v) state, that in situations of high inflation, which are the only ones in which real interest rates can become severely negative, it is difficult to keep real interest rates positive unless one attacks the inflation problem itself. But experience in a number of countries, such as Brazil and Israel, shows that this problem can be handled by indexation. Indexation is not a satisfactory solution to the problem of inflation, but on the crucial aspect of ensuring high enough real interest rates it certainly provides a better answer than the policy followed in other countries of keeping nominal interest rates well below the rate of inflation for fear that high interest rates will fuel cost-inflation.

Against the clear political attractiveness to governments of low interest rate policies and the fallacious arguments marshalled in support of such policies, the case for market-related sufficiently positive real interest rates should be put forward squarely as being critically important for attaining high rates of economic growth. Only interest rates that meet that test will achieve the three broad objectives of financial sector policies put forward by Hanson and Neal (1986, pp. 34-35): "(1) to mobilise adequate amounts of resources, both domestically and internationally; (2) to allocate credit to its socially most productive use, and (3) to provide a stable financial environment, which will encourage development". Against this general background one can also agree with the suggestion that greater reliance should be placed on market forces to determine the multitude of interest rates in the light of maturity, risk and administrative costs. And one can acknowledge that in developing countries, too, there may occasionally be situations where negative real rates would clear the market (Hanson and Neal 1986, p. 35) in which cases the principle of positive real rates should cede to the principle of a market-related rate. It is suggested, however, that these are the exceptions that confirm the rule, and that very few of the cases of negative real rates one would encounter in the 1980s would qualify as such exceptions.

The experience of recent years indicates, on the contrary, two further classes of situations in which high — indeed extremely high — real interest rates occurred.

The first is in the immediate aftermath of stabilization from hyper-inflation. At that stage, the actual increase in prices may have been brought down to a very moderate rate of inflation through a combination of policies such as price freezes, fiscal measures and tight money, but inflationary expectations, which dominate interest rates, have not yet been turned around. In such situations the difference between expected and realised rates of price increases keeps *ex post* real interest rates high. This was the experience in Argentina and Israel in the first months of their 1985 stabilization plans — as it was the general experience in the stabilization plans in Europe in the 1920s. *Ex post* real interest rates of 3 or 4 per cent per month proved necessary for a number of months in both countries to prevent undue expansion of credit and protect their newly stabilized exchange rates. High real rates are detrimental to investment activity, and to economic activity in general, but they are, at least for a short period, an inevitable cost to a country that needs to shake off

77

hyper-inflation. That cost can only be minimised by making the design and the execution of the policy package as convincing as possible, with a view to bringing down as rapidly as possible the expectation of future inflation. Lowering the interest rate and raising the supply of money before the reversal of inflationary expectations has increased the real demand for money would be counterproductive and might prove disastrous if it reignited inflation.

The second situation producing extremely high interest rates, which may, but need not, coincide with the first, relates to deregulating the banking system without assuring proper financial supervision. In Chile in 1981 and 1982, real interest rates (in a period of low inflation) exceeded 3 per cent per month as banks granted and rolled over masses of bad loans. Similar symptoms of banking systems in disarray were encountered around that time in Argentina and Turkey. The remedy against those cases of high interest rates was the institution or re-institution of essential prudential supervision over the banking system, which, in Turkey at least, included regulation of interest rates (Corbo 1985; McKinnon 1986).

NOTES AND REFERENCES

1. This point was first made in Van Wijnbergen 1983. Van Wijnbergen also argues that any substitution of bank deposits for curb market deposits must reduce the capital available to business, because the former deposits are, and the latter are not, subject to reserve requirements. This is not a necessary effect, however. Unless the government has good reason to channel additional required reserves into government expenditure (which may be high-priority government investment), it can readily ensure the full pass-through of any additional deposits received by the banks through a lowering of reserve requirements against bank deposits.

2. Twice as high an effect of interest rates on growth was also reported in World Bank WDR 1987, p. 118, *viz.* that an increase of the real interest rate toward the equilibrium level by 10 per cent would raise the growth rate by a figure in the order of 5 per cent. This finding, by Maxwell Fry, for a group of developing countries in Asia does not strike me as having a solid foundation. The figure of about 5 per cent is an average of twelve country figures, eight of which are below 4 per cent and one, for Singapore, as high as 28 per cent (Fry 1981).

3. I want to acknowledge the help received from Daniel Oks of the World Bank staff in the preparation of this section.

4. Data problems stand in the way of adding variables for other factors of production. The attempt by Sherman Robinson (1971) to use population growth as a proxy for the labour supply was not very successful; inspection of the data suggested that the inclusion of this variable would in any event not contribute much to the correlation.

5. For earlier attempts to use export growth in the explanation of GNP growth, see Feder (1983) and literature therein cited.

6. On the disastrous experience of some Latin American countries that relied on a *laissez-faire* approach rather than prudential supervision to manage the banking system, see Diaz-Alejandro (1983). In Turkey, the attempt in 1980 to do away with financial repression by deregulating interest rates produced a major financial crisis two years later and induced the authorities to resume setting maximum interest rates while introducing more stringent and more effective banking regulation. The rates for deposits were intended to be positive in real terms, but tended to lag behind changes in the rate of inflation in periods of accelerating inflation. This problem was overcome as inflation was brought under better control (Kopits 1987, pp. 12 and 18 and chart on p. 21).

7. If the equilibrium real rate were 10 per cent (incidentally, the World Bank's and IDA's minimum yield for a project to be acceptable), the inflation rate implied in Chart 3 would be 20 per cent and the real rate corresponding to G'F' would be -10 per cent.

8. Calculations of real interest rates for recent periods tend to include strings of years in the 1970s when almost all interest rates, in the industrial as well as the developing countries, uncontrolled as well as controlled, were negative or barely positive. This may have contributed to a feeling that the issue was one of *de minimis*. Thus, in Hanson and Neal, the real US six months deposit rate for 1970-82, based on the inflation rate for six months after the date for which the nominal interest rate was taken, is quoted at -0.7 per cent, and the real prime lending rate at 1.9 per cent. But the negative real rates of the 1970s were an abnormality, just as much as the high positive real rates in the early 1980s were.

Chapter 4

DETERMINANTS OF THE DOMESTIC SAVINGS RATE

4.1 Savings and Investment Revisited

In a seminal paper, Feldstein and Horioka (1980) showed for the industrial countries that differences in the rate of investment to GNP over the period 1960-74 were predominantly explainable in terms of differences in savings rates. International capital movements, it appeared, did not perform the function of transferring savings from countries with low to those with higher productivity of capital on a scale sufficient to remove a strong correlation across countries between savings rates and investment rates. The origin of this correlation may be that savings have a strong tendency to stay in their country of origin, with investment, like charity, beginning at home; or that — in a reverse causation — good investment opportunities in a country encourage high levels of saving while a pessimistic business outlook discourages both investment and savings[1].

Later studies (Dooley *et al.* 1987, and literature cited therein) have confirmed that the high correlation between investment and savings rates was not a statistical fluke. It did not decrease in the period after 1974, in spite of the removal of capital controls and the rapid growth of international lending by commercial banks; and — which is of greatest interest in the context of this study — the correlation applies to developing countries as well as to OECD countries. The only clear exceptions are those developing countries that depend primarily on aid to finance current account balances: for the category of "official borrowers," the correlation between savings and investment ratios is much weaker since 1974 than for the "market borrowers," in spite of the obvious fact that the latter group of developing countries is more closely integrated in international capital markets than the former.

For the developing countries as a group, the association of investment and saving is so high that domestic savings financed about 90 per cent of their investment in the period from 1960 to 1983 (World Bank WDR 1985, p. 4). Only in the countries in which foreign aid played a large role in the provision of resources could countries achieve and maintain an investment rate far in excess of the saving rate. Thus the low-income countries in Africa have been able to afford a combined excess of investment over savings of some 10 per cent of GNP throughout the 1980s, after excesses of only about 3 per cent in 1965 and 1973 (World Bank WDR 1986, Table A7).

The authors of the 1987 study also provide a plausible explanation for the strong association between saving and investment ratios even among the industrial countries, where capital movements are not subject to important restrictions. The existing degree of mobility of capital will even out covered interest rates for *financial* claims in different currencies, and spending spurts, for example large government deficits, in one country that can be financed by such claims can thus absorb the savings of other countries without necessarily crowding out domestic investment or forcing up savings in the deficit country. But claims on physical capital arising from investment in the private sector are much less substitutable from one country to another. These are more nearly in the category of non-tradeable claims, for which the law of one interest rate does not operate — in much the same way as the law of one price does not operate for non-tradeable goods, as is evident from wide divergencies of exchange rates from purchasing power parity (Dooley *et al.* 1987, pp. 522-528).

Thus, high investment ratios can materialise only in countries that provide the necessary resources by high savings ratios and where investment opportunities are limited, as in some countries in a predevelopment stage, the tendency to save may be "frustrated," to use Hirschman's term (1958, p. 37) and any discretionary income may flow into consumption. In modern developing countries there is, however, an alternative to frustrated saving that may appear extremely attractive to the owners of capital in such countries: investment abroad. Whether seen from the perspective of asset diversification or capital flight, the export of savings can bring about a large excess of savings over investment. The most striking example of a persistent reverse flow of capital is Venezuela, which had an excess of savings over investment of 5 per cent of

GNP in 1980-85, after smaller but persistent excesses in the preceding fifteen years.

Subject to the qualifications mentioned, however, domestic saving is the major, and in many cases the overwhelming, determinant of domestic investment. This is also strikingly evident if one compares countries such as India and Pakistan. India's saving ratio from 1973 to 1985 was about $22\frac{1}{2}$ per cent and its investment ratio about $23\frac{1}{2}$ per cent; Pakistan's saving ratio over the same period was in the 11-13 per cent range, and its investment ratio around 16 per cent.

4.2 Domestic Determinants of the Savings Rate

What, then, determines the savings rate in a country? Table 4.1 shows enormous variation in national savings rates, with almost as many observations lying above 25 per cent as below 10 per cent of GNP. The table, which is derived from the *World Development Report 1988* (World Bank), is organised by geographic groups of countries; yet the spread of the numbers within these groups is almost as wide as among them.

Savings data are notoriously weak even in developed countries and some of the wide differences in numbers for what would appear to be similar developing economies may be attributable to statistical errors. However, while the savings numbers deserve to be approached with a fair amount of scepticism, the same may also apply to the search for errors in these numbers. Such errors tend to be discovered when cases of unusually high savings rates, such as in India (Rakshit 1982, pp. 561-572), or of unusually low savings rates, as in Chile (Levy 1979, p. 294) are made the subject of special investigations — which makes one wonder whether such investigations might not themselves be biased in the direction of what might be called "centripetal corrections".

But clearly, beyond errors in measurement, there must be a wide range of factors that play a role in determining countries' saving rates. Before exploring the literature on this subject, it is worth noting that development economics has a sort of vested interest in one causal factor. The profession has grown up with models, going back to Harrod-Domar, that were based on the savings rate being a positive function of per capita income i.e., on an excess of the marginal

Table 4.1.   RATIOS OF GROSS NATIONAL SAVINGS TO GNP, 1965 TO 1986
Per cent

Country	1965-73	1973-80	1980-86
Latin American and Caribbean			
Argentina	19.7	21.2	10.0
Bolivia	25.2	18.0	− 0.1
Brazil	19.5	19.1	17.3
Chile	12.8	12.2	7.0
Colombia	17.2	19.0	15.3
Costa Rica	16.8	13.8	16.6
Ecuador	16.3	21.2	18.1
Guatemala	12.9	16.4	9.7
Jamaica	25.6	13.6	10.5
Mexico	19.9	21.3	23.3
Peru	27.2	24.7	22.3
Uruguay	11.7	11.3	9.9
Venezuela	30.1	34.5	23.9
Africa			
Cameroon	—	16.8	22.2
Cote d'Ivoire	—	16.6	10.0
Ethiopia	12.6	6.6	4.0
Ghana	12.1	6.9	1.4
Kenya	18.7	16.4	17.1
Liberia	—	27.5	9.6
Malawi	—	13.2	8.8
Niger	—	8.6	4.5
Nigeria	19.4	28.3	15.7
Senegal	—	4.1	− 3.4
Sierra Leone	11.1	− 1.2	3.0
Sudan	11.2	10.2	5.0
Tanzania	16.9	13.3	9.2
Zaire	10.0	8.8	8.4
Zambia	30.2	19.9	2.6
South Asia			
India	17.9	22.2	23.1
Pakistan	—	11.6	13.5
Sri Lanka	14.6	13.4	16.4
East Asia			
Indonesia	13.7	24.6	25.2
Korea	20.4	25.7	28.3
Malaysia	21.6	29.4	27.3
Papua New Guinea	—	11.5	2.6
Philippines	20.6	24.3	19.0
Thailand	22.6	21.5	19.3
Europe and North Africa			
Algeria	29.9	38.9	36.6
Egypt	13.2	22.4	14.1
Morocco	14.5	16.4	13.5
Portugal	—	25.9	25.9
Tunisia	21.5	23.2	22.8
Turkey	19.1	18.1	18.5
Yugoslavia	30.0	32.9	38.1

Source: World Bank WDR 1988, Table All.

propensity to save over the average propensity to save. Such an excess is indispensable in order to solve what Sir Arthur Lewis (1954) once called "the central problem in the theory of economic development", *viz.* "to understand the process by which a community which was previously saving and investing 4 or 5 per cent of its national income or less, converts itself into an economy where voluntary saving is running at about 12 to 15 per cent of national income or more".

An income elasticity of saving in excess of unity is also a prerequisite for a happy ending to a model that starts with a poor country borrowing to overcome an initial shortage of saving. Only if savings rise faster than income is there a built-in mechanism to ensure that at some stage in the future saving will first become equal to investment, then become equal to investment *plus* the interest borrowed on the cumulative use of foreign savings, then exceed even this level so that the borrowings can begin to be repaid. It is true that one can construct debt-cycle models that assume a constant marginal propensity to save, but then some extraneous change is necessary to prevent the country from getting ever deeper into an unsustainable pattern of debt. The *1985 World Development Report* (World Bank) presents such a model (Box 4.1, pp. 47-48), based on consumption at a constant 80 per cent of GNP, but after ten years of export growth at 3 per cent per annum, "a surge in exports is required to finance interest payments and amortization", and a jump in the export growth rate to 14.1 per cent per annum conveniently comes to the country's (and the modeler's) rescue.

While a savings ratio that rises with per capita income is, thus, an essential component of the development modeler's tool kit, it is not strikingly obvious that it is a dominant feature of reality, either among countries or in individual countries over time.

Among the figures for individual countries, the most striking savings rates are those of India and China, the two largest developing countries. Both are among the low-income countries, yet both have for many years had high investment and saving rates, with no more than a rather marginal reliance on foreign capital. Indeed China, for which fully comparable statistics are not available for earlier years, had an excess of saving over investment (a current account surplus) of about $13 billion in 1982-84[2].

Since China and India are both very large countries, it is perhaps understandable that they cannot count on foreign capital in amounts that are large in proportion to their own resources. They are typical "Feldstein" countries in which domestic investment would in any event have to be financed predominantly by domestic savings. (Presumably, the United States, an even larger economy, represents a still more special case as it can finance payments deficits in its own currency.) But this in itself does not readily explain a high savings rate; many smaller countries, some helped by substantial foreign savings, have nonetheless settled for investment rates well below the figures for the two sub-continents.

But China and India are by no means the only outliers in their relationship between savings and income. As shown in the first two columns of Table 4.1, in Latin America in the 1960s and 1970s some of the lowest saving ratios (in the low teens) are found for two countries that rank among the highest in per capita income: Uruguay and Chile, while Argentina and Brazil, at similar income levels, had savings ratios that were about twice as high. These simple, statistically unsophisticated, comparisons throw some doubt on the prevalence, or at least on the dominance, of per capita income as an explanatory factor of the savings rate. It is now time to turn to a brief visit with recent econometric exercises on this subject.

These exercises predominantly deal with household savings, rather than with total domestic savings, which also include business savings and government savings (the latter defined as the difference between government revenue and its expenditure on current goods and services). We shall concentrate here on various attempts to explain private or household savings and raise some questions concerning the concept of government savings in the next section[3].

One of the peculiarities of current literature on saving is that much of it is devoted to establishing the impact on saving of this or that particular variable, with other variables merely taken along for the ride to ensure a respectable correlation coefficient[4]. Thus there is for example, the literature that explores the effect of the real interest rate on savings (Rossi, forthcoming, and papers by Fry and Giovanni cited therein). That effect is uncertain *a priori*: on the one hand one can expect higher interest rates to encourage saving by enabling the saver to buy more future consumption in terms of current consumption forgone (the "substitution effect"); on the other hand, higher interest rates reduce the amount of saving needed to provide a desired future income level (the "income" effect). The broad result up to now of this branch of the savings literature seems to be that a positive effect on saving (or a negative effect on household consumption) of the real interest rate can be discerned, but that it is not very strong: "The effective mobilization of domestic savings through changes in savings incentives is likely to require changes in real interest rates which, given the existing constraints, may prove unfeasible, especially in low-income developing countries" (Rossi 1988, p. 126)[5]. Against the weak positive effect of interest rates on personal saving found by these cross-country correlation exercises one should also give attention to certain individual cases where the introduction of positive real interest rates has been associated with sharp increases in the personal savings rate. In Korea, the increase of the real return on one-year time deposits from slightly negative in the early 1960s to positive figures in the order of 10 to 20 per cent in the period 1965-71 brought about a rise in personal savings from about zero to 8 per cent of GNP (McKinnon 1974). Taiwan, where high positive real rates were introduced earlier, has since then consistently enjoyed a high personal savings rate and, as a result, has had to rely much less than Korea on foreign capital to finance a high level of investment. The conclusion would thus seem justified that for an individual country considering the transition to pronounced positive real interest rates both the general experience and that of the few highly successful countries would be relevant.

The general findings of the weak response of total private savings to interest rates are fully compatible with the evidence that financial savings in developing countries are strongly responsive to the real deposit rate. This has been shown by cross-country analysis by Lanyi and Saracoglu (1983, p. 29) and quite strikingly for four individual developing countries over time in the *1987 World Development Report* (World Bank, Chart 7.2 on p. 119). For reasons indicated in Chapter 3, increases in the proportion of savings channeled through financial institutions brought about by higher interest rates have an economic benefit of their own in that they would tend to encourage a more rational use of these savings.

A second branch of savings studies explores the effect of social security on savings. Here, too a number of opposite tendencies can be expected to be at work. On the one hand, the assurance of a certain minimum income after retirements tends to reduce the need for planned savings. On the other hand, the introduction of social security may lead to a reduction in the retirement age (it has done so in the United States) and hence to the felt need for a larger stock of savings for retirement (Munnell 1974, pp. 553-565). The empirical answer for developing countries as to the net effect of these two influences appears to be that the retirement effect and the wealth-substitution effect approximately offset each other (Kopits and Gotur 1980, p. 186). A similar finding was made for the industrial countries: "Social Security variables have no effect on household saving" contradicting Martin Feldstein's earlier finding that "Social Security depresses savings" (Koskela and Viren 1983, p. 215). The implication of these findings — which may of course need corroboration — is that any net savings of the social security system would be an addition to the savings flow coming from households.

The extent to which social security and other forms of organised savings produce a net savings surplus depends on the financing structure and the investment policy of the savings institutions.

Private forms of insurance, such as provident funds, private pension funds, or life insurance companies can perform their function only by building up a stock of capital that guarantees participants' future or contingent payments. Insurance schemes run by the state may also operate on the principle of capitalisation or funding, or they may be financed on a pay-as-you-go basis. The funding technique of social security will typically recommend itself for programmes confined to relatively restricted benefits, directly linked to contributions[6], for a homogeneous group of participants. Social insurance schemes that are based on these principles in a number of low inflation Asian countries (Malaysia, India, Sri Lanka and Singapore) have been quite success-ful not only in providing their participants the security promised, but also in running a savings surplus. In the most recent year for which data are available, that surplus amounted to between 1 and 2 per cent of GNP in India and Sri Lanka, more than 3 per cent of GNP in Malaysia and as much as 7 per cent of GNP in Singapore (ILO 1981 and 1985), although the built-in dynamics of the system imply that this high contribution to savings in Singapore will not continue (Wallich 1983, p. 89). However, as insurance schemes are expanded to cover larger parts of the population and additional risks so that the linkage between the premiums a participant pays and the benefits he may receive becomes less direct, the tendency is to shift to pay-as-you-go financing. This tendency will become inevitable where inflationary developments and the need to adapt benefits to them make past premiums irrelevant to current benefit claims. The development of Chile's social security system over the past sixty years presents a textbook case of a system that first built up reserves (added to national saving), then ran down its surplus, and finally became highly dependent on government subsidies to maintain the payment of entitlements to its participants (Wallich 1983, Chapter 3).

The ultimate benefits to capital formation deriving from the various forms of social insurance depend further on the purposes to which the accumulated funds are devoted. Governments tend to set investment policies not only for official social security schemes but also for private insurance plans. In many countries, government securities are the main investment outlet for insurance surpluses, either by the investors' choice (because of the quality of the assets and the limited availability of alternative investments) or by government prescription. This method of investment may raise the availability of resources in industries or social services designated as recipients by the government — such as steel and transport in Argentina and hospitals in Mexico and Ecuador (Wallich 1983, p. 65) — or it may have little other effect than that it raises the ability of the government to run budget deficits. Finally, where surpluses are channeled back to participants through mortgages or personal loans, as occurred on a large scale in Chile, the savings may at best promote housebuilding and at worst may neutralise collective saving by increasing consumption financed by policy loans.

We must return to the question raised earlier in this chapter as to whether there is a clear positive difference between the marginal and the average propensity to consume. The modern (post-Keynesian) consumption/savings theory based on the life-cycle hypothesis and introduced by Franco Modigliani carried the logical implication that this would *not* be the case, in other words that the marginal propensity to save should not be a function of (per capita) income. The original statistical exercises conducted by Modigliani on savings data for a combination of 24 developed and 12 developing countries found confirmation for this hypothesis: the constant in the cross-country savings equation did not differ significantly from zero (Modigliani 1970, p. 204). As far as the developing countries in this sample are concerned, however, this finding may well have been due to the combination in a single calculation of a limited number of LDCs (and a not particularly representative selection at that) with a much larger number of developed countries. When the two groups of countries were analysed separately in a later study (Kopits and Gotur, 1980), the finding that per capita income had virtually no impact on the propensity to save was indeed confirmed for the industrial countries; but in a sample of 40 developing countries an increase in income did have the effect of raising the savings ratio.

Again, however, the treatment as a single group of 40 developing countries (all those for which sufficient data were available to the authors) may have missed important differences among these countries. In an analysis of 17 Latin American countries from 1950 to 1966, Landau found a clear correlation between income and the marginal propensity to save for the 12 "poorer" countries, but no correlation for the five "richer" ones (at that time: Argentina, Chile, Mexico, Uruguay, and Venezuela). Per capita income rankings in Latin America have changed somewhat since the 1960s, but the absence of any positive association between per capita income levels and savings ratios continues to this day, as was noted with reference to the data in Table 4.1.

Such cross-country findings do not necessarily preclude the possibility that savings rates for individual countries would move over time as a function of per capita income. Here again, however, the absence of a clear positive relationship can be established without recourse to correlation calculations. Because of the disturbances related to the debt crisis it may be preferable to use information that is limited to the 1960s and 1970s, which were on the whole years of persistent growth in most Latin American countries. From 1960 to 1980, GNP per capita increased in all thirteen countries shown in the first group of Table 4.1. Yet the savings rate in the period 1973-80 exceeded that for 1965-73 in only six. It declined between the two periods in the seven others, including Brazil with the highest growth rate in per capita GNP. The lack of evidence on the presence of a high marginal propensity to save raises doubts concerning approaches to the debt problem that rely heavily on a steep marginal savings curve. We return to this question toward the end of Chapter 10.

4.3 "Government Saving" — A Useful Concept?

It is natural for a developing country to use foreign savings in addition to its own, that is to say to run a current account deficit. The policy issue that faces the country is how large that current account deficit can safely be set, given the immediate and medium-term outlook with respect to the resources available from abroad.

The net use of foreign resources implies an excess of absorption over output at home. Accordingly, the current account deficit can be described — and from a certain point of view explained — in terms of the domestic excess absorption. It is interesting to observe the two distinct definitional approaches that are used to describe this linkage between domestic and foreign macroeconomic streams.

Under the first approach, which tends to be used in the analysis of problems of industrial countries, the current account deficit is viewed as the outcome of two internal balances, each of which is the net result of a positive and a negative stream, *viz.*

1. The balance between private saving and private investment, and
2. The balance between government receipts and expenditures.

Thus in explaining the current account balance, this approach would focus on the government fiscal balance, private saving, and private investment. Indeed the concern frequently expressed in recent years about the current account deficit of the United States has focused primarily on the fiscal deficit, although the low rate of private saving has also been commented upon.

In the alternative approach, which is frequently applied in the study of developing countries, there appears to be a tendency to group the same variables in rather different combinations. Here, the current account deficit is equated with the excess of investment over saving, both variables conceived as the sum of their private and official components. Hence current account deficit = (private and official) investment — (private and official) saving. There can of course be no conflict between the two approaches since one can readily be transformed into the other by the use of further identities and the introduction of the concept of "government saving" as equal to government receipts — current government expenditures[7].

Yet in spite of the identity between the two approaches, the choice of one rather than the other tends not to work out as policy-neutral.

The first approach is, as such, neutral between measures that lower expenditures and measures that raise revenues. It is also neutral among categories of expenditures and categories of revenues. The second approach is neutral between changes in revenues and changes *in current* expenditure. Government investment expenditure, on the other hand, is merged with private investment expenditure into an undifferentiated "investment" category that tends to benefit from a discriminatory bias in its favour.

The logic of the distinction between the two approaches cannot, of course, be carried very far, if for no other reason than that, at the level of logic, there can be no difference between two identical approaches. But in periods of rising government expenditure, the authorities in developing countries show a tendency to discriminate in favour of investment expenditure. The concept of "government saving" certainly does not discourage such discrimination. Part of this tilt toward physical capital formation may be due to the fact that this variable was featured as the determinant of the growth rate in standard growth models. Often, investment is favoured over other inputs by overvalued exchange rates (which make imported capital goods unduly cheap), subsidised credit, and freedom from sales taxes and import duties on investment goods. As against the revered position of official (as well as private) capital formation, current expenditures by the government fall under the derogatory classification of "government consumption" (Goode 1984, pp. 237-238)[8]. This discriminating distinction affects the availability of funds even though capital and current expenditures (for offices and officials, for schools and teachers, etc.) are equally necessary to produce the output of government services. By contrast, when expenditure needs to be cut, discrimination often works in the opposite direction: for employment reasons, current (especially wage) expenditure is better maintained than capital expenditure, especially in so far as capital goods are imported.

The evidence of tendencies toward distortion in governmental expenditures would seem to put into question whether the concept of "government saving" has been a particularly useful addition to the development lexicon. Officials and politicians should be encouraged to consider expenditure items on their merits without any preconceived notion that expenditures that can be classified as "capital" have any innate superiority over those that cannot claim that distinction.

NOTES AND REFERENCES

1. This direction of causation was not mentioned in the article cited.

2. The current account figures for China for recent years, which agree with figures for changes in reserves, appear reliable. It is not clear whether the same can be said about the savings and investment figures. Although the *World Development Report* (World Bank) lists such figures for 1965 and for recent years in Table 5, it omits them for the period starting in 1965 presented in Table A.11. Hence there is no figure for China in Table 4.1.

3. It is, of course, possible to argue that the proper variable to explain is total savings, e.g. on the ground that private savers take the government's saving or dissaving into account in framing their own savings decisions. But even if private savers were intent on doing this, how could they? Conceivably private savers might respond to government borrowing by preparing for the additional taxes they or their progeny will have to pay to service the debt. But in contrast to the reasonably well known figures for the changes in the government debt, which reflects contractual obligations, "government saving" is nothing but a statistical construct that not all governments consider of sufficient importance to provide as part of the budget.

4. A notable (not recent) exception is the unpublished Harvard doctoral thesis by Luis Landau, *Differences in Savings Ratios Among Latin American Countries,* Cambridge, 1969.

5. In a similar vein, Lanyi and Saracoglu 1983, p. 6: "The available empirical evidence ...

suggests that the substitution effect is more important than the income effect in developing countries, although not overwhelmingly so".

6. For example provident funds, where each participant receives his own contributions plus accumulated interest in a lump sum upon retirement, provide more direct linkage than pension funds, where the participant receives payments for the rest of his life.

7. The transformation runs as follows: Government expenditure - government receipts government investment expenditure + current government expenditure - government receipts government investment expenditure - government savings.

8. The predeliction for "capital budgets", and the assumption that capital expenditures always qualify for borrowing, and current expenditures never, also work in the same discriminatory direction (Goode 1984, pp. 30-31).

Chapter 5

GOVERNMENT FINANCE AND THE DEBT PROBLEM

5.1 The Government Deficit as the Primary Cause of the Deficit in the Current Account of the Balance of Payments

From the narrow point of view, the problem that many developing countries have experienced for six years or more with the service of their foreign debt can appear as simply a balance-of-payments problem. The balance-of-payments statistics showed that credit items in the current account, such as exports and remittances by emigrants did not provide enough foreign exchange to pay for necessary imports and also to pay in full the interest on the foreign debt — let alone any repayment of that debt. Thus it appeared that the debt problem would be much relieved, and perhaps become manageable, to the extent that growth in the industrial countries became more buoyant, export prices improved and import prices (e.g. of energy) came down. It was acknowledged, of course, that these external factors would need the support of sound domestic policies and realistic exchange rates in the debtor countries themselves, but the emphasis remained nevertheless on external variables[1].

Such a view of the debt problem, however, in particular as that problem persists over a long period, is inadequate because it does not look beyond the immediate effects of higher exports or cheaper imports on the balance of payments. It ignores the fact that these favourable effects on the current account are accompanied by an equal increase in domestic real income, which in turn, and with some lag, will lead through a multiplier process to a stream of additional imports[2]. On assumptions that seem plausible for developing countries[3], the resulting stream of additional imports will absorb a large proportion of the initial positive change in the balance of payments. Accordingly, the search for a *lasting* positive change in the balance of payments will have to go beyond exogenous current account improvements (Polak 1957, pp. 1-50)[4].

To put the same proposition in national account terms that are relevant to the medium or longer run, one should look to the domestic, rather than to the foreign, half of the national accounts identity in order to find lasting corrections for major current account disequilibria. With respect to the industrial countries, it is now widely recognised that the solution to the balance-of-payments problem of the United States must be found in correcting the large deficit on the government's account. For the highly indebted developing countries, too, one has to look at the sources of domestic dissaving to find the underlying causes of persistent current account difficulties.

In principle, the excess of absorption over income that shows up as the domestic counterpart of a current account deficit can come from any sector of the economy. In practice, there is in almost all of the countries with serious debt problems little question as to which sector bears the main responsibility. In all these countries, business investment is not only far below the level of the 1970s, when it was stimulated by low real interest rates and the ready availability of capital from abroad, but probably even below the level of the 1960s. There are various reasons for this, depending somewhat on the individual country, such as a bleak economic outlook, high real interest rates, and crowding out of business investment by the pre-emption of a large part of national savings by governments. In the sector of private consumption, even though real wages are below the levels of a decade or longer ago, the possibilities for consumers to maintain consumption by borrowing against future income are limited, and indeed the rationale for such borrowing may be lacking as evidence mounts that "permanent income" may well be lower than the level of earlier expectations.

There remains the official sector as the underlying source of excess absorption and thus not merely the counterpart, but the cause, of the deficit in the current account of the balance of payments. It should be noted at once that this is not obvious from readily available public finance data. Indeed, in 1979 and 1980 the fiscal deficits of the central governments of the 15 heavily indebted countries (all but one of which ended up with debt service problems) were remarkably low: 0.8 per cent of GDP in both years (IMF WEO 1987, Table A19). A number of these countries actually had central government surpluses (or were in fiscal balance) in many recent years: Brazil from 1975 to

1980, Chile from 1975 to 1981, Uruguay in 1979 and 1980, Venezuela in 1975, 1976, 1979, 1981 and 1985, and Yugoslavia from 1982 to 1984.

5.2 Wide Swings in Government Deficits, and Their Causes.

The trouble here is with the statistics. The fiscal figures for central governments are typically seriously deficient as an indicator of the extent to which governments as a whole acted as net absorbers of resources. In many of the prospective problem countries other official bodies, including in particular state enterprises, ran large deficits for which they borrowed at home or abroad. In a few countries, moreover, central banks ran losses by selling foreign exchange for the service of private foreign debt at rates lower than they were then paying to acquire foreign exchange.

But while data on central government finance exist for practically all countries, figures on consolidated public sector deficits are much harder to obtain. Data for selected Latin American countries are brought together in Table 5.1. The figures presented in this table measure, for all countries except Brazil, the conventional ("overall") consolidated fiscal balance. In recent years, the relevance of this concept of the deficit has been questioned in connection with certain cases of high inflation; we shall return to the question of the best way to measure the expansionary impact on the economy of the fiscal balance in Section 5.3.

Table 5.1. CONSOLIDATED PUBLIC FISCAL SURPLUS (+) OR DEFICIT (−)
FOR CERTAIN LATIN AMERICAN COUNTRIES

Per cent of GDP

	1979	1980	1981	1982	1983	1984	1985	1986
Argentina	−6.1	−7.5	−13.3	−15.1	−16.8	−12.8	−5.5	—
Bolivia	−8.4	−9.0	−7.8	−14.7	−19.1	−27.4	−9.1	—
Brazil[a]	—	—	−5.2	−7.0	−3.5	−2.7	−4.3	−3.7
Chile	−4.7	+6.1	+0.8	−3.4	−3.0	−4.3	−2.6	—
Colombia	−0.2	−2.8	−5.2	−6.0	−7.6	−6.3	−3.9	−0.5
Ecuador	−0.5	−4.5	−5.8	−7.5	−2.2	+1.6	+0.9	—
Mexico	−7.4	−7.9	−14.7	−17.5	−8.9	−9.0	−10.0	−16.1
Peru	−1.5	−5.4	−6.7	−7.2	−9.5	−6.8	−3.7	−6.2
Venezuela	+3.8	+4.4	+3.6	−5.6	+0.4	+8.6	+5.0	—

a)   For Brazil, "operational deficit", see Section 5.3.
Source: World Bank.

This table shows for all the countries covered a sharp rise in public sector deficits measured on a consolidated basis in the early 1980s. For a number of the countries shown, namely Argentina, Bolivia, Chile, Mexico, Peru, and Venezuela, the deterioration reached 8 to 10 per cent of GDP in a few years. The ready availability of foreign credit permitted this radical change in absorption by the official sector. It probably could not have been sustained for any length of time even if credit conditions in the capital markets of the world had remained comfortable. As it was, the abrupt change in these conditions brought about the need for a sharp fiscal adjustment in many of the highly indebted countries.

Two major factors forcing this adjustment were the increase in interest payments abroad and the declining availability of capital from abroad, which could not readily be replaced by borrowing on a similar scale in domestic capital markets. Figures on the changes in the net availability on account of foreign capital and interest payments combined are shown in Table 5.2. Disbursements on public and publicly guaranteed debt declined from more than $40 billion a year in 1981-82 to about $20 billion in 1985-86, while repayments declined by a few billion dollars only. During the same period, interest payments continued to rise, in spite of the fact that the six-month Libor rate for dollar loans was halved between 1982 and 1986 as indebtedness continued to increase and governments became responsible for the service of a larger proportion of the total[5]. These factors combined made for a $27 billion shift (from +$9 billion to -$18 billion) in the availability of finance from foreign capital and interest on that capital. That figure represents over 35 per cent of the imports of these countries in 1986[6].

In order to link these figures to government finance data, it is necessary to take the figures for individual countries and express them as percentages of GDP, like the figures in Table 5.1. This is the approach followed by Reisen and van Trotsenburg. They arrive at a negative shift in "net transfers," comparing 1980-81 with 1983-85, of 8.7 per cent of GDP for Argentina, 9.4 per cent for Mexico and 9.9 per cent for Venezuela[7]; in other words, figures of the same order of magnitude as the increases in consolidated deficits noted above[8]. The two authors conclude that "the budgetary burden ... imposed on the Latin American debtor countries in recent years was heavier than the demands for adjustment in the historical transfer cases", citing Machlup's estimate for Germany's reparation burden, 1924 to 1932, at 2.5 per cent of GNP (Reisen and van Trotsenburg 1988, p. 26).

Table 5.2. SEVENTEEN HIGHLY INDEBTED COUNTRIES: NET CAPITAL
FLOWS AND INTEREST PAYMENTS ON PUBLIC AND PUBLICLY
GUARANTEED DEBT

$ billion

	Disbursements	Principal repayments	Net flows	Interest payments	Net flows less interest payments
1970	4.0	1.9	2.1	.9	1.2
1975	13.6	4.5	9.0	3.0	6.0
1980	35.6	15.2	20.4	14.3	6.2
1981	42.7	16.2	26.5	17.2	9.3
1982	45.1	15.4	29.7	20.7	9.0
1983	36.1	13.3	22.8	20.7	2.0
1984	28.1	12.5	15.6	23.1	−7.5
1985	21.0	13.3	7.6	25.5	−17.9
1986	20.0	13.6	6.4	24.8	−18.4

Source: World Bank, *World Debt Tables, 1986-87 Edition*, pp. 26-27 and *1987-88 Edition*, pp. 30-31.

The authors have performed a service by recalling the discussion, over half a century ago, of the German transfer problem as being relevant to our thinking on the adjustment problems that the heavily indebted countries have been undergoing in recent years. In particular, they draw the correct parallel on the role of government finance: now, as in the German case, the transfer can only take place if the government of the paying country first puts itself in a position to collect the necessary purchasing power domestically (Machlup 1976, p. 425). Thus, in a fundamental sense, the international debt problem is in the first instance a problem of government finance in the indebted countries. Another valuable inference from the older discussion is that debtors can only pay if creditors are willing to accept their commodities: protectionism in the industrial countries will negate any solution to the debt problem. It will, of course, also be necessary for the industrial countries to maintain an adequate level of aggregate demand, i.e. an adequate growth rate. This condition can be seen as a modern and more general counterpart to the requirement formulated in the transfer debate that the receiving government must make an expansionary budget adjustment equal to the transfers it receives.

On a few major points, therefore, the earlier discussion of the transfer problem can be of help in our search for an understanding — and hence for a basis for the solution — of the current international debt problem. But it is also important to remember the very important differences between the earlier

German reparations problem and the current debt problem. The reparations problem raised the question whether, or how, an economy recovering from the dislocations of war and inflation could be expected to shoulder a transfer burden equal to a few per cent of its GNP. The adjustment problem that faced certain developing countries in the 1980s related to their ability to reverse a number of years of heavy government borrowing abroad for investment and consumption purposes and resume growth — while paying interest on borrowings that have not made a corresponding addition to output. The magnitude of the adjustment in this case — in the order of 10 per cent of GNP for some of the countries in the most exposed positions — may appear much larger than the reparation problem that so preoccupied the profession fifty years ago. But, as our very fragmentary figures show, the adjustment imposed by the recent end of the borrowing phase was of a similar order of magnitude as the burst in government deficits that preceded it.

The fact that the adjustment period had been immediately preceded by an expansionary burst that was strongly import-oriented implied that it would be appropriate for the balance-of-payments correction to be slanted more in the direction of import compression, and less in the direction of export expansion, than would have been the indicated response to a transfer burden imposed on an economy that was more nearly on a long-run growth path. The bloated level of imports of some Latin American countries in 1980 and 1981 did not constitute a proper point of reference for the decline that took place in the following years. Much has been made of the fact that the dollar value of imports in recent years was about half the pre-crisis level in Argentina, Brazil and Mexico. But this occurred after imports more than tripled between 1977-78 and 1980-81 in Mexico, rose by 150 per cent in Argentina and by 70 per cent in Brazil. At least as relevant, therefore, is the fact that the import value, in 1984-85, was close to the 1977-78 level in the first two countries, nearly double that level in Mexico and more than 50 per cent above that level in Chile, Colombia and Peru. It was only in Venezuela, of the major Latin American debtors, that imports did not increase much from 1977-78 to 1980-81 and still declined sharply thereafter[9]. Moreover, since in a number of the countries affected the real exchange rate was much lower in the later than in the earlier years, import substitution can be expected to have played an important role[10].

Perhaps because the deficit had become so enormous in so short a time the need for a large fiscal adjustment was promptly recognised — and if one bases one's judgment on the pace of fiscal adjustment in industrial countries — acted on forcefully and with considerable speed in some countries. Argentina, Bolivia, Mexico and Venezuela all managed fiscal corrections of 8 to 10 per cent or more of GDP two years after reaching their peak deficits. And, not surprisingly, just as fiscal deterioration had its counterpart in a worsening of the current account of the balance of payments, fiscal adjustment tended in most cases to be accompanied by notable improvements in the current account[11]. But in the countries mentioned, as in other heavily indebted countries, the fiscal improvements frequently did not stick.

In some countries, the reasons for fiscal backsliding came from abroad. The large increase in Mexico's fiscal imbalance in 1986 as a result of the fall of the oil price, and in spite of further real adjustment in expenditure and non-oil taxation, has already been referred to. In other countries, the nature of the expenditure cuts was such that they could not be sustained over the long run as essential capital spending, maintenance costs, social services, or real government salaries were reduced below levels that were economically or socially acceptable. Some of the adjustment measures taken to raise revenues also proved to be unsustainable. In some countries, political pressures, understandable after a string of years of declining real per capita consumption, overcame the best intentions of the authorities to restore fiscal order. And finally, and perhaps most disconcertingly, there are indications that, in some countries at least, the adjustment process itself has started to produce a negative impact on government finance. A number of causal strands that have interacted to produce this effect can be discerned:

1. In the period when foreign capital was readily available, many countries allowed their currencies to appreciate in real terms, absorbing the balance-of-payments effects by larger foreign financing. Adjustment to the debt crisis forced a reversal of this policy by means of a sharp depreciation of real exchange rates. The immediate consequence of this was a proportionate rise in the real cost of the service of the foreign debt, which was expressed in foreign currency (mostly US dollars). The impact of a real depreciation on the non-interest part of the government's fiscal position is much more difficult to determine. It depends, essentially, on the relative roles of tradeables and non-tradeables underlying government revenue and government expenditure, and on the response to the shift of the real exchange rate of the relative magnitudes of these flows (Reisen 1988). A country that relies heavily for its revenue on the *ad valorem* taxation of exports and imports, and whose government expenditure is predominantly for domestic labour and non-tradeable goods, may see its non-interest fiscal position improve as a result of a

real depreciation of its currency so as to outweigh the increased real cost of the debt service (depending, of course, also on the ratio of debt service to foreign trade). It would take a good deal of empirical work to determine which of the highly indebted countries are in this relatively favourable position. It may well be that only those countries in which the government acquires close to the full foreign exchange value of certain major exports (petroleum!) would find themselves in that category. In general, countries with interest payments abroad running at, say, 35 per cent of exports, may not find a full offset to the increased real cost of interest payments in greater revenue from taxes on international trade, after deducting the increase of the cost of tradeables — both imported and domestically produced — used in government investment and consumption.

2. An aggravating factor is that the increased cost of the debt service owed by the private sector to foreign creditors may threaten massive defaults which could both be domestically disruptive and undermine even further the country's creditworthiness. Where such debt was guaranteed by the government it had to assume the service itself; and even in many instances where no guarantee had been given, the government felt it necessary to "nationalise" private debt (Tanzi and Blejer, forthcoming).

3. The transition to a far more competitive real exchange rate was accompanied in some countries by a sharp rise in inflation. Not in all countries: Korea, for instance, managed a substantial real depreciation in the 1980s while keeping inflation at a low level. Other countries, such as Argentina, Bolivia, Brazil and Chile had high inflation rates over much of the post-war period or even before, which were unrelated to the debt crisis. But in some countries, such as Mexico and Yugoslavia, it would appear that real depreciation (supported by an accommodating monetary policy) played an important part in the burst of inflation during these countries' adjustment processes.

4. Inflation itself, whatever its initial cause, may worsen the government's fiscal position. It is a widespread practice among economists to treat a government's recourse to the printing press as simply the use of another source of finance: whatever part of expenditure cannot (conveniently) be covered from conventional taxes plus foreign or domestic borrowings is financed by "the inflation tax". While it has been realised at least since the experience with inflationary finance in World War I that inflation shifts real purchasing power from the holders of money to the government (Keynes 1923), it is confusing — to say the least — to present government finance data treating "the inflation tax" as just another tax, like the income tax or the VAT. That approach totally

blurs the concept of a fiscal deficit; with inflation treated as a source of revenue, the budget is on its way to being balanced!

More important is the practical consideration that the revenue from legitimate taxes does not remain unaffected if the government meets part of its financing need by inflating the money supply. This proposition was elucidated by Tanzi (1978, pp. 417-451) a decade ago, but it continues to be mostly ignored in calculations of the optimum inflation rate. As Tanzi shows, in developing countries with considerable tax collection lags and much reliance on specific rates that lag inflation (in other words, with a revenue elasticity below unity), the real yield of traditional taxes is likely to decline with inflation[12]. As a consequence, the additional real command over resources that a government can achieve by recourse to the printing press may well peak at a very low rate of inflation, and at that point may be only little higher, if any, than at zero inflation. It is thus quite likely that the high rates of inflation observed in many highly indebted countries are not only a reflection of the difficulties of fiscal adjustment encountered by the authorities, but also, in turn, add to the severity of these difficulties.

Against the background of these considerations it is not surprising to note the irregular pattern shown by the budget deficit figures for many problem countries since the peak deficits that, for most of them, occurred in 1982 or 1983. One can also note a somewhat similar irregularity in the improvement of the current account, (Figure 2.2) with balance, or indeed a surplus, being achieved in some years which then again disappeared. Some part of the current account fluctuations may be due to external causes, and the effects on the current account of the net absorption by the government may up to a certain point be offset by the crowding out of private investment demand, as the government starves the market for credit to the private sector. But in general one would expect the multiplier effects on the rest of the economy of an expansionary policy by the government to be dominant, and to be reflected in the current account.

Accordingly, there is still every reason, in modern circumstances, to respect the theorem carried over from the historic transfer debate, *viz.* that the country's first step toward meeting its payments obligation abroad is to mobilise the necessary domestic resources via the budget. Without this step by the government, it is unlikely that the country will attain the balance-of-payments position that would make the transfer possible. Even if it did, as a result of some fortuitous development in the net foreign transactions of the private sector, the attempt by the government to acquire these resources by borrowing from the Central Bank would be likely to undo the favourable payments position in a short time.

5.3   How to Measure the Government Deficit

The subject of the definition of the government deficit has many facets (Chellia 1988, Tanzi 1978), but I shall limit myself here to the one that is most relevant in the present context. That is the question as to whether it is advisable to correct the conventional measure of the deficit for the inflation component of interest payments that is included in this measure, i.e. whether to consider the "operational deficit" rather than the overall deficit. In periods of high inflation, the interest paid to creditors consists of a small, real, component and a much larger component that serves to compensate creditors for the reduction in the real value of their claims. Thus, seen in real terms, a large part of the government's interest cost constitutes in fact repayment of principal. If this amount is paid in the form of a "monetary correction" — i.e. a write-up of the nominal value of the claim — the amount repaid is at the same time reborrowed, so that the real value of the government debt remains unchanged. Why then include this repayment in the measure of government expenditure, and hence in the measure of the deficit, since loan repayments in the traditional form are excluded from both measures?

The question is particularly acute because at present national practices with respect to the measurement of budget deficits in high inflation countries differ sharply, thus hampering the comparability, and indeed the understanding, of national figures. In Israel, a country where debt in local currency was until recently universally indexed, the only available measure of the government deficit includes only the payment of the real interest rate. In other words, Israel's budget data provide information on the operational deficit only. In Brazil, government debt is also mostly indexed, which results in a figure for the operational deficit; but the amount of the "monetary correction" is also published, and can be added in to arrive at the overall deficit. In Mexico, with a shorter history of rapid inflation, government debt has in general not been indexed and in recent years the interest paid thus contained a large inflation premium. By making an estimate of the real interest rate that the government would have to pay, a figure for the operational deficit can be constructed and in the last few years the government has increasingly emphasized this latter measure as the more significant indicator of the stance of fiscal policy (Mancera 1987, p. 2). In Argentina and Chile the question has hardly arisen because most

104

of these countries' government debt is denominated in foreign currency and thus in a way automatically indexed. Yet in Mexico and Brazil, with large domestic currency debt and high inflation, the differences between the two definitions of the deficit are enormous. In both countries, the operational deficits in recent years have been of the order of a few per cent of GDP, with the overall deficit some 15 per cent of GDP higher.

These figures for the magnitude of the monetary correction (MC) can readily be understood on the basis of a simple formula based on the debt and inflation characteristics of the two countries. MC can be seen as the amount of money that needs to be paid to maintain the real value of the existing domestic currency debt; the correction over any period equals therefore the inflation rate over that period times the nominal value of the debt. During the same period, and disregarding any changes in real GDP, money GDP will increase in the proportion of (1 + the inflation rate). Hence, putting the initial ratio of domestic debt to GDP as d and the inflation rate as i, we find[13]:

$$\frac{MC}{GDP} = \frac{di}{1+i}$$

For example, with domestic debt at 30 per cent of annual GDP and inflation at 100 per cent per annum, MC/GDP would be 30/200 = 15 per cent of GDP; with debt at 20 per cent and inflation at 250 per cent, the correction would be 50/350 = 14.3 per cent of GDP. The first set of figures might roughly apply to Mexico in 1986, the second to Brazil in 1985. (Domestic debt/GNP figures from Reisen 1988, Table 3.) Note that at extremely high rates of inflation, the inflation correction approaches the ratio of domestic debt to GDP: at the end of the adjustment period almost nothing would be left of the real value of the debt existing at the beginning of the period, so that nearly the entire real amount would have to be reborrowed.

With the operational and the overall deficits so far apart, how can a sensible choice, or a compromise, between the two be made? One suggestion has been to abandon in such cases the concept of a single number for "the" deficit and merely to consider the two measures as constituting the lower and upper bounds of the "true" deficit (Tanzi et al. 1987, p. 731). This approach also seems to be reflected in recent IMF practice where, in standby arrangements for high inflation countries, both measures are monitored as indicators, though not necessarily as formal criteria, of performance.

This approach constitutes a half-way recognition of the analytical importance of the operational deficit. This recognition may go far enough in the case of countries with moderate inflation, but it is clearly unsatisfactory in cases where the inflationary component has become quite large. Take the case of Israel, where the stock of indexed government debt was well in excess of the annual GDP and where inflation, in the period shortly before the mid-1985 stabilization programme, ran at 1 000 per cent a year or more. Would anyone want to argue that the conventional deficit (which Israel wisely did not calculate in that period) at somewhere over 100 per cent of GDP was a figure with any economic meaning?

For countries such as Brazil and Mexico, with an inflationary component of some 15 per cent of GDP, the conventional deficit has not yet reached a magnitude that makes it self-evidently irrelevant. Yet, for these countries, an attempt should be made to do better, on the fiscal side, than to rely on a wide range. It may be helpful for that purpose to go back to the rationale for the established exclusion of debt amortization from the fiscal deficit. The argument there is that the recipients will consider amortization as a return of investment funds and thus, unlike the amount received as interest, will not consider it as available for consumption. It would seem plausible that in both countries money illusion is no longer important, although this is a point that deserves further investigation. In any event, this is not the full story. With high interest rates and money very scarce, the receipt of money from the government, even when considered as a return of capital, may well be used for investment expenditure that would not otherwise be financed. The periodic write-up of holdings of government debt for the inflation correction may also be considered as a good occasion to sell part of the debt in order to finance other investments. Indeed, as inflation proceeds, the public may become less and less willing to hold government debt; even the payment of higher real interest rates may not be sufficient to offset increasing fears of radical measures, such as additional taxation of capital or income, or indeed de-indexation. For all these reasons, running from the remnants of money illusion to capital flight, it is not sufficient to assume, as the advocates of the concept of the operational deficit do, that payments made in whatever form for the purpose of maintaining the real value of the government debt will in fact achieve that result. Thus it will be necessary to verify the extent to which that real value is maintained, and to adjust the measure of the deficit for any shortfall.

The conclusion from this analysis would seem to be that the conventional deficit, inclusive of the monetary correction, does not constitute a useful measure in highly inflationary conditions. At the same time, it is possible to envisage a relevant measure of the deficit in these conditions. This would be *the operational deficit increased by any decline in the real value of the government's internal debt.* There would be no reason to reduce the operational deficit for any increase in the real value of the debt, since such an increase would almost certainly be due to the government crowding out private demand for credit by changing various features of government borrowing[14].

It should be recognised that the special measure of the fiscal deficit just described is suggested as being of some value only in the context of high rates of inflation, i.e. in situations where the conventional measure has become clearly inappropriate. In these circumstances also, even more than in others, any measure of the deficit is, as Tanzi and his colleagues correctly point out "a crude tool for assessing the impact of fiscal policy on the economy" (1987, p. 729). In particular, it cannot, for a variety of reasons, be equated with the magnitude of the fiscal adjustment required for a successful stabilization plan — a subject that cannot here be pursued.

NOTES AND REFERENCES

1. A typical example of this approach is Cline (1983). Larry A. Sjaastad was one of the earliest to point out the weakness of this approach: "One of the key errors of some current thinking about the debt problem is the idea that it is fundamentally a trade problem ..." (Sjaastad 1983). He directed the focus to the underlying problems of government finance.

2. The situation is somewhat different with respect to the benefits arising from falling world interest rates. Insofar as the saving in interest costs accrues to the government, there is no reason to assume counteracting secondary effects.

3. The assumptions relate to the relative size of the marginal propensities to save, to invest, and to import. On the special assumption that the first two propensities are equal (and that there are no other domestic "leakages") the induced imports will, over time, offset the whole of the initial exogenous improvement in the balance of payments.

4. Cf. Polak 1957. The following quotation from that paper is applicable to the subject under discussion here: "When a country is running a balance-of-payments deficit, it is far too often believed that any measure or event that will increase exports or decrease imports (oil discoveries, higher world market prices, the entry into production of some import-replacing industry, etc., etc.) will by itself relieve the deficit ... These events will by themselves produce a *temporary*, but not a *lasting*, improvement in the balance of payments" (p. 30, emphasis in original).

5. When private borrowers became unable to service their debts, governments were pressed by creditors to take over or guarantee loans to the private sector that had fallen into arrears. Governments were generally not in a position to resist such demands by the banks, which made the "nationalisation" of (non-guaranteed!) international credits to private borrowers a condition for their rescheduling of official debt. Consequently, 85 per cent of the total long-term external debt of the highly indebted countries was public or publicly guaranteed by 1986, as against 72 per cent in 1982.

6. The figures in the last column of the table are presented as "Net Transfers" in the World Bank source cited. Although the term is widely used in the literature on the debt problem and is more concise than the heading of the last column in the table, I am afraid that it can give rise to misunderstandings. I have two difficulties with it. First, as a general matter, I would always be concerned about the loss of information and the risk of mistaken inference, when some special balance is struck across various entries in the balance of payments, and when, in addition, that balance receives a title of its own that somehow suggests a deeper meaning for it. There is no obvious reason why, of all debit items in the current account of the balance of payments, one in particular — interest payments — should be singled out to be paired against net new loans. Why this item rather than, say, energy imports, capital goods imports, or shipping costs? Second, and more in particular, it is evident that the term is being used to turn a reasonable proposition on the normal direction of the flow of capital to developing countries into an unreasonable norm for the magnitude of that flow in every year. It is reasonable to expect capital to flow from the high income countries that are well endowed with capital to the lower income countries where capital is scarcer. But this need not happen at all times, especially not immediately after a period of excessively large inflows, such as that in the years before 1983. There is even less reason to expect net inflows to increase every year by at least the amount of the additional interest to be paid on the net inflow of the previous year. That expectation would imply an unlimited exponential increase of the debt of developing countries as the norm. It would also mean that the capital exporting countries would forever plough back the earnings on their capital exports and would never enjoy any return from their savings invested abroad. It might be pleasant for developing countries if creditor countries assumed a responsibility for that type of "reverse debt service"; but no one could posit this as the normal state of affairs, either for the aggregate flow from the capital exporting countries or for groups of capital exporters, such as the commercial banks or the multilateral development banks.

7. Reisen and van Trotsenburg 1988, Table 1.2. Their figure for Brazil on the same basis is -5.1 per cent; no figures for other Latin American countries are provided.

8. The two elements mentioned are, of course, not the only large factors of foreign origin affecting the government's financial position. To cite one other influence that hit Mexico slightly later: the drop in the oil price from 1985 to 1986 reduced government revenues by $8.5 billion, or 6.7 per cent of GDP (Mancera 1987, p. 2).

9. All data from IFS. For a rough conversion to imports in real terms: export prices in dollars of the industrial countries were about 20 per cent higher in 1984-85 than in 1977-78.

10. This was noted for Mexico by Ortiz (1985, pp. 88 and 91), where the very large decline in imports in 1982 is to a large extent attributed to "an unusually strong process of import substitution, especially at the intermediate goods level".

11. See Chart 4.1 comparing public deficits and current account balances for nine developing countries in WDR 1988 (World Bank).

12. Government expenditures are, of course, also affected by inflation. Heller found that expenditure adjusts more rapidly to inflation than revenue (i.e. that the net effect of inflation is to worsen the fiscal balance) in about 60 per cent of the 23 countries analysed and that the fiscal response varied according to the stage of the inflationary process. Hence "the impact of inflation on the net fiscal position of the public sector is not *a priori* predictable" (Heller 1980, pp. 712-748).

13. The same result is derived more labouriously under a number of restrictive assumptions by Tanzi and his colleagues at the IMF (Tanzi *et al.* 1987, pp. 711-738).

14. The crowding out consideration is brought in by Tanzi *et al.* (1987, p. 724) as a qualifier to the reliability of the operational deficit as the indicator of the government's net absorption of resources. The qualification is justified where, through improved terms on its liabilities, the government crowds out other demand for credit. It seems to me not justified where the government, defensively, improves the terms to maintain the competitiveness of its own real debt.

Where there is evidence of crowding out, one should in principle make allowance for it, which may be difficult or impossible; but I can see no reason to follow Tanzi *et al.* in their suggestion that this can be done by the reinclusion of the monetary correction, or some large part of it, in the measure of the deficit.

Chapter 6

DOMESTIC AND FOREIGN SAVINGS

6.1 The Issue in General

Much of the early post-war literature on the contribution that foreign capital could make to development was built on rather special assumptions on how the financial systems of the developing countries were (or were not) linked into the international market for capital, a concept in which I include here both private capital movements and aid. These assumptions, which often remained implicit, saw saving in a developing country determined by domestic variables, especially income and its distribution, and thus unaffected by the magnitude of the supply of foreign savings. At the same time, such linkage as there was between the domestic "capital market" — if one could stick this euphemistic label on the highly compartmentalised rivulets of saving and investment in the economy — and the world capital market was assumed to function in one direction only: money might flow in, primarily as official grants, official credits, and direct investments, but very little attention was paid to the notion that it might also flow out.

The first assumption — that domestic saving was unrelated to the supply of foreign saving — may have been "curiously naïve" from the start (Papanek 1972, p. 934). The second was perhaps justified in the early post-war years when exchange controls were still reasonably effective in most developing countries. Since then, it has lost most, if not all, of its justification as international banks are not only investing the world-wide pool of capital in any country in the world that offers attractive investments, but also seek to draw capital into that same pool from any country in which resources can be found. In this setting, it is not surprising at all that sophisticated savers in developing countries will, if they can, channel capital towards the markets in the high-income countries, unless the obvious qualitative attractions that these markets offer are offset by higher yields in developing countries. In contrast to most developing countries, the capital markets in developed countries offer a wide variety of financial assets to suit the tastes of different categories of foreign as well as domestic investors. In addition, the banks in developed countries offer many financial services that may not be available in developing countries. Indeed, seen from this angle, there are good reasons for business firms and wealthy investors in developing countries to conduct a large part of their financial operations through one or another of the major financial centers in the industrial countries, either directly or via a local office of an international bank. The extent of the reliance on foreign banking centres may differ widely among developing countries, as well as over time, and spurts of private capital outflows from these countries may draw sudden attention as evidence of "capital flight," but the underlying tendency for capital to flow not only from rich to poor, but also from poor to rich, countries should be recognised.

Indeed the largest, the most general, and the most persistent flow toward the markets of the developed countries comes from the authorities (central banks and governments) of the developing countries, in the form of the foreign exchange reserves kept by these authorities in the financial markets of the main industrial countries. In mid-1988, these reserves stood at some SDR 120 billion (not counting the reserves of the Middle East oil countries), a figure of the same order of magnitude as the amount of private LDC "flight capital" held in the industrial countries[1].

The various issues that relate to the linkages between domestic and foreign savings briefly touched upon here will be developed in the rest of this chapter.

6.2 Does the Supply of Foreign Savings Affect the Supply of Domestic Savings?

This question looms rather large in the development literature; almost certainly, it does not deserve all the attention it has received.

Initially overlooked as an issue, the question was then pursued for some years with a vengeance by those who took a negative view of foreign aid and were anxious to prove that $1 million worth of aid added much less than that, indeed perhaps nothing, to investment and, hence, to growth. They tried to prove their point by running correlations — across countries or for individual countries over time — in which the ratio of foreign savings to GDP was one of the factors explaining the domestic saving ratio. It has been well established by Papanek (1972) that these correlations are essentially worthless, for a variety of economic and statistical reasons. The statistical reasons are all reducible to the fact that foreign savings, domestic savings, and investment are linked through national account definitions. These linkages invalidate the results of treating them as independent variables. The economic reasons are more interesting. Let me mention a few[2]:

1.   If a country uses foreign savings well, it needs less of them as time proceeds and its own savings increase. The negative correlation between foreign and domestic saving over time proves nothing about the existence of a response mechanism that might induce a country to save less in any particular year if it received more aid or larger capital flows in that year.

2.   If foreign countries allocate aid in some measure on the basis of need, if that need is measured by poverty, and if poverty is attributable in part to a low saving ratio, cross country statistics will show a negative correlation between aid and savings, which again proves nothing about country behaviour in response to possible changes in aid.

3.   Fluctuations in a country's crops, the demand for its exports, or its terms of trade or political vicissitudes may affect at the same time its saving ratio and the extent to which it has access to foreign credits or makes use of its reserves (both of which are captured in the standard comprehensive definition of foreign savings). Thus a whole range of events may influence domestic and foreign savings in opposite directions, without any implication of a causal connection between the two savings streams.

4.   If consumption aid (food, technical assistance, military aid) is used by the recipient country as intended, it will raise the country's consumption total without a rise in its income, thus producing an apparent fall in domestic saving equal to the rise in foreign saving brought about by the same transaction: another meaningless instance of negative correlation.

These examples should suffice to disqualify as *prima facie* irrelevant the simple correlation exercises published around 1970 — whether correlations over time or across countries — that were intended to "prove" the small or non-existent benefit of foreign capital or aid. Unfortunately, the ease with which these calculations can be made seems to continue to tempt new researchers on the same path (Schattner 1986, p. 245; Holthus and Stanzel 1986, p. 292).

The fact that the evidence provided by unsophisticated correlation exercises proves nothing about the possible negative impact of foreign saving on domestic saving should not, however, be taken as proof that there have not been important instances where precisely such negative impacts occurred. Some such instances were adduced in Section 2.2 — referring to the period of excessive borrowing by some countries in the late 1970s — a period about which the *1985 World Development Report* (World Bank) commented that "many governments ... borrowed abroad to postpone adjustment at home" (p. 65). Similarly, there is evidence that some African countries combined high per capita aid inflows with a rising tax effort, and achieved high rates of growth, while other countries, which also received large aid, but had a falling tax effort, experienced low growth rates (Mosley 1980, pp. 86-88). This last observation suggests at the same time that here — as in so many putative relationships in development economics — it is counterproductive to look for general rules of behaviour that hold over long stretches of time or across widely different countries. The same relaxation of a supply constraint — be it food aid, budget aid, suppliers' credits, commercial bank credit — may have a positive effect on growth in one country and a negative effect in another, depending both on the terms on which it is made available and the policy stance of the recipient country[3].

6.3 Private Capital Exports and Capital Flight

In the context of the desirability of enhancing the supply of capital available to developing countries, attention naturally focuses on the stream of capital *toward* these countries, and on measures to enlarge that stream. But in a highly integrated world economy it cannot be assumed that capital moves along a one-way street. *Official* capital movements — from donor countries and international lending institutions — can be expected to move initially from developed to developing countries, but at a later stage loan repayments may become quite important and may indeed ultimately exceed new loans as the receiving country comes to "graduate" from its status as an international borrower. In addition, official capital exports from developing countries occur as these countries acquire needed reserves of foreign exchange. For movements of *private* business capital, such as direct investment and commercial bank credit, the natural direction would also be expected to be overwhelmingly into, rather than out of, the developing countries. The large multinational corporations are typically located in the industrial countries, and while most of their foreign assets are in industrial countries too, they have also contributed — and are still contributing — large amounts of capital to the developing countries. There is a reverse stream of business-related capital exports from developing countries, including export credits and the finance of foreign subsidiaries, but the magnitudes involved are not large. While the great expansion of offshore banking encouraged business firms in developing countries to transact a large part of their financial business through these centres, it is not obvious that this institutional change produced major net outflows of business funds. Commercial banks in the industrial countries gave huge credits to the developing world in the 1970s and early 1980s, based in part on the deposits these banks were accepting from the oil surplus countries; again the reverse flow of outward banking money from developing countries is likely to be small (Cumby and Levich 1987).

There is, however, one category of private capital movements for which the balance of inflows and outflows could be expected to be in the outward direction. These are the movements of *private non-business* capital. Until recently, few individuals in industrial countries were interested in investing their savings in financial assets in developing countries; the active demand for Mexdollars by United States citizens a few years ago was a clear aberration from prudent investment. The development of mutual funds for developing countries is a hopeful new development that may ultimately channel important capital flows into the stock markets of these countries. For the time being, however, the quantitative importance of these funds is still limited. Wealthy individuals in developing countries, on the other hand, may have a variety of strong reasons to move their assets (which may not be sharply distinguishable from the assets of business firms under their control), to other countries: to diversify their portfolios, to hedge against expected devaluations of national currencies, to get better yields, to avoid taxes or confiscation, to seek anonymity, etc. Some movement of funds from developing to developed countries has probably gone on for many years. It appears to have intensified in the last decade or so, partly because the incentives for such movements became greater and partly because the facilities for these outward movements of capital were enhanced by the active solicitation of these funds by banks in the industrial countries. It is essentially these private funds that constitute the flight capital from the developing world. Although capital flight is far from a new phenomenon, it has drawn a great deal of attention in recent years, and has been presented as a major obstacle to a resumed flow of bank credit to the developing countries.

Capital flight among the industrial countries was a major source of international financial disturbance in the 1920s and again in the 1930s, when these movements began to be referred to as "hot money" (Kindleberger 1987). Capital flight from the developing countries was widely commented upon in the early 1960s as capital was moved out of newly independent countries on a large scale (Little and Clifford 1965, p. 218). The Fund was sufficiently concerned about the subject in the middle 1960s to try to estimate the magnitude of the problem, which was found to be by no means small (Kafka 1967, p. 214). The outward flows from the developing countries did not cease then — on the contrary, they were quite important in some countries in the 1970s — but they somehow dropped out of the picture until after the outbreak of the debt crisis. In the last few years, they are widely cited as evidence of financial mismanagement in a number of debtor countries and as a reason (or perhaps an excuse) for the unwillingness of banks to lend fresh money to these countries. These are, of course, as a 1987 IMF staff study points out, the same banks that are competing for deposits from flight-motivated investors resident in developing countries (Deppler and Williamson 1987, p. 49).

The magnitude of the problem of capital flight from developing countries in recent years — and in earlier years as well — is extremely difficult to determine with any degree of precision. There are three reasons for this. First, there is the question of definition: what categories of non-official capital exports are to be regarded as not made on the basis of ordinary business considerations, and should therefore be qualified as "capital flight"[4]. Obviously, a question with such emotional overtones has no precise answer. Indeed, enormous amounts of capital move among the industrial countries on the basis of interest and exchange rate considerations and it is not customary nowadays to label these movements capital flight[5]. Second, capital flight, even if it takes place within the law of the source country, is by its very nature conducted with a maximum of secrecy. And third, the balance-of-payments statistics on various categories on capital movements, as well as the statistics on the year-to-year changes in countries' outstanding debt that some observers have used as a substitute for balance-of-payments statistics, are notoriously poor — indeed so poor that most compilers of estimates of capital flight proceed on the assumption that the residual item in each country's balance of payments, "Errors and Omissions", consists predominantly of capital movements that escaped the statistical net. But that assumption is not tenable in at least some of the countries concerned where import and export transactions are systematically misreported by traders[6].

Given the abundance of estimates made on many different bases, I shall limit myself here to the reproduction of a single one that draws, in an eclectic way, on a judicious combination of a variety of techniques. This is the "preferred estimate" of Lessard and Williamson (1987), which attempts to measure the total of non-official capital outflows.

Table 6.1.   "PREFERRED ESTIMATE" OF CAPITAL FLIGHT, 1976-84

$ billion

Argentina	16
Brazil	9
Korea	0
Mexico	27
Philippines	4
Venezuela	30
Total six countries	86

Source: Lessard and Williamson 1987, Table 9.2.

Although these figures are about a third lower for Argentina and a half lower for Brazil and Mexico, than those published by Morgan Guaranty, they still account for a large proportion of the foreign debt of Argentina and Mexico, and about the whole of Venezuela's foreign debt.

For countries in which capital and foreign exchange are scarce, the outflow of capital on a large scale is without a doubt a most serious matter. The observer who characterised capital flight as "the temporary privatization of official reserves" deserves an award for the understatement of the decade (Stuetzel 1973, p. 42). It can be assumed that most of it constitutes a diversion of resources from domestic real investment to foreign financial investments — though if the alternative would have been larger consumption expenditure abroad the cost to the country would have been even greater. Even if the yield of this financial investment is repatriated at some time, the country loses the additional benefits that would have been brought about if the money had been productively invested at home: entrepreneurial income, additional workers' earnings, taxes. There is a loss to the country even if the country's credit standing permits it to draw in additional foreign loans to offset the effect on the reserves of capital flight, and thus not interrupt its growth rate. That did happen in a number of countries in the late 1970s and this may be one of the reasons for the limited attention that the subject of capital flight received in these years. But foreign credit, as became painfully evident soon thereafter, is a limited resource with a rising, and beyond a certain point an almost vertical, supply curve (Section 2.4). As capital flight induced some borrowing countries to venture on to increasingly risky stretches of this supply curve, it contributed in a major way to the outbreak of the debt crisis[7].

There are wider consequences of capital flight. The simultaneous assumption by the state of foreign debt and acquisition by private residents of foreign assets brought about a massive redistribution of wealth as the national currency depreciated, with a consequent income redistribution as this debt had to be serviced. The tendencies in this direction were reinforced as the government assumed liability for private foreign debts or made foreign exchange available at subsidised rates for the service of private debt (Rodriguez 1987, pp. 129-144).

Much of the recent literature on capital flight displays a major effort to explain and understand why private capital moves out of developing countries. In its most extreme form this effort is found in Khan and Ul Haque's (1985, p. 608) attribution of capital flight to the "expropriation risk" prevalent in developing countries: "the domestic resident faces the possibility that his assets may be expropriated by the government, whereas the risk on similar assets held abroad is assumed to be negligible. The domestic investor would thus have an incentive to transfer resources abroad to avoid the domestic risk". Lessard and Williamson (1987 pp. 235-238) see the nature of the tax systems of developing countries as a fundamental cause of capital flight and an obstacle to the return of flight capital. Ize and Ortiz (1987, pp. 311-332) have developed a most ingenious model showing how the deterioration of the fiscal position of Mexico (itself in part an effect of the debt crisis) enhanced the risk for investors in peso claims (and even in Mexdollar claims) to a greater extent than that of the holders of dollar claims on Mexico. The latter could expect that the Mexican government would do everything within its power to meet its foreign debt service, but this effort — in the face of a serious deterioration of the country's fiscal bind — would make it practically inevitable that the government would not be able to meet the real service of its domestic debt. Thus it could be expected that the real value of domestic claims would have to be sharply reduced by inflation as a way out of this dilemma, as indeed happened. (As mentioned in Section 2.3, the implied exchange rate guarantee of Mexdollars was repudiated by the imposition of a non-market exchange rate unfavourable to the holder.) Domestic investors foreseeing these developments were thus induced to take their capital abroad while they could, even though foreign investors continued to accumulate the more secure dollar-denominated claims on the country.

These and other "structural" explanations of the advantages to residents of developing countries of moving and holding part of their wealth abroad rather than at home touch on important weaknesses in the economies of these countries. Each of these factors can contribute to an explanation as to why equilibrium real interest rates in countries afflicted with these structural weaknesses are higher than they need be, and why growth is held back. But as explanations of the phenomenon of capital flight they are seriously incomplete. The evidence to support this judgment is both factual and theoretical.

If the operationally relevant cause of capital flight lay in certain structural characteristics of most, or at least many, developing countries, the evidence of capital flight should be general across countries, as well as persistent in individual countries. Neither of these two propositions applies. On the contrary: capital outflows vary enormously both from country-to-country and from year-to-year. Even the three countries most criticised for their large cumulative outflows over the past decade or so have experienced years of very substantial inflows; and at least some of the countries that appear as mostly immune to the disease of capital flight if one looks only at cumulative figures over a decade (such as Peru and South Korea) have experienced certain years of very substantial outflows. Moreover, the causes of the ups and downs in capital outflows do not appear to lie in factors in the industrial countries (Lessard and Williamson 1987, p. 215). In 1966, when conferences and papers on the subject of capital flight seemed to be reaching a peak, each of three major past sources of capital flight (Argentina, Mexico, and Venezuela) had a net inflow of residents' capital, according to Morgan Guaranty[8].

Now for the economic argument. The factors mentioned as "causing" capital flight are determinants of part of the residents' demand curve for foreign exchange. A further explanation is needed to indicate why this demand was met and the country actually lost the foreign exchange through capital flight. There are two elements to this piece of the puzzle. Capital flight (on a net basis) takes place when residents buy foreign exchange from the central bank against delivery of domestic currency. Given the magnitude of certain bouts of capital flight, the withdrawal of the corresponding amounts of domestic currency would have caused a severe shortage of domestic currency, unless the central bank had continuously replenished the domestic money supply by credit operations. Without the co-operation of the central bank, the *attempt* at capital flight would have pushed up interest rates sharply; the resulting enhanced relative advantage of domestic over foreign interest rates would have deterred some from going through with their plans to export capital and induced others (residents or foreigners) to bring capital in. That lesson was well learned by Argentina and Israel when they entered upon their stabilization policies in the second half of 1985. Both countries calibrated their interest rate levels (through adjustments in the degree of tightness of their monetary policies) so as to ensure neither a net capital inflow, which would have had undesirable inflationary effects, nor a tendency toward a net capital outflow which would have manifested itself by a premium in the market for the dollar and which would have undermined national confidence in the nominal anchor of the countries' respective stabilization exercises. Secondly, the ability on the part of residents to buy, on a net basis, foreign exchange from the authorities presupposes that the latter were willing to sell foreign exchange at an exchange rate that the capital exporters still considered as favourable. Whenever the demand for foreign assets was large, this could only happen on a protracted basis if the authorities replenished their reserves by borrowing abroad. A country that was unwilling to reduce its reserves or to borrow to accommodate the demand for foreign exchange from would-be capital exporters would allow the exchange rate to depreciate in a free market. In that event, the attempt of some to acquire foreign exchange would have depreciated the exchange rate of the country's currency to the point where others saw an advantage in bringing an equal amount of foreign exchange into the country[9].

Thus, from a policy point of view, it is important to focus on those causes that can be remedied by measures that are readily available to the authorities. If this approach is taken, the question as to why capital flight takes place in some countries at some times, and a reflow in the same countries at other times, is not essentially complicated. As the Brazilian economist Alexandre Kafka put it more than twenty years ago: "The rules under which many developing countries choose to operate are often quite sufficient to explain the capital exports which take place" (1967, p. 214-15). The main "rules" to which he referred were overvalued exchange rates and interest rate control, particularly in the face of inflation[10].

Whenever currencies are overvalued or interest rates are kept well below equilibrium levels, mobile capital will try to take advantage of the situation and seek investment abroad. Exchange control on capital movements can make capital flight more difficult but it is unlikely to succeed for any length of time in preventing it where the exchange rate and interest rate incentives are strong. It has been noted that two Latin American countries that have not suffered seriously from capital flight (Colombia and Brazil)[11] also had restrictions on the export of capital (Hommes 1987, pp. 168-174). But the main reason for their success in keeping capital at home has been the maintenance, by both countries most of the time, of sufficiently high real interest rates and the avoidance of overvaluation of their currencies. The pursuit of similar policies has prevented capital flight from Chile without the benefit of extensive exchange controls. And there have been a sufficient number of instances of a return flow of capital when exchange rates and interest rates were brought into line to confirm the significance of these two variables in the struggle to keep capital at home. Admittedly, the return flows so far have been small compared to the estimated stock of assets held abroad, part of which may indeed have become permanently uprooted from its home soil (Rodriguez, 1987). But the pursuit of correct policies from now on can, as a minimum, ensure that capital flight does not further sap the stock of savings available for investment in the country of its origin.

NOTES AND REFERENCES

1. Neither the official nor the private holdings abroad represent net LDC saving channeled to industrial countries, since both together are far smaller than the total LDC debt outstanding — a figure in the order of $1 000 billion.

2. Papanek 1972, *passim*. For a similar analysis, in considerably more detail, cf. Kessler and Strauss-Kahn 1984.

3. Papanek 1983, p. 177, comparing changes in aid and changes in defense expenditures in India and Pakistan, concluded that the consequences of aid seem to depend less on the quantity of aid provided or on the projects financed by the aid donors, than on how the government receiving aid wanted to use it.

4. That is the way in which most observers have put the question. But some have tried to define "flight capital" rather than "capital flight", by asking what capital held abroad is at any time held for non-business considerations. This approach permits capital that is held in foreign countries to change its spots, so to say, as its owner's motives change. For a discussion of this approach, which was pioneered by Michael P. Dooley in the IMF, and the technique of

measuring flight capital derived from it, cf. Deppler and Williamson 1987, pp. 43-4. While the approach may be as these authors state, intuitively appealing, it involves the use of further tenuous assumptions that undermine the credibility of its statistical findings.

5. It *was* some fifty years ago, when the Governor of the Banque de France complained about "these modern freebooters who, with their gangs, have exhausted one market after another" (*Revue des Deux Mondes,* 1st April 1937).

6. The question is discussed in Lessard and Williamson 1987 and capital flight statistics are corrected for errors in trade figures.

7. Deppler and Williamson (1987, p. 52) present too sanguine a slant on capital flight before the debt crisis by viewing it as "the internationalization of the intermediation between domestic savings and investment" and by positing that the harmful effects do not result from "capital flight *per se*" ... (but only if) "another condition (is) met, namely, that nonresidents be unwilling to indirectly finance the capital flight through the acquisition of offsetting claims on the country in question".

8. The same applied to Chile, Nigeria and Peru, but not to Brazil, Ecuador and the Philippines. Cf. Morgan Guaranty, *International Capital Markets,* June/July 1987. (Calculated on a definition different from that of Morgan Guaranty's, Venezuela still suffered capital flight in 1986.)

9. I disregard here any effect on non-capital transactions arising from changes in the exchange rate.

10. Statistical exercises to find explanations for capital flight by multiple correlation have not been too successful because of poor data, short periods for which the relevant data were available, and difficulties of specification. As far as they go, however, they point to overvalued exchange rates and low interest rates as primary explanatory factors of capital flight (Cuddington 1986).

    The same can be said about the findings by Conesa; perhaps the influence that the latter finds for capital flight to decrease as domestic growth increases may be attributable to tension in the domestic credit market (essentially: interest rates) that accompanies growth, rather than growth as such (Conesa 1987). Note in this connection the reflux of capital into Mexico in 1986 and 1987, provoked *not* by high growth but by financial stringency brought about by monetary policy.

11. Capital flight from Brazil has picked up in recent years, in particular since the 1986 Cruzado plan did away with most of the indexation of financial assets.

Chapter 7

THE SEARCH FOR FOREIGN SAVINGS

7.1 Aftermath of the Debt Crisis

The discussion on capital flight, which occupied the last section of the previous chapter, highlights a number of interesting aspects of the international mobility of capital that the developing countries face in the latter years of the this century. To a much greater extent than was the case even twenty years ago, these countries are financially linked to the capital market of the developed countries (note the use of the singular "capital market": for many purposes, the once separate capital markets in the industrial countries can now best be regarded as a single market with which the developing countries have to deal). To the extent that each developing country has something approaching a capital market of its own, that market has its linkages with the world capital market, subject to constraints arising from often severe market imperfections and from governmental controls. Where local markets are too anaemic to provide an efficient matching of savings surpluses and investment demands in the country, some international linkages still function. The government, assuming that it has at least some degree of access to foreign capital, can balance the costs, advantages, and disadvantages of borrowing abroad against the alternative of acquiring resources at home, be it by taxation, domestic borrowing from a limited number of captive lenders (such as banks and insurance companies), or paying its way by use of the printing presses. Wealthy individuals have a choice between holding assets (real or financial) at home or abroad; they may also be able on their own credit to attract foreign capital for their domestic business ventures.

Thus, even countries that can hardly boast of having an organised financial market take part in the process of international financial intermediation. Major international banks are active in this intermediation process, channeling money to and from developing countries: lending to governments and individuals in these countries as long as they consider them creditworthy, and soliciting the deposits of individuals who prefer to hold assets abroad — the two processes not infrequently running side by side in opposite directions in the same country.

In some respects, the process of international financial intermediation as it functioned in the last few years before the debt crisis could be described as the *summum* of financial efficiency. Through the mechanism of syndicated loans credits of billions of dollars each could be channeled from the banking systems of all the industrial countries into one or another of the megadebtors (Mexico, Brazil, etc.) in a minimum of time, and at practically no real cost: no serious economic reports, a few airplane trips, mainly the clatter of hundreds of telex machines. At the same time, other billions of dollars in developing countries that had been accumulated in private savings or borrowed from banks could readily find their way into bank deposits in the United States or Switzerland. This, however, as experience has shown, is hardly the kind of financial efficiency that is conducive either to the optimum allocation of the world's savings or to the rapid development of the countries that have found themselves hooked into these financial circuits. The debt crisis has put a crimp into the excessively easy flow of megacredits to many LDC deficit countries. It has not, unfortunately, stopped the drainage of resources through capital flight, but countries can adopt financial policies (discussed in Chapter 6) that make this perverse flow of capital costly instead of remunerative and may thus stop or reverse it.

The fact that some of the overly smooth, but far from optimal, forms of capital flows have been, or can be, turned off still leaves the question wide open on how to enhance the growth process in the developing countries by means of a truly efficient process of financial intermediation. The debt crisis has left many developing countries seriously short of inflows of foreign capital that could — together with structural measures — help revive their economies. Hence the search for new, or the revival of old, techniques for the transfer of capital to developing countries.

How much foreign capital do the developing countries need to complement their own savings? How much capital can the industrial countries make available from their savings to speed up development in the rest of the world? Are these two amounts compatible, or how can they be made compatible?

124

It would be reassuring if the three questions could be answered *seriatim,* thus giving us a solid base on which to build a policy approach to North-South co-operation in this major area. But the experience of the last twenty years or so with respect to the international flow of capital provides us with little hope for easy answers. We start out from the second question, the supply of capital.

7.2   The Supply Situation in World Capital Markets

A number of shocks have disturbed the traditional view that the mature industrial countries could serve as a reliable source of capital for the rest of the world. That view was firmly grounded in the experience of the 19th century and the pre-World War I period of this century, when high savings rates in Western Europe (and later in the United States as well) produced a regular surplus of savings over investment. Efficient capital markets channeled this surplus to the newly developing countries of that time — the United States and Canada in the Northern Hemisphere, Australia, Argentina and other "new" countries in the Southern Hemisphere (Lessard and Williamson 1985, p. 1). The main instrument for these flows was the long-term fixed-rate bond, appropriate to an era of low secular inflation. This rather harmonious mechanism collapsed with the outbreak of World War I.

After 1914, it took some forty years of almost perpetually disorganised international finance until the traditional pattern of excess savings in the developed world began to re-establish itself in the 1950s. After the capital stock and the savings ability of the European countries had been rebuilt with the help of the Marshall Plan, the industrial countries in Europe joined the United States and Canada as the traditional net savers in the world economy.

Thus, the OECD countries together tended to run a substantial current account surplus to cover aid and the export of capital to the non-OECD world. Indeed, some in the OECD would regard it as "normal" for each industrial country to produce, if not every year, at least on average over a cycle, a current account surplus from which its international obligation to the poorer part of the world could be discharged. The expectation of a current account surplus was even quantified in the 1960s: a respectable figure was at least 1 per cent of GNP, a figure that would be ample to cover a country's contribution to foreign aid, which gradually came to be regarded as subject to international monitoring and target setting. If the savings surplus was in excess of the rough 1 per cent target, it would allow, beyond aid, for the outflow of private capital to the developing world. In the 1950s and 1960s, aid and direct investment accounted for the bulk of transfer of savings from North to South and (as noted in Section 2.1) the size of the flow that materialised in those years was regarded as roughly compatible with the needs and absorption capacities of the developing countries. Whether that view was fully accurate or not is hard to establish in retrospect; in any event, growth observed in the developing countries was rapid beyond expectations.

That exceptionally calm period in the world supply and demand of savings did not last. In the 1970s it was twice disturbed by oil shocks: sharp increases in the world price of petroleum in 1973 and 1979, which raised the income and savings of the oil exporters and pushed the industrial countries into large collective current account deficits in 1974 and 1980[1]. Now, the net flow of savings to the non-oil developing countries had to come from oil surpluses, partly in the form of OPEC aid, but mostly via the banks in the industrial countries, where the oil exporters deposited their surpluses.

The current account surpluses of the oil exporters, while spectacular immediately after the oil price increases ($67 billion in 1974 and $103 billion in 1980) could not be maintained. They melted away as the real price of oil eroded and the oil countries adjusted their imports quickly to their newly acquired levels of exports (thus incidentally providing a massive confirmation of the observation made at the beginning of Chapter 5 on the transient character of current account surpluses arising from increases in exports).

But these changes did not restore the *status quo ante,* in which the industrial countries served as a reliable source of capital for the developing world. For in the 1980s, it was the United States that initiated a large savings deficit through an expansion of its budget deficit, not accompanied by a rise in private saving or the crowding out of private investment. Thus, in part through a rise in interest rates, which spread all over the world, the United States became a massive absorber of the savings of the rest of the world. Current account deficits for the LDCs in the order of $100 billion in 1981 and 1982 could not have coexisted with the deficits that the United States developed immediately afterwards: $47 billion in 1983 and figures in excess of $100 billion since 1984. The savings surplus in the rest of the industrial world could not be stretched to finance *two* massive deficits elsewhere, for a combined total of $200 or $250 billion. Thus, even if there had been no over-extension of credit to developing countries in 1980-82, these countries collectively would have found it much more difficult thereafter, in the new world setting, to get credit for large current account deficits. If they have to compete for available capital with the United States, the developing countries are greatly handicapped. They cannot run current account deficits unless they have first lined up the matching financing — the only exception being running up unpaid bills, but "arrears" constitute a method of financing that is certain to cut off future credits. The United States, on the other hand, can finance its deficits in dollars, through a mechanism that raises interest rates all over the world.

Clearly, the assets that the United States can offer to foreign suppliers of capital are superior, category by category, to anything any developing country can offer: claims on the largest government of the world or on giant banks backed by the Federal Reserve system; shares in dynamic corporations; real estate in a country whose capitalist future (in the eyes of many) compares favourably to that of the other industrial countries, and certainly to that of the developing countries.

To the extent that the world economy made room for the US fiscal deficit by increases in world interest rates, investors and consumers in the United States were the least exposed[2]. High interest rates are deductible for tax purposes, as business costs or as mortgage rates for private houses; the tax treatment in many other countries is less generous. In any event, foreign government borrowers (the obligors of the bulk of LDC debt) have no tax obligation from which the cost of interest can be deducted. In those major industrial countries that are net international creditors, having acquired increased creditor positions as US deficits cumulated, high dollar interest rates made some positive contribution to GNP. In those LDCs where the large international debt was concentrated, by contrast, high interest rates produced a proportionally much larger reduction in GNP.

The negative influence that the United States economy exercises on the supply of capital available to developing countries will not subside until its payments situation is brought under control. In other words, the problem will at best improve gradually, over a number of years. Action by the United States is an indispensable element toward the achievement of that end. The United States, through fiscal or other action to reduce total (private and official) consumption, will have to make room in its economy for an improved current account position. There must also be complementary action on the part of the other industrial countries, in particular the countries with large current account surpluses. One possible form of such action would consist of expansionary fiscal, monetary and other measures, aimed at reducing the national rate of saving with a view to raising these countries' absorption of resources as compared to GDP. Most of the international pressure exercised by the United

States on Germany, Japan and other surplus countries reflects this approach to adjustment. But this is not the only, nor from a world point of view the optimal, method of adjustment. There is no indication that aggregate saving in the world is unduly high: the prevailing unusually high real interest rates would rather signal an insufficiency of world saving (in which the low savings rate in the United States is, of course, a major element). Most evidently there is a large unmet need for savings in the developing world, both in the low-income countries where this is a chronic phenomenon, and in the middle-income highly indebted countries as an aftermath of the debt crisis. From a world welfare point of view, therefore, the high saving industrial countries (as well as the high saving NICs in East Asia) should not merely be encouraged to consume more. It may well be in their own interest to raise consumption levels, e.g. by allowing their wage earners to enjoy more of these nations' increased productivity, and by raising national housing standards. But the adjustment process would be served as well, and the plight of the developing countries would be served much better, if the surplus countries continued to save in the form of current account surpluses but directed these resources as capital flows to the developing countries, rather than to the purchase of government paper, real estate or corporate stock in the United States. In this connection, particular attention is deserved by proposals, initiated by Dr. Saburo Okita of Japan, to raise Japan's capital exports to the developing countries. In the World Institute for Development Economics Research plan that elaborated the Okita proposal, a yearly amount of $25 billion or more would be set aside out of the Japanese current account surplus for the next five years for deliberate recycling to developing countries and specific actions would be taken by instrumentalities of the Japanese government to bring about this recycling (WIDER 1987).

To the extent that such actions by Japan and other surplus countries relieve the capital shortage in developing countries, these countries will be able to relax their import restraints. The United States, as a major exporter of capital goods, which has suffered heavily from import restrictions in countries contending with extreme shortages of foreign exchange, would be a main beneficiary of a more generous supply of capital to the developing countries.

To return to the adjustment action required from the United States, it is of course by no means self-evident that resources no longer drawn into the United States would automatically become available for investment in the developing world. We have noted earlier (Chapter 4) the strong tendency, laid bare by Feldstein and Horioka, for a large proportion of the savings of any industrial country to be invested at home. If this tendency has been somewhat distorted in recent years by high interest rates in the United States, it is only logical to expect it to snap back as that tension subsides. Certainly as long as there is a large US current account deficit, and probably even after that deficit has been eliminated, it will take the positive attractiveness of investment in particular LDCs to make capital flow into those individual countries. The frantic search by the international banks, overwhelmed by the inflow of Euro-deposits, for a place — any place — to relend this money surely was a one-time occurrence; no regret is in order for the expectation that it will not return.

While the developing countries collectively could, even with the best of records, hardly hope to attract foreign resources at the 1978-81 level, the implication of the preceding is *not* that as long as there is a large US deficit, no developing country should expect to add substantially to its own saving by drawing on foreign capital. The United States is not the sole importer of capital and in the queue for foreign capital the developing countries do not necessarily rank behind the industrial countries. In the last few years a number of developing countries in East Asia, as well as the smaller industrial countries, have been able to borrow large amounts from commercial banks. But of course these borrowers have had to overcome the high real interest rates that still prevail in world capital markets. Other developing countries would no doubt find it possible to join their ranks once they had established or re-established their creditworthiness, but even then they would have to offer investment opportunities that could compete with those offered by the aggressive current importers of capital.

7.3 The Demand for Capital Imports

Assuming that the global supply situation in the world's capital markets will gradually be returned to balance by the necessary action on the part of the United States and its major trading partners, will there be enough capital available to meet the needs of the developing countries? And if so, in what form, by what capital instruments, will these needs then be met?

On this subject, one is faced by a bewildering multitude of attempts to measure the developing countries' need for capital from abroad. International institutions such as the IMF (in its *World Economic Outlook*) and the World Bank (in its *World Development Report*) regularly produce projections for the current account deficit (the flip side of the need for foreign capital) for the developing countries, with sub-divisions for main regional or analytic sub-groups. The Fund typically looks a few years ahead, the Bank about a decade.

The Inter-American Development Bank and UNCTAD have similarly made these kind of projections, as have a number of unofficial students of the debt problem (Cline 1984; Lessard and Williamson 1985; Fishlow 1987). When made at about the same time, many of these projections come to rather similar results, but over time estimates for future years tend to change considerably. Lessard and Williamson, writing in 1985, found a near-consensus projection for the 1987 deficit for all non-oil developing countries at around $45 billion, less than half of the 1981 deficit but reasonably close to the 1983 figure — presumably the latest actual figure available to those making the projections. Fishlow, writing two years later, encountered about equal Fund and Bank projections for 1990 (at some $60 billion), and about equal Bank and UNCTAD projection for 1995 (at about $100 billion) (Fishlow 1987, p. 248). Such similarity among the various numbers indicates by no means that the projections are robust. What it implies, rather, is that different projectors tend to use similar objectives, e.g. the desired rate of economic growth for the developing world; similar assumptions, e.g. with respect to the expected OECD growth rate, and similar coefficients, such as the elasticity of imports with respect to GDP growth. Quite likely, moreover, the choices of the various parameters, all of which contain a fair dose of arbitrariness, are made in such a way as to produce a "reasonable" result for the combined current account deficit, that is to say one that seems within reach of being financeable. As the figures cited tend to confirm, this means projected deficits rather close to the recent past for the near future, but higher projections further ahead.

A careful sensitivity analysis made by Fishlow of the range of deficit projections shows that they are extremely sensitive, both to some of the targets built into them and to the elasticities assumed in the behavioural equations. One percentage point difference in export growth rates makes a difference of close to $100 billion in the projected annual combined current account deficit if the growth rate of imports is not adjusted (1985, p. 256). The export growth rate itself is defined as equal to the OECD growth rate, multiplied by the marginal elasticity of developing countries' exports with respect to that growth rate. Estimates for that elasticity range from a figure of about 1.5 used by most observers to Cline's highly optimistic 3.0 (p. 259). Thus differences in the assumed OECD growth rate of 0.5 per cent lead to differences in the capital need ranging from $75 to $150 billion. Again, if the import elasticity is unity, the deficit works out some $100 billion less than if it is 1.5 (Fishlow 1985, p. 98). While differences in coefficients could in principle perhaps be narrowed by improved techniques of measurement, the high sensitivity of balance-of-payments projections for a series of year ahead is unavoidable: it arises from the attempt to project the relatively small difference between two variables (e.g. exports and imports), both of which are assumed to be growing at compound rates of interest. The growth rates assumed may be plausible but they cannot be known or specified within narrow margins[3]. There is no way out of this problem, although there are various ways to protect oneself — and the reader — from the worst pitfalls of exercises of this nature.

One of those ways is to remain aware, through the iterative process of calculations, of the crucial importance of the starting point. As Fishlow points out (1987, p. 247) starting from a trade surplus in 1985 (but one smaller than the interest cost) leads to a reasonable growth rate for the next few years with relatively little foreign finance; but heavier borrowing would be needed thereafter to maintain the same growth rate, under the same assumptions for the world economy. As shown in Chapter 9, GDP growth at the same rate as export growth is affordable, starting from current account balance, without the need for foreign savings at all.

A second way to free oneself from the unpredictable effects that result from combining (even mildly) arbitrary targets and assumptions with (even moderately) uncertain coefficients is to approach the question of foreign capital not from the angle of need but from that of a plausible safe path of using foreign capital. Lessard and Williamson (1985, p. 27) derive a guess of a sustainable annual current account deficit in the late 1980s of $80 billion (of which $64 billion borrowed and $16 billion obtained from official transfers) for all non-oil LDCs combined, based on projected exports (in 1987) of $600 billion, growing at 8 per cent year, (3 per cent inflation, 5 per cent real growth), and a safe debt level of 133 per cent of exports (1 1/3 × .08 × 600 = 64). One can argue about each of the few steps in this calculation, but at least it does not rest on a combination of spuriously precise objectives and assumptions. The authors point out that the extra $20 billion or so borrowing a year over what was implied in the consensus estimate cited above ($45 billion) would permit the developing countries an extra rise in output on the order of $100 billion, based on marginal import propensities of some 20 per cent. They do not predict an actual growth rate that could be achieved by this addition. That rate would continue to depend on the combination of the two fundamental ingredients that always shape a country's economic success: how favourable is the world economy, in terms of growth, openness of trade, etc., and how well does the country itself exploit its surroundings, in terms of competitiveness, cost-effective import substitution, flexibility in output, effective economic management, economical use of available capital, attractiveness to foreign capital, and similar growth-promoting features.

Once having established a target figure for the flow of capital to the developing countries, the authors proceed to see how this figure could be built up from various components: aid, direct investment, portfolio investment, bank loans, etc. Fishlow follows a comparable approach. Both studies conclude that with a great deal of good will and innovative thought about financial instruments, and large lending by multilateral institutions, the targets should be attainable.

The conclusions with respect to good will, innovation and the activities of the multilateral institutions are all well taken, and we shall have more to say on these aspects below. But the underlying assumption of a normative figure of capital transfers that the developing countries need, and that the developed countries should therefore try to meet, is far less solid.

The capital market is both more homogenous and less homogenous than this approach would seem to imply. To put it differently, the world capital market is segmented along different lines than implied by this approach. At the one extreme, there is foreign aid. It constitutes the sum of the amounts made available for this purpose in annual national budgets in donor countries. In most cases, year-to-year changes in those amounts are marginal. Consequently, the total changes only gradually too, except when sharp exchange rate fluctuations affect the conversion factor into a common unit of measurement, e.g. the US dollar. Aid is, moreover, overwhelmingly concentrated on the low-income countries, among which each donor distributes a total amount that is substantially predetermined by the donor's budgeting process. Thus with respect to the foreign aid component of the international flow of capital, it can fairly be said that the needs of individual low-income countries are met insofar as the aggregate supply of aid funds suffices for this purpose.

Supply-side considerations also determine the availability of foreign savings to the developing countries via the highly concessional credits extended by the MDBs, such as the World Bank's IDA. It applies much less to the credits granted by MDBs at close to market interest rates. Over the longer term the volume of these credits is determined by the ability of these institutions to raise their capitals. But for shorter stretches of time, these agencies have considerable leeway to enlarge or contract the total flow of lending, which also means that there is no clear necessity to offset increased lending to one group of countries by reduced lending to another. [The year-to-year flexibility of total lending, and even more of total net lending, is even greater for the IMF (see the next chapter) but we stick here to the view that Fund credits do not qualify as development finance.]

As one moves away from official sources of finance, the concept of an aggregate supply of funds from abroad available to the developing countries essentially ceases to be applicable — whether one considers commercial bank lending, direct investment, portfolio investment or any of the other market-determined components of the capital account of the balance of payments. The commercial banks may have a target for the reduction in their exposure in problem countries, from which they may have to deviate from time to time to provide some "new money" in the context of a major rescheduling operation. But credits to countries in good standing are treated in a very different compartment of what was described as a "split market" (IMF 1984, p. 31), *viz.* a market for credits to creditworthy developing and developed countries at notably lower interest rates than the banks charge to problem countries. The split in interest rates has tended to disappear as banks (starting with the 1986 credit to Mexico) have begun to charge concessional rates problem countries; but the markets remain no less split. Thus, Korea's move to repay part of its bank credit does nothing to enhance the availability of bank credit to Mexico or Brazil, although it may well enhance the supply of credit for Malaysia or Thailand.

Direct investment is perhaps the clearest example of a form of foreign capital actually or potentially available to developing countries that is not in an important way supply-controlled. Fundamental considerations of long-run profitability will determine whether corporation X, Y, or Z will want to operate in, or be closely associated with operations in, country A, B or C, and on what scale. If the answer to this first question is positive, second-order considerations of profitability, as well as national direct investment and taxation provisions in A, B or C will determine whether a corporation's move into the country takes the form of direct investment — i.e. is associated with a substantial provision of capital — or some other form, such as licensing. Assuming that X, Y or Z are large corporations in the industrial countries — as they would normally tend to be — they would have access to the capital markets in these countries to provide as much or as little foreign capital as they considered most advantageous.

Given the wide variety of factors that determine the multiple flows of capital to (and *from*) the developing countries, and the many ways in which the sub-markets for capital are segmented, little can be achieved by treating the supply of capital, and the growth rate in the developing world affected by this

133

supply, as a single aggregate problem. A more fruitful approach would start out from a sub-division into three groups of developing countries, without any attempt to classify all developing countries into one or another of the three groups:

a)   The countries that have preserved their creditworthiness — a group that, one might hope, would some day expand by those countries now in group (b) that had regained their creditworthiness. This group includes the Asian NICs (Korea, Taiwan, Hong Kong, Singapore), both India and China, and a number of other Asian countries such as Thailand, Malaysia and Indonesia (and perhaps Pakistan). In Latin America, probably only Colombia falls in this group. For most of these countries, the supply of foreign capital is not a serious problem. Indeed, a major concern for them is not to take in foreign capital too rapidly or indiscriminately and to remain alert to the risk of overexposure that might manifest itself under future unfavourable cyclical conditions. Some of the new ideas to facilitate the flow of capital to developing countries will yield the greatest benefits to this group of countries. The benefits may arise not only in the form of broader flows of capital but also through lower costs, or more effective creditor-debtor relationships.

b)   The middle-income countries suffering from the debt crisis — i.e. approximately the "Baker countries" plus some smaller Latin American countries in similar circumstances. For as far as one can now foresee, those countries are unlikely to have significant access to "voluntary" credit from the commercial banks and this is likely to restrain also their access to other private sources of credit. Thus, for example, a relaxation on the rules for insurance companies in industrial countries, allowing them to invest more freely abroad, would probably help the group (b) countries very little. Enlarged lending by MDB's is crucial for these countries, but even with such lending they are likely to remain short of capital for many years to come, their interest rates will remain relatively high, and investment/GDP rates below the level of the 1970s. This does not necessarily imply slow growth. But, more than in the group (a) countries, the attainment of high growth rates will depend on the economical use of capital. The decline in real wage rates in the course of this decade, in conjunction with the prevailing high interest rates, may well have created the economic conditions that will permit fast growth rates for these countries from here on out, provided political and financial conditions become propitious to more stable expectations.

c)   The low-income countries, most of which are in Sub-Saharan Africa, but including also a few in Asia (Bangladesh, Nepal) and in the Western

Hemisphere (Haiti). As far as foreign savings are concerned, these countries are almost entirely dependent on aid, although aid alone, without structural reform, cannot put them on a new growth path. Innovations in the flows of private or official credits at market interest rates are, at least for the time being, of little interest to this group of countries.

7.4 Supply Meets Demand

Table 7.1 attempts to put together the manner in which the supply situation in the capital markets of the world interacted with the demand for this capital exercised by the capital importing developing countries.

Any table of this nature deserves to be surrounded by a number of cautionary remarks. The first warning to be issued is that the separation of the items into those that need financing and those that provide financing indicates in no way a causal order, which may well run in the other direction. Thus the abundance of bank credit in 1980 and 1981 was in many ways the cause of the large current account deficits, and the shortage of bank credit in the later years forced the cuts in that deficit. In both periods, supply to a large extent determined demand. Secondly, the reader has to be aware that the grouping of individual items on the demand or supply side (or in the residual category of "Swing items") is to some extent arbitrary. The practice followed in the design of this table has been to start out from the categories distinguished in the underlying IMF table and sort them by sign: all three items under "Financing need" involve net payments in every year; all items under "Financing", net receipts; and every one of the four components of the last category shows positive figures in some years, negative in others. Under this approach, the "Financing need" is seen as including not only the current account deficit, but also two items of the capital account: the credits extended by developing countries to move their exports and the unrecorded capital outflows, part of which may represent capital flight. The principle of selection followed in this table might not prove suitable for other periods, or might lead to different sub-totals if the basic material were available in a finer breakdown. Nevertheless, while one must be aware of the risks of misunderstanding that are involved in any analytical presentation such as that given in Table 7.1, it is better to run these risks than to work from the basic unstructured data provided by the Fund.

The largest component of the supply of capital in recent years, commercial bank credits, has been extensively commented upon in this and other chapters, and the role of IMF and World Bank credits will be discussed in Chapter 8. Some other, rather more specialised, components (not necessarily shown separately in Table 7.1) will be analysed in the remaining sections of this chapter: foreign direct investment in Section 7.5, other forms of equity

Table 7.1.   NET FLOW OF EXTERNAL FINANCE TO CAPITAL
IMPORTING DEVELOPING COUNTRIES

$ billion

		1980	1981	1982	1983	1984	1985	1986
1.	Financing need							
1.1	Current account deficit	76	117	108	65	38	41	44
1.2	Export credit extended	13	26	10	10	15	11	2
1.3	Unrecorded capital outflows	16	19	25	10	2	5	3
1.	Total need	105	162	143	85	55	57	49
2.	Financing:							
	(Official sources)							
2.11	Transfers (aid)	13	14	13	14	14	17	17
2.12	Loans	24	33	32	31	32	23	30
2.1	Total	37	47	45	45	46	40	47
	(Private sources)							
2.21	Direct investment	9	14	13	11	10	10	10
2.22	Net borrowing	78	90	43	17	11	14	—
2.2	Total	87	104	56	28	21	24	10
2.	Total financing	124	151	101	73	67	64	57
3.	Balance (2-1)	19	−11	−42	−12	12	7	8
4.	Swing items							
4.1	Arrears	− 1	6	16	12	3	—	4
4.2	Fund credit	1	6	7	11	5	—	−2
4.3	Minor items	4	−1	1	−1	—	4	4
4.4	Use of reserves	−23	—	18	−10	−20	−11	−14
4.	Total	−19	11	42	12	−12	7	8

Notes:
1.1   Defined here as deficit on goods, services, and private transfers, i.e., excluding official transfers.
1.2   Includes other asset transactions.
1.3   Recorded errors and omissions.
2.12   Net disbursements by official creditors.
2.22   Calculated as a residual. Except for discrepancies in coverage, reflects mainly net external borrowing from private creditors and short-term flows.
4.3   Sum of SDR allocations, valuation adjustments and gold monetisation plus short term borrowing by monetary authorities from other monetary authorities. Includes rounding errors.
4.4   Negative figures indicate reserve increases.
Source: IMF WEO April 1987, Table A40; items rearranged, rounded, and relabeled to bring out in the table (rather than only in the notes) the main economic content of each item.

136

investment in Section 7.6, and official export credits in Section 7.7. The one other major financing category, transfers and concessional official loans, has been extensively analysed in recent literature (OECD 1985; Cassen 1986; Krueger 1986).

7.5 Direct Investment

Net flows of direct investment (FDI) from industrial to the non-oil developing countries were below $2 billion a year in the early 1960s, around $5 billion in the middle 1970s, and around $10 billion in the 1980s (IMF 1985, pp. 3-4, and Table 7.1, above). With a rough adjustment for price changes over the twenty-five year period, this would suggest a rising trend in real FDI through the 1960s, but no pronounced trend thereafter. In relative terms, whether compared to other private flows or to development aid, FDI declined in importance. (Not much attention should be paid to sometimes sharp yearly fluctuations. These fluctuations do not necessarily indicate wide swings in direct investment activity in the economic sense: the balance-of-payments figures on FDI incorporate all shifts of capital between head offices and dependent companies, some of which may be essentially speculative in nature.)

In recent years — since the debt crisis — a widespread policy view has been that the role of direct investment in the flow of capital to developing countries should be raised, with the inference drawn that countries should be less restrictive on the entrance of FDI than many of them had become in the 1970s (Group of Thirty 1984, pp. 1-2). One argument for this switch is the greater safety of direct investment for the capital importing country, and the side benefits it tends to entail.

In periods when the service of international credits encounters difficulties, observers are quick to point out the smaller risks attached to the importation of capital by means by equity investment. "Safety through direct investment" was the prevailing counsel learned in the 1930s[4]. It was repeated by United States Treasury Secretary James A. Baker III in his initiative on the debt crisis in Seoul in October 1985, when he reminded his audience: "Foreign borrowings have to be repaid — with interest. Equity investment, on the other hand, has a degree of permanence and is not debt-creating. Moreover, it can have a compounding effect on growth, bring innovation and technology, and help to keep capital at home" [IMF Summary Proceedings (SP) 1985, p. 55].

The second argument in favour of direct investment is the decline in the availability of bank credit to countries with debt problems. A Fund staff study on FDI concluded that "the long-term possibilities for substitution between direct investment and commercial bank debt can be significant". ... "These countries (those for which net bank lending is likely to be particularly constrained) could find it advantageous to encourage a greater inflow of direct and portfolio equity capital ... to support an adequate growth rate, as well as to reduce vulnerability to any future deterioration in economic conditions" (IMF 1985, pp. 1, 26). The Managing Director of the Fund went even further in a December 1983 speech to the Economic Club of Chicago, stating that "foreign direct investment could play a far greater role in resource transfers than in the past".

The advice to show greater openness towards foreign enterprises is generally well taken and it is indeed being heeded in many countries. But whether this will be of significant help in strengthening the balances of payments of the countries that have lost access to bank credit is more questionable. One important reason for this is that there is only a weak link between a country's receptivity to the operations of foreign companies and the actual entry of foreign capital under the heading of FDI; and the link is even weaker between the import of "innovation and technology" from abroad and the import of capital.

One can readily envisage the traditional example of FDI, where a foreign company starts a mine or a manufacturing plant in a developing country and brings in state of the art machinery, management, technology and all the money necessary for the local outlay on land and construction and the operating expenditure (for wages, taxes, local materials, etc.) in the start-up period. Only after the enterprise has become profitable is there the possibility of a return flow of remitted profits, and even then part of the profits may be retained in the host country — ploughed back into further FDI.

That is one possible option for the foreign company, but it is not the only one. Variants are possible, and have increasingly been used, with respect both to *(a)* the financial structure of the enterprise in the host country and *(b)* the organisation of the enterprise itself.

a) On the financial side, the foreign company may make every effort to minimise the amount of foreign exchange it brings into the country and to maximise the amount it takes out. Instead of building an expensive factory, it can rent an existing one; instead of buying new machinery abroad it can send over second-hand equipment from its plants at home. This was typically how the American (and European) automobile companies started production abroad (Maxcy 1981). Foreign companies can reduce profits in some countries by selling part of their output to the parent company or affiliates in third countries at artificially low prices (Vaitsos 1974, Chapter 6); it has been claimed that international pharmaceutical companies engaged in this practice on a large scale (Dunning 1981, p. 208). Transfers to cover local expenditure (and, at the same time, exchange risks) can be minimised by borrowing as much as possible in local currency from host country banks. Through these and other practices, companies can own and operate foreign subsidiaries without the host country balance of payments receiving any important contribution to the capital account of its balance of payments.

b) Alternatively, the financial commitment of the mother company can be minimised without a significant reduction in its ability to control its involvement in production in the host country by *not* owning and operating a foreign subsidiary, but by relying instead on "new forms of international investment" (Oman, 1984). These new forms involve a wide spectrum of techniques that have been developed most actively in the last two or three decades (although none of them were unknown before) and that permit participation in host country production without owning a majority participation in a local company. These mutations of direct investment include: joint ventures, licensing agreements, franchising, management contracts, turnkey contracts, production-sharing and risk service contracts in conjunction with the host country's state-owned company (both used primarily in the oil industry)[5], and international sub-contracting (Oman 1984, pp. 14-17).

Starting out from traditional direct investment, all these new forms of investment can be described as "unbundling" its various components (provision of management, transfers of technology, risk taking, exploitation of rents, provision of finance), with each participant — the foreign firm, the local entrepreneur, or the host country government assuming those components it considers itself best equipped to assume. In the 1970s, with finance readily available through syndicated loans (and in the case of oil producers, from their own earnings), host countries were often anxious to seek "new forms" that did not make them financially dependent on foreign corporations. The unexpected increase in world interest rates may well have upset that calculation. For many countries, moreover, the resulting debt crisis meant that they had managed to avoid the frying pan of the oligopolistic power of multinational firms only to land in the fire of the international banks and the IMF (Oman 1984, p. 35). Not surprisingly, many host countries would now be more ready to seek association with foreign companies in a rebundled form, including in particular the capital component. It is far less certain, however, that the foreign companies that have learnt the new techniques of risk shedding will also be anxious to turn back the clock. They may find themselves supported by their governments in their predilection for the unbundled approach; Fred Bergsten suggested ten years ago that, "American policy ... should abandon entirely the idea of direct ownership ... and encourage the provision of production and marketing skills through service or managements contracts ... because they offer a highly leveraged return on corporate assets" (Bergsten *et al.* 1978, pp. 159-160).

The structural changes that have taken place in the forms in which corporation in the industrial world can extend their activities (in the broadest sense of the word) to the developing world suggest that it may not be easy for countries that have lost access to bank credit to replace this by direct investment flows. A further factor to be considered is that direct investment, unlike bank credit, has always been heavily concentrated in a few countries — those with large domestic markets, those that were rich in natural resources, and those that provided a base for export-oriented production. Outside of the oil countries, five countries (Brazil, South Africa, Mexico, Singapore and Malaysia) accounted for almost half the stock of foreign direct investment in 1983 (IMF 1985, p. 4). Moreover, an inquiry made in 1984 by the Group of Thirty of a sample of major international companies found that 75 per cent of them took the view that, in the past five to ten years, the climate for foreign investment had deteriorated in Latin America, blaming increased government controls, arbitrary government intervention and nationalism as the main reasons for their negative views (Group of Thirty 1984, p. 34). Changes in policies, some of which have already taken place in the last few years, may over time bring about a change in these views. Moreover, the establishment in 1988 of the Multilateral Investment Guarantee Agency as part of the World Bank family will help encourage foreign direct investment by providing investors the opportunity to purchase insurance against non-commercial risks from an international agency. As movement towards the restoration of creditworthiness proceeds, the attractiveness of the countries concerned in the eyes of all investors — at home and abroad, direct investors and bank lenders — will no doubt improve. What is less obvious is that direct investment flows can be expected to fill the gap much before other forms of investment (including the reflux of flight capital) begin to recover.

7.6 Other Forms of Equity Investment

In the period from 1974 to 1982 developing countries could with extreme ease attract foreign savings through credits from the world's banking system. Since then, the risks of this financing technique have become painfully obvious. Moreover, the commercial banks, having become aware of the deterioration of a good part of their overseas loan portfolio, turned overnight from pushers of new loans to unwilling, overextended, creditors. They would agree to new lending to the highly indebted countries only under pressure, and even then only for the defensive purpose of ensuring that the debtor obtained means to meet the debt service. Thus, even when the debtors were still willing to borrow more from the banks, the latter were no longer prepared to lend to them on the old model. In the early phase of the debt crisis this refusal by the banks to lend on a voluntary basis was sometimes regarded as a temporary phenomenon that would pass over as the debtor countries straightened out their policies and improved their debt service ratios by raising exports. After that, it was hoped, voluntary lending to the erstwhile problem countries could be expected to resume on a prudent scale. But six years of the debt crisis have by now convinced even optimistic observers that voluntary lending to the problem debtors on a significant scale still lies in a distant future.

Against this background there is every reason to explore the possibilities of alternative forms of cross border capital flows that, first, could originate with other sources of capital in the developed countries than the banks, and, second, could take other forms than loans.

As far as sources of capital are concerned, the natural place to look would be the institutional investors of whose aggregate assets, which are a multiple of those of the banks, so far only a small proportion has been invested abroad (and an even much smaller proportion of *that* amount invested in developing countries). The alternative form would be equity participation (direct or indirect) instead of loans or bonds.

These considerations underlie the major efforts made in recent years by the International Finance Corporation (IFC) and the OECD Development Centre to encourage equity capital flows (other than direct investment) from the developed countries to developing countries. These efforts were not especially directed toward the heavily indebted countries; the development of a broader cross-border stream of equity investment holds out promise for all developing countries, whether they have the option of attracting bank credit or not.

The largest and (what is especially relevant) the most promising approach to equity finance from abroad would be by investment in the equity markets of developing countries (Lessard and Williamson 1985, pp. 50-60; Wellons *et al.* 1986, pp. 76-79). In some degree, the ground has been prepared for a move in this direction by a sharp increase in recent years in the willingness of investors in industrial countries to buy equities in other industrial countries[6]. This development was supported by the realisation that stock markets in different countries were — at least in part — subject to different risk factors, so that diversification of a portfolio over a range of countries could effectively reduce its risk exposure, even if markets in some individual foreign countries might be more volatile than in the home country.

Once institutional investors — such as pension funds and life insurance companies — had made the initial step of investing in foreign equities, the principle of risk diversification could be carried further by expanding this policy to include the stock markets in developing countries. The fluctuations in these markets tend to be less intercorrelated with those in the industrial countries, thus providing a better spreading of risk[7], while the total return, measured over the period 1976-83, has been about twice as high as in the industrial countries[8]. The preferred technique of equity investments has been through investment trusts, which provide built-in diversification within each investee country.

Calculations can be made to show that the potential for an inflow of capital into developing countries stock markets is substantial. First, stock markets themselves in some of these countries may have a large growth potential. At the end of 1985, equities accounted for 5 per cent or less of all financial assets in such diverse developing countries as Venezuela, Korea, Argentina, Thailand, Nigeria and the Philippines, compared to 28 per cent in the United States, 32 per cent in the United Kingdom and 20 per cent in Japan. The low figures quoted would appear to be related to a lack of financial, rather than economic, development; the ratios for Malaysia, (24 per cent), Jordan (24 per cent) and Brazil (17 per cent) are close to those of the industrial countries, and the figure for India (12 per cent) was twice as high as that for France (6 per cent). Second, foreign participation in emerging stock markets is still very small, perhaps only one-fifth proportionally of the investment of industrial countries in each others' capital markets. And, third, the growth rates of the countries that have received most of the foreign equity investment so far, such as South Korea, Brazil, Malaysia have been — and are likely to remain — impressive.

Nevertheless, all this relates to potential. The actual investment in these new markets through investment trusts has not been large as measured on the scale of the capital needs of developing countries in general, or even those of the particular countries to which most of the equity investment has gone. In the four years 1984-87, the total inflow into LDC stock markets through this medium was just below $1 billion, most of it in 1986 and 1987[9] . Thus, aggregate LDC figures of $1 or 2 billion a year, as calculated as potential flows by Lessard and Williamson (1985, pp. 54-55) may well lie some distance in the future. In connection with this source of capital, as with others, the implications of what individual capital importing countries can do to enhance their attractiveness to equity investment may be more important than speculation on the potential future total of such investment. Many developing countries sharply restrict the access of foreigners to their capital markets, presumably out of fear of foreign control of some of their major corporations. But if this is the source of concern, a percentage limit, rather than a prohibition, on foreign holdings will achieve the desired end. Beyond permitting foreign purchases of equities, much can be done to make such purchases more attractive by improving corporate reporting standards, restricting insider trading, etc. Improvements in a country's equity market may, in fact, be as important to attract a wider group of domestic investors into equities as it is to bring in foreign investors. Either way, such improvements could raise the efficiency with which investment in the country would be matched with available savings, whether domestic or foreign.

There are other forms of equity investment from abroad than those relying on the purchase of shares in emerging stock markets. Mention may be made here of venture capital operations, either by specialised institutions or as a (relatively minor) activity of commercial banks; investment banking, and leasing operations. Under each of these headings, foreign companies may bring capital into developing countries, in most cases through local subsidiaries. But again, as in the case of investment through the stock market, the benefits to an investee country are not limited to the amount of capital brought in from abroad. Equally important would be the establishment of such things as local venture capital or leasing companies that would introduce more efficient techniques of matching the supply and demand for savings. The IFC has been instrumental in promoting the spread of some of these investment vehicles. Over the last ten years, it has poured $17 million of its own money into venture capital companies in developing countries, which had a total capitalisation of $110 million. It has also invested in a number of LDC leasing companies; the total leasing activity of these companies in 1986 amounted to $400 million. Leasing as a form of domestic financial intermediation has, moreover, sprung up independently in many countries (in Mexico and Brazil as early as the 1960s).

7.7 Official Export Credits[10]

Official export credits have, until recently, not received the attention they deserve as a source of development financing. In part, the reason for this may lie in the fact that these credits cut across other balance-of-payments categories: to the extent that they reflect credits initially granted by official export agencies or taken over by export guarantee agencies, they appear as part of official long-term lending; but in so far as they refer to officially guaranteed private credits on which the guarantee has not been invoked, the actual credits are recorded in the balance of payments under bank credit or suppliers' credit. Traditional balance-of-payment statistics, which tend to be structured by debtors rather than by creditors, do not record a number for official export credits, and data under this heading have been assembled, with considerable difficulty, in the last few years only; the quality of these statistics is recognised as poor[11].

Up to the debt crisis, export credit agencies had been successfully (and profitably) promoting national exports. Propelled by competitive motives, they had continued to provide or ensure export credit even when it appeared likely that the policies pursued by some of the debtor countries would to lead to future difficulties. Then, when arrears emerged or the debtor asked for rescheduling, the agencies typically abruptly ceased to provide cover, and stayed "off cover" for a number of years until they considered that the debtor's payment difficulties has been overcome and its creditworthiness re-established. This meant that just when a country began to implement a Fund adjustment programme in conjunction with a Paris Club debt rescheduling, it lost its access to official export credits from the main industrial countries.

The statistics (such as they are) on the activities of official export promotion through credits and credit guarantees testify to the importance of this source of foreign capital but suggest that its time path may have been broadly in parallel with the general credit extension by the commercial banks, taking into account the long lags inherent in the export credit business where disbursements tend to run some three years behind the agencies' offer of credit insurance. In 1984, (the first year for which a consistent series of stock data is available) official export credits to all developing countries (measured as the net increase in the credit agencies' exposure) have been estimated as in excess of $15 billion[12]. The amounts in the preceding years must have been of a similar order of magnitude to build up to a stock of outstanding credit of $145 billion at end 1983[13]. Note that the net flow of $15 billion in 1984 represents about 30 per cent of the financing need as defined in Table 7.1, and is about as large as foreign aid in the same year.

This figure, however, still reflected the generous export promotion of the early 1980s. As the agencies tightened access in 1982 and 1983, net flows in 1985 and 1986 declined sharply below the 1984 level (by about $1 billion and $4 billion respectively).

Against this background, official export credits would deserve particular attention as a means of promoting capital flows to the developing world when other sources of credit dried up. In principle, at least, the authorities in the industrial countries could help to overcome the difficulties of highly indebted countries and, at the same time, give a fillip to their export industries, by pushing the export credit mechanism into higher gear. It was natural, therefore, that the Interim Committee, searching for some constructive contribution that it could make to the debt crisis, in early 1985 came up with a recommendation for an early resumption of export credit cover. The wording of the recommendation may not look particularly impressive[14]; but at least in this case, unlike most of the advice of the Interim Committee, which is addressed to others, the assembled ministers of the industrial countries were advancing a policy that they themselves could implement in their respective countries.

And, indeed export credit agencies have, over the past few years, been adopting a progressively more open stance. They will now typically resume cover after a debtor country has come to terms with its Paris Club creditors and will continue cover through subsequent annual Paris Club reschedulings[15]. Unfortunately, this change in practice has not led to the resumption of a larger flow of export credits. In part this is still the after-effect of the tightening of access that took place in 1982-84. But the low level of new commitments in 1985 and 1986, which presage low net flows in 1987 and 1988, appears to be indicative of a decline in demand in the face of a more open supply. Developing countries, even those without payment difficulties, have cut back sharply on large public sector investment projects for which export credit insurance has traditionally been sought. Reasons for the cutbacks have been the desire to limit external indebtedness as well as the scarcity of matching domestic budgetary funds — the same reasons that reduced the demand for project loans from the World Bank. In conclusion, therefore, the negative implication of the shrinkage in official export credits in recent years lies not so much in the reduced amount of balance-of-payments credit as in the disconcerting implications for long-run growth of the sharp cut in investment that used to be financed by such credits. The positive implication is that once investment demand revives official export credits are likely to be available.

NOTES AND REFERENCES

1. In recent years, and in particular from 1981 onwards, the figures for the combined current account deficit of the industrial countries, as well as those for the United States referred to below, are inflated by the systematic under-reporting of invisible income items. These and other weaknesses of the data underlie also the large negative figures (reaching in some years about $100 billion) for the current account balance for the world as a whole. Cf. IMF, *Final Report of the Working Party on the Statistical Discrepancy in World Current Account Balances,* Washington, 1987.

2. The sentence is phrased in the past tense. Important reductions in corporate and personal tax rates introduced in the United States in 1987 mitigated somewhat the extent to which the United States economy is protected from high interest rates.

3. The author first ran into this problem many years ago when he attempted a sensitivity analysis of the current account effect of different uses made of investment financed by borrowing from abroad (Polak 1943, pp. 208-240). It was there found that the foreign balance as calculated on the basis of slightly different assumptions was substantially affected by what seemed to be innocuous rounding-off procedures (Footnote 8 on p. 230).

4. When a committee of the League of Nations studied the interwar experience for guidance on better management of the post-war economy, it had this to say on the nature of foreign investment:
    There are certain principles concerning long-term foreign investment on which we insist. The first of these principles is that, whenever possible, preference should be given to equity investment over debt ... there is real danger, in our opinion, of attention being so concentrated on the satisfaction of immediate and pressing capital needs that subsequent effects will be ignored. To pump capital into stricken areas by the most perfect pumping mechanisms will benefit no one in the long run if the strain imposed by the reverse movement later, when amortization and interest payments exceed new lending, leads to a breakdown similar to that of 1929 (League of Nations 1943, pp. 95-96).

5. Under a production-sharing contract, the foreign company receives a fixed proportion of the

physical output; under a risk service contract, a fixed proportion of the money value of the output.

6. United States pension funds, with assets of about $2 000 billion at the end of 1987, held some $120 to $140 billion in foreign securities, of which only $1 to $2 billion was estimated to be in LDC securities or LDC country funds.

7. The diversity of fluctuation for the emerging markets held even through the October 1987 crash, when all OECD stock markets fell more or less in unison. By February 1988, the stock markets in four of the emerging markets monitored by the IFC (Korea, Venezuela, Zimbabwe and Jordan) were above their 1987 highs, while the markets in three others (Mexico, Hong Kong, and Malaysia) had declined substantially more than in the main OECD countries.

8. Total return, 1976-83, reported as 25.5 per cent for the IFC "emerging markets index" as against 12.1 for the *Capital International* world index (Lessard and Williamson 1985, p. 56-57).

9. This figure does not include inflows into investment trusts established through debt-equity swaps, which amounted to some $600 million in the eighteen months through June 1988, but which, of course, do not in the main represent new capital inflows.

10. See Dillon and Duran-Downing, *Officially Supported Export Credits* (IMF 1988, p. 24). This section draws heavily on this IMF publication.

11. The reasons why the statistics available from the creditor countries are difficult to interpret are extensively discussed in Dillon and Duran-Downing (1988, Appendix II). Debtor countries' statistics, to the extent that they have been tested in the context of Paris Club reschedulings, are considered even less informative — if for no other reason than that some official export credit guarantee agencies make every effort to ensure that the debtor is not informed of the existence of a guarantee.

12. The figure of $15 billion is found in Dillon and Duran-Downing (1988, p. 15), with the comment that it understates the net flow by the amounts of rescheduled credits not reported. Such amounts have become increasingly important since 1984.

13. Outstanding credits at the end of both 1983 and 1984 are estimated at about $145 billion at current exchange rates. The stability in the total is compatible with a large net flow during the year since the value of outstanding credits in currencies other than the dollar declined with the appreciation of the dollar. About one-third of the total outstanding represented guaranteed bank credits and the remainder direct official export credits and insured suppliers' credits.

14. "For those countries whose external debt has been rescheduled, whose prospects of economic progress are good, and which are undertaking satisfactory adjustment policies, the industrial countries should consider resuming export credit cover, subject to standard national policies." Communiqué of The Interim Committee of 19th April 1985, last sentence of paragraph 7 (*IMF Annual Report, 1985*, p. 129).

15. This change in policy required a prior change in the technique of Paris Club reschedulings. Until early 1984, the Paris Club followed the practice, in second or subsequent reschedulings for the same country, to "advance the cut-off dates", i.e. to subject to rescheduling any new export credits that might have been granted after a previous rescheduling. This practice

147

entailed a degree of risk that the agencies were not willing to bear. To permit an early resumption of cover, and the maintenance of cover through subsequent Paris Club meetings, it was necessary to switch to a practice of keeping the original cut-off date through successive reschedulings, and this change was adopted in the course of 1984.

Chapter 8

FINANCIAL FLOWS AND FINANCIAL POLICIES: THE IMF AND THE WORLD BANK

8.1   Introduction

In the post-war period, the International Monetary Fund and the International Bank for Reconstruction and Development have been the two major official institutions concerned with both financial flows to the developing countries and the financial policies of these countries.

As conceived at the 1944 Bretton Woods Conference, neither institution's functions were limited to the developing countries. The World Bank made large loans for reconstruction of industrial countries in the early post-war years. Once that task was finished, its financial activities were concentrated entirely on the provision of loans to promote — and in recent years also to maintain the momentum of — the economic growth of developing countries. The Fund's field of activities, both regulatory and financial, covers its whole membership, with no formal distinction between developed and developing countries. As a matter of practice, however, the Fund's financial policies have been increasingly directed towards the needs of the developing countries. These policies included the creation of the Compensatory Financing Facility (CFF, 1963), the Extended Fund Facility (EFF, 1974), the Structural Adjustment Facility (SAF, 1986) and the Enhanced Structural Adjustment Facility (ESAF, 1988), all of which were designed to assist the non-industrial members of the Fund. Moreover, no industrial country has used the Fund's regular financial resources in the last ten years. The reason for this is not that the industrial countries have avoided balance-of-payments difficulties, but that they have found convenient sources of finance elsewhere: in the Eurodollar markets; in the credit mechanisms of the European Community and, as far as the United States is concerned, in large-scale purchases of dollars in the exchange markets, mostly by other industrial countries anxious to mitigate the appreciation of their own currencies. Whatever the circumstances that have enabled industrial countries to avoid the need to approach the Fund for credit, the effect has been to restrict the financial activities of the Fund to the developing countries.

The financial purposes of the two institutions are different; the Fund extends credit for a limited number of years to enable a country to meet balance-of-payments deficits of a temporary nature, while the Bank gives long-term development credit. Hence, the Fund's credits revolve much faster than those of the Bank, and even though the amount of credit extended by the Fund exceeds in some years loan disbursements by the Bank (for example in 1982, 1983 and 1984), the amount of the Bank's outstanding loans (in the order of $100 billion) is about $2\frac{1}{2}$ times the amount the outstanding Fund credit to developing countries.

With respect to the interest taken in the broad financial policies of their members, the relative roles of the two institutions were, at least until recently, the reverse: the Fund was much more active than the Bank. The Fund's relations with all its members have always put much emphasis on the pursuit by members of financial policies that contribute to growth and adjustment[1]. These relations are intensified when the Fund provides balance-of-payments credit to a member, as it has been doing to many developing countries in recent years. In the Bank, by contrast, policy discussions with members on macroeconomic issues played only a subsidiary role as long as the Bank's lending activities were overwhelmingly directed toward the financing of individual projects; but more recently, since programme and sector lending has assumed a larger proportion of the Bank's lending operations, the Bank has become more active in the field of its members' macroeconomic policies.

After these introductory observations of a comparative character, I shall discuss the two institutions separately in their twin roles of contributing finance and influencing members' financial policies — the IMF in Sections 8.2 to 8.4 and the IBRD in the next two sections. The final three sections of this chapter are devoted to a discussion of the role of the two institutions in the debt crisis.

8.2 The Fund and the Policies of Its Members

Under its statutes as agreed at Bretton Woods, the Fund was charged with a double task consisting of (1) promoting certain features of the international monetary system, such as balanced growth of international trade, exchange stability, multilateral payments and the elimination of foreign exchange restrictions and (2) extending credit to its members. These two fundamental aspects of the Fund's mission — the regulatory and the financial — are not to be seen as separate or competing. On the contrary, they are complementary. Specifically, the Fund was equipped to extend balance-of-payments credit to enable its members to continue to pursue, even under adverse conditions, policy objectives laid down in the Fund's purposes. In the absence of financial support from the Fund, balance-of-payments difficulties might have induced countries to weaken their pursuit of these objectives and, for example, to abandon exchange rate stability or resort to discriminatory payments arrangements or the imposition of exchange restrictions.

When a member decides to use Fund finance, a second set of linkages between the provision of the Fund's money and the member's policies comes into play. The Fund's concern is now no longer limited to the member's observance of the general rules of conduct in the international monetary system; indeed, on this score the Fund may be willing to grant some temporary dispensation, such as approval of a multiple exchange rate or some exchange restrictions, if the member's situation appears to require that. But at the same time the Fund will want to satisfy itself that the country's macroeconomic policies are sufficiently strong to make it plausible that they will bring the payments position of the country into balance within a reasonable time; "to shorten the duration and lessen the degree of disequilibrium in the international balances of payments" is listed as the sixth and last of the Fund's Purposes. If a country's polices are successful in this respect, it will also be in a position to repay the Fund within a limited number of years. The intended turnaround period differs somewhat depending on the "facility" under which credit is made available. It is three to five years for regular Fund credit and five to ten years for credit under the Extended Fund Facility; but in any event the expectation must be credibly established that the use of the Fund's money will be temporary.

The requirements of the Fund with respect to policy action necessary to make a country's use of the Fund's resources temporary are captured in the code word "conditionality". In contrast to the situation some years ago the concept of conditionality is no longer controversial; in the large body of literature on this subject (Williamson ed. 1983, Guitian 1981, Kenen 1986, Killick 1984, Dell 1981, Myers 1985) it is generally agreed that lending by the Fund must be predicated on policies by the borrowing country that will correct its payments position. Critics of the particulars of the Fund's conditionality fall rather neatly into two groups: those who fault the Fund for too much interference in members' domestic affairs, and those who fault it for too little. The former critics want the Fund to disinterest itself from the specific corrective policies needed to bring about the desired payments improvements, while the latter want the Fund to extend its conditionality to cover such issues as income distribution or human rights. It has to be recognised in this connection that areas of disagreement are probably inevitable in the confrontation between an international organisation with the power to lend or withhold money in critical situations and member countries in the throes of political tensions often springing, at least in part, from failed economic policies. To review the debate on conditionality would take us outside the scope of this study. What is relevant in the present context is the influence that the Fund's conditionality attempts to exercise in steering members' financial policies towards the objective of economic growth.

Not all cases of balance-of-payments deficit require changes in policies. When the causes of a country's problems can confidently be expected to reverse themselves before too long, it is reasonable for the country to wait out the process of self-correction and, in the meantime, to finance, rather than try to correct, the deficit in its international payments. This was the philosophy that underlies the Fund's "Compensatory Financing Facility" under which members could obtain, with a minimum of policy conditions, additional Fund credit to meet temporary shortfalls in their export proceeds if these were primarily attributable to factors beyond the member's control.

But payments deficits that can be considered fully self-correcting are the exception rather than the rule[2]. In most cases of deficits, some adjustment is indicated: not only in situations where unduly expansionary policies had caused excessive domestic absorption, but also in cases where a lasting change coming from abroad — e.g. an increase in the cost of energy — made policies that might have been perfectly adequate before insufficient to meet the new circumstances.

To bring about adjustment, the country has to reduce its total absorption and/or increase its supply of goods and services to a combined total change that reduces the deficit in payments to an amount that can be financed on a durable

152

basis. Finance from the Fund, from the country's own resources, or from other sources will permit some relief during a transitional period, thus easing to some extent the pain of adjustment. The country's financial policies will have to be designed in such a manner that the necessary adjustment is achieved within the time constraint set by available financing possibilities.

If the level of demand was initially excessive, the policies to achieve this objective have to contain a component that brings down aggregate demand. Depending on how far the level of demand is being compressed, these policies may be labeled anti-inflationary or deflationary (contractionary). The policies can consist of budgetary measures, such as expenditure cuts or higher taxation, or measures that limit the amount of credit the banks can extend. Often, where the initial expansionary cause resided in the fiscal situation and the budget deficit was financed by the banks, budgetary and credit measures may be complementary instruments. These or other measures aiming at the compression of aggregate demand are likely to bring about rather promptly the desired improvement in the current account of the balance of payments, though frequently at the cost of an initial decline in output.

It is fair to say that in its first decade or so of operations the Fund's advice on how to correct payments disequilibria did not go beyond the demand restricting component. This was the component that was almost always necessary in an adjustment programme to achieve the objective for which the Fund was most directly responsible: the correction of the payments situation. It was recognised that the introduction of "monetary stability" was often "only the beginning of the efforts needed to achieve growth". But at the time these latter efforts were believed to fall largely outside the sphere of activities of the Fund, although the Fund stated that it was anxious to assist these efforts insofar as it could[3].

Obviously, countries undergoing an adjustment process want to do more than correct their payments position. They also want, as quickly as possible, to resume economic growth. The additional measures needed for this purpose fall in the broad category of supply policies, such as the stimulation of farm production by setting or allowing more remunerative prices, the stimulation of exports and import substitution by a more competitive exchange rate[4], or the more effective use of capital by raising the interest rate to a market-related level. Over the years, the Fund has increasingly been urging members to include in their adjustment programmes a wide range of supply policies (Guitian 1981). Emphasis on supply policies on the part of the Fund has not always been welcomed by the members concerned. It is indeed tragic to observe how in a number of developing countries suffering from protracted payments difficulties the process of adjustment is prolonged, and growth delayed, as the adoption of supply-promoting measures is resisted and excessive reliance continues to be placed on demand restraint and highly distortionary import restrictions.

The strongest move toward recognition of, and insistence on, adequate supply policies as part of the Fund's conditionality in making finance available is to be found in the joint Fund-Bank preparation for credits under the Structural Adjustment Facility (SAF) and its enhanced version, the ESAF, both facilities exclusively available to low-income countries[5]. The beneficiaries of these facilities are mostly the countries in Sub-Saharan Africa but a few low-income countries in Asia and Latin America also qualify. India and China, both of which qualify on the basis of their per capita income levels, have generously forgone applying, thus raising very substantially the amount available for other, smaller, low-income countries. In the preparation for obtaining SAF credits, member countries are required to submit three-year policy frameworks prepared in co-operation with the staff of the Fund and the Bank. As a result of this approach, structural adjustment (i.e. adjustment on the supply side) policies are given full weight, in SAF and ESAF programmes, in conjunction with policies to contain aggregate demand within the limits the country can sustain. These limits, in turn, have been raised materially as a result of the resources available from SAF or ESAF, other Fund credits that the country concerned may negotiate in the same context, credits from IDA and other funds administered by the World Bank, and in some cases enhanced aid from bilateral donors.

8.3 Quantitative Aspects of Fund Credit

One of the Fund's principles is that the revolving character of its resources must be safeguarded. This means, in the first place, that each credit[6] granted by the Fund must be reimbursed over a specified period, which may be three to five years or five to ten years, depending on the lending facility under which the country has borrowed. As a matter of principle, the Fund does not renegotiate or extend the terms of credits previously granted. It has found that some debtor countries were unable — and in at least one case, that of Peru, unwilling — to make repayments when these were due, or to pay interest on time; in all these cases it has urged the country to come into compliance with the rules. When this did not occur after a number of increasingly strong messages that might

154

stretch over a period of a year or so, the Fund has declared the country ineligible to use its resources. At the end of June 1988, eight member countries were in the ineligible category (Guyana, Peru, Vietnam and five African countries) and the overdue payments owed by these countries and others with arrears to the Fund in excess of six months totaled about SDR 2 billion.

But the concept of the revolving character of use of the Fund goes beyond payments of interest and principal being made on time. It also includes the notion that members should arrange their international financial affairs in such a way that indebtedness to the Fund is not a lasting situation. A period of indebtedness is expected to be followed by one in which the member is not indebted to the Fund and may well have a creditor position, financing through the Fund the credits outstanding for the benefit of other members. This broader view of a revolving Fund, which was a prominent element in early descriptions of the institution, implied the connotation of a mutual credit association in which the members would alternate between debtor and creditor positions.

The industrial members that used the Fund, as well as the largest developing members, have generally conducted their financial relations with the institution in accordance with this wider concept of a revolving Fund. Of the nine developing countries with the largest quotas, three (Saudi Arabia, Venezuela and Nigeria)[7] have never drawn on the Fund and the other six all followed an in-and-out pattern. Thus India was out of debt to the Fund from 1971 to 1973 and again in 1978-79; China, since 1983; Brazil, from 1968 through 1981; Mexico never drew before 1976 and was out of debt in 1980-81; Argentina had a debt-free period from 1967 to 1971 and again from 1978 to 1982, and Indonesia, from 1974 to 1982. But among the other LDC members, prolonged use was the rule rather than the exception. By the end of 1987, 18 African countries had been uninterruptedly in debt to the Fund for more than ten years, including three for over twenty years. Eight countries in the Western Hemisphere, eleven in Asia and four in Southern Europe were also in the over ten-years group. Thus, if one looks at the pattern of total outstanding Fund credit to developing countries over the years, the trend is strongly upward, from about SDR 1 billion in the mid-1960s to about SDR 30 billion in 1987 after declining from the 1984-85 peak; a thirty-fold increase over a period during which these countries' imports increased roughly ten-fold and their quotas about five-fold.

There have so far been only two periods during which Fund credit to developing countries showed important declines: from 1968 to 1970, when the reserves of virtually all countries in the world increased as the counterpart to the payments deficit of the United States, and in the last two and a half years, following the rapid expansion of credit that led to a peak value of SDR 37.7 billion at the end of 1985; by mid-1988 the amount outstanding was down by one-fourth to SDR 28.6 billion[8]. In one sense, these interruptions of the trend can be attributed to the Fund's rules on repurchase, which have the purpose — and normally the effect — that particular credits are fully repaid in five years (and for some facilities in ten years). The repurchase rules thus impart a cyclical component to the amount of credit outstanding.

Table 8.1.   OUTSTANDING FUND CREDIT TO DEVELOPING COUNTRIES, 1950-88

SDR billion

End of period	General resources account	Trust fund loans	Structural adjustment facility	Total[a]
1950	0.1	—	—	0.1
1955	0.1	—	—	0.1
1960	0.4	—	—	0.4
1965		—	—	
1970		—	—	
1975		—	—	
1980	7.4	2.6	—	10.1
1981	12.8	3.0	—	15.8
1982	19.2	3.0	—	22.2
1983	29.9	2.9	—	32.8
1984	34.9	2.8	—	37.7
1985	35.2	2.5	—	37.6
1986	33.4	1.9	0.1	35.3
1987	28.8	1.4	0.5	30.6
1988 (June)	26.8	1.1	0.6	28.6

a)   May differ from sum of three preceding columns due to rounding.
Source: IMF.

But other factors are at least as important. Countries that repay the Fund can negotiate new credits if their payments position is still weak provided they can reach agreement with the Fund on the associated policies. The two conditions are not independent; countries may allow arrangements to lapse before having drawn the full amount available if their payments outlook improves (as India and Brazil did in 1984)[9] and may revert to the Fund as their situations worsen as Brazil, after a long interlude, did in the summer of 1988. Thus, there is an important demand element in the degree to which the Fund's resources are used, which is further supported by the historic tendency of the Fund to broaden members' opportunities for access in response to new evidence of need; ESAF is the most recent example of this[10]. Over the medium term, these considerations of demand tend to dominate the amount of Fund credit outstanding. Fluctuations in the payments pressure that countries experience will be reflected in the degree of interest they attach to entering into discussions with the Fund on new credits and will thus, with a lag, result in fluctuations in drawings. That lag can be long: countries' attitudes towards the Fund, like supertankers at full speed, are not quickly turned around.

The attachment of the Fund to the principle of temporary use derives not only from the Fund's concern that payments imbalances be corrected without undue delay; it is also related to the confidence that creditor countries have in the liquidity of their asset position in the Fund. The counterpart of credits extended by the Fund is held by creditor countries (usually their central banks) as part of their reserves. Even though it is only a small part of reserves, its liquidity must be beyond question. In particular on the occasion of the quinquennial reviews of the Fund's quotas, the issue of the revolving character of the Fund's assets tends to arise as a factor in the willingness of certain creditor countries to enlarge their quotas.

There is, thus, every reason for the Fund to stress the revolving character of its credit and to encourage measures by debtor countries that make this a reality. This attitude does not, of course, mean that after a surge in use the Fund must by any means available reduce the level of its outstanding credit, either to individual countries or in total. In any concrete situation, the Fund's first tasks are the protection of its members and of the international monetary system; but even in difficult times these tasks do not necessary conflict with substantial repayment to the Fund by some part of the membership. In the light of past experience, if the weakness in the world economy that has been evident since 1985 persists, there is little reason to expect a further sharp reduction of the outstanding amount of Fund credit to the developing countries; indeed, it may well resume its upward trend.

In this general context, Fund credit to African countries deserves particular attention. In a few years, from 1980 to 1984, the Fund's outstanding credit to its African members quadrupled, from SDR 1.8 to SDR 7.1 billion. In these years, the Fund was forthcoming in responding to the needs of that continent

157

while bilateral and multilateral aid donors were less quick to react. The infusion of so much Fund money, at approximately market interest rates, did certainly not constitute the optimum solution to the needs of these poor countries but it was perhaps the only solution available at the time. Now that other, less expensive, sources of assistance to the African countries have come on stream — including the Fund's own Structural Adjustment Facility and ESAF — there is no reason to expect further increases in the amount of regular Fund credit; indeed some reduction will be desirable from these countries' point of view if they can apply some of the low-interest loans from other sources for this purpose. But to the extent that that is not possible, the Fund should not seek a reduction of outstandings in the face of the overwhelming problems of most of these countries, merely to demonstrate the revolving character of its resources. As mentioned, the Fund does not "refinance" or "extend" credits, but provided the countries concerned can agree with it on new programmes, the Fund can make new loans while older loans are being repaid as scheduled.

8.4 The SDR Mechanism and the Developing Countries

In 1969, the entry into effect of the First Amendment to its Articles of Agreement extended the responsibilities of the Fund to watching over the adequacy of the supply of international liquidity in the international monetary system. In that context the Fund was given the power to create new reserve assets in the form of "Special Drawing Rights" (SDRs) if it judged this necessary to supplement existing reserves assets, which at that time consisted mostly of gold and US dollars[11]. The Fund has only twice decided to "allocate" SDRs to its members, in 1969 for the three-year period 1970-72 and in 1978 for the period 1979-81. As a result of these actions, members hold about SDR 20 billion (equivalent to about $26 billion at mid-1988 exchange rates), less than 5 per cent of their holdings of foreign exchange. A sharp division of views among members on the advisability of SDR allocations in present circumstances has stood in the way of allocations since the beginning of the decade.

Would a more positive attitude on the part of the major industrial countries (in particular the United States, the United Kingdom, Germany and Japan), leading to resumed allocations, be of assistance to the developing countries? Two distinct issues arise in this connection: *(a)* the potential benefits to developing countries of SDR allocations as envisaged under the Fund's current Articles of Agreement, *viz.* to help them finance the secular growth of their reserves, and *(b)* the use of SDR allocations to finance a larger flow of development capital to these countries — a subject that has long been discussed as "The Link" (between reserve creation and development finance). We shall discuss these two issues in the following two sub-sections.

a)   SDR allocations to facilitate the build-up of countries' reserves

One of the main factors in the declining interest in SDR allocations that has gradually spread among the industrial countries is the expansion in the activities of commercial banks over the past twenty years. In the 1960s there was good reason to fear that the growing need for reserves would not be met within the existing par value system, either by a substantial flow of dollars from the United States or by increases in gold production. A potential world-wide reserve shortage, leading to strains on economic growth and on the further liberalisation of trade and capital movements, was therefore seen as a realistic risk, to which the creation of SDRs was conceived as the answer.

Since then, a major change has taken place in the international monetary system. The Bretton Woods par value arrangements have been blown away, and international banking has assumed enormous proportions. These developments have enabled many countries, developing as well as developed, to meet their need for growing reserves by borrowing from the international banking system. Even though the debt crisis of the 1980s has put a crimp in the flow of bank loans to one large group of countries, the stock of reserves in the world has resumed its upward trend, even in many countries that were affected by the debt crisis.

The risk of a general shortage of reserves — the original reason for which the SDR was designed — is thus no longer clearly in evidence. This fact does not constitute a bar to the resumption of SDR allocations; indeed the second decision to allocate was taken at a time (in 1978) when the change in the system was fully recognised. A number of valid reasons for allocation can still be cited (Polak 1988). While the risks to the system with respect to the quantity of reserves have been much reduced, there remains an element of qualitative risk: large-scale borrowing to build up national reserves is risky because banks may refuse to roll over loans in the very circumstances in which the reserves are most needed. The acquisition of a sufficient buffer stock of reserves is, moreover, a costly matter for many developing countries, in particular for those that do not have access to international bank credit. For them, the acquisition of reserves competes with the growth in their imports and hence the growth rate of their economies and an allocation of SDRs would be important

159

in reconciling what could otherwise be a painful conflict between growth and reserve adequacy.

The resumption of general annual allocations would thus provide benefits both to the system, in the sense that it would reduce the importance of borrowed reserves, and to many individual members. The developing countries have been strongly demanding allocations; while some industrial countries may not see this as a matter of great interest to themselves, they could remove a contentious North-South issue by agreeing to allocations on an appropriate scale.

b)   The link between SDR allocation and development finance[12]

Ever since the question of the creation of a new type of reserve asset surfaced in the 1960s, it has been suggested that any new mechanism of reserve creation could at the same time be used as a source to finance the payments needs of developing countries. This suggestion was actively discussed at ministerial level in the Committee of Twenty (Committee on Reform of the International Monetary System and Related Issues) between 1972 and 1974. The developing countries hoped to achieve receiving a much larger share in allocations than their share in Fund quotas (about one-third), which to the extent that it exceeded their need for reserves could be used to finance a higher level of imports. Some industrial countries approached the broad concept of the Link in a different way: not to give developing countries control over a larger proportion of allocated SDRs, but as a relatively painless way of channeling resources to development agencies, such as IDA, without the need for budgetary approval by parliaments. That version of the Link was, however, of no great interest to the developing countries.

At one stage of its deliberations, the Committee of Twenty came close to agreeing on the principle of a Link between reserve creation and development assistance, with only the United States and Germany holding out against it. Since then, however, the opposition to the concept has broadened to include by now almost all industrial countries. The fundamental objection on their part is that decisions on the desirable amount of reserve creation should not become entangled in an entirely different matter, the appropriate amount of official credit flows to the developing countries. At the same time, the potential benefits that developing countries could reap from an SDR Link have been substantially reduced. The SDR is an interest-bearing asset; users of SDRs pay interest and countries that acquire SDRs through transactions earn interest on them, as they do on their holdings of reserve currencies. When the discussion on the Link started, the SDR interest rate was very low, so that allocations had a high "grant content". Gradually, however, the rate has been moved up to market levels to raise the attractiveness of the SDR as a reserve asset. While this has not eliminated the interest of developing countries in allocations, it has reduced it. Thus, for example, the replacement of any part of IDA money by Link money would be to the detriment of low-income countries. It is noteworthy in this connection that recent communiqués (September 1987 and April 1988) of the Group of Twenty-Four no longer mention the Link. Previously, the persistent advocacy of the Link in pronouncements by developing countries had probably raised antagonism to any SDR allocations on the side of the developed countries. The latter had, indeed, been instrumental in getting acceptance of a set of words in a communiqué of the Interim Committee that implied that the Link was incompatible with "the monetary character of the SDR"[13]. This appears to seal the demise of the Link — and perhaps thereby to raise the chances for the resumption of regular SDR allocations.

8.5   The World Bank and the Policies of Borrowers

Like the Fund, the World Bank has command over large financial resources — its paid in capital and much larger amounts borrowed in the world's capital markets — that it can put at the disposal of its members for purposes stated in its Articles of Agreement. Like the Fund, too, the Bank has always had a deep interest in the economic policies of the members borrowing its resources, both (in the early years perhaps primarily) for the parochial reason of ensuring that its loans would be serviced, and increasingly, as the Bank grew in stature, for the broader reason that sound economic policies were the principal key to a country's ability to develop. But the Bank has found it more difficult than the Fund to establish a close and efficient integration between the provision of resources and the promotion of desirable policies by its members.

For the Fund, there is a natural link between the financial and the policy dimensions of its purposes. There is an obvious connection between the granting of balance-of-payments loans that are expected to be repaid in a few years and policies to promote creditworthiness. It took the Fund a few years to make this connection clear; in the early years of the Fund the complaint of its potential borrowers was not (in today's terminology) that the Fund's "conditionality" was too demanding, but that members lacked any certainty as to where they stood with the institution (Horsefield 1969, pp. 190-191). But, by the early 1950s the Fund had found a way to integrate its credit extension with its concern about the borrowing member's policy, using the process of negotiated conditionality to this end.

There was no obvious parallel for the Bank. True, the Bank began, like the Fund, by giving balance-of-payments loans (to finance the imports needed for reconstruction) to a few European countries in whose policies it had sufficient confidence (France, the Netherlands, Denmark and Luxembourg, all in the spring and summer of 1947) (Mason and Asher 1973, p. 154). But these were exceptions to the general rule of the Bank's Articles of Agreement that its "loans shall, except in special circumstances, be for the purpose of specific projects of reconstruction or development" [Article III, Section 4 (vii)]. And not all its members were considered by the Bank as such prime borrowers to which loans could be extended without dialogue about the countries' economic policies. Yet it could hardly seem natural to mix discussions on macroeconomic policies with the negotiation of a wide range of technical and organisational particulars concerning some development project; indeed, later experience taught the Bank that this approach would be unsatisfactory if tried (see below).

This put the Bank in a dilemma. It was deeply concerned about the creditworthiness of its borrowers, probably more so than the Fund[14]. The Bank observed (AR 1948) that in many countries the social, economic and political conditions for development were lacking, raising serious questions about the ability of these countries to service foreign loans, from the Bank or other creditors. In its early years, "the Bank merely observed these obstacles (in sorrow — it is true)" (Adler 1977, p. 31). They led it to adopt a non-negotiating, arms-length approach in its judgment on a country's macroeconomic performance: if that performance was considered acceptable, the country would be treated as creditworthy for individual projects; if not, it would not receive Bank financing, however meritorious an individual project might be.

If a country was judged creditworthy the Bank sometimes entered into important policy negotiations that could greatly influence the scale and content of a country lending programme; but it was only much later — in the 1970s — that the Bank set out as a general policy to remove the fundamental obstacles to development in its member countries, through policy advice, technical assistance, proposals for institutional reform, and greatly expanded lending operations (Adler 1977, p. 31); this approach was reinforced when the Bank introduced lending for "structural adjustment" in 1980 (see below).

When the Bank started its operations the emphasis in development theory was overwhelmingly on investment as the crucial factor in accelerating growth. Among potential investment projects, those financing infrastructure fitted most comfortably with the Articles and the private enterprise philosophy of the Bank. "The absence, or severe inadequacy, of infrastructure facilities was one of the clearly identifiable differences between developing and developed countries, and infrastructure investment lent itself ideally to the 'specific project' financing called for in the Articles. Infrastructure projects, too, were considered well suited for debt financing, as distinct from equity financing, which would be at least partially required for 'directly productive' investment in industry and agriculture" (Adler 1977, p. 32). In accordance with this approach, more than 70 per cent of the Bank's lending to developing countries[15] in its first two decades went for infrastructural projects broadly defined, with the percentage only gradually declining from the early 1960s (Table 8.2).

Table 8.2. COMPOSITION OF IBRD AND IDA LENDING TO DEVELOPING
COUNTRIES, BY FIVE-YEAR PERIODS

Per cent

	Infrastructure	Directly productive sectors	Programme loans
1948-52	77.1	21.4	1.5
1953-57	68.9	20.5	10.9
1958-62	87.0	13.0	—
1963-67	72.9	16.9	10.2
1968-72	66.9	28.2	5.0
1973-77	55.5	38.2	6.3
1978-82	59.2	33.9	6.9
1983-87	56.1	25.2	18.7

Source: Adler 1977 p. 33 up to 1977; World Bank data thereafter. The three categories of lending were defined as follows: Infrastructure: power, railways, highways, ports, telecommunications, irrigation, education, water supply, agricultural research, population and urbanisation. Directly Productive Sectors: agriculture and rural development (excluding irrigation and agricultural research), industry, development banks and tourism. Programme Loans: includes technical assistance loans and, from 1978 to 1987, all adjustment loans.

In the 1970s the Bank became increasingly conscious of obstacles to rapid growth other than the lack of capital, and of other development objectives than the growth of GDP or GDP per head. Both processes of discovery in the development field led the Bank to widen the aspects of the economy, or indeed of society, in which it took an active interest: employment and unemployment,

163

income distribution, literacy, health, population control, ecology, the role of women, etc. It also broadened greatly the scope of the projects for which it was willing to lend, beginning in the mid-1960s and expanding rapidly in the 1970s to include training, education, urban services, small-scale industry and agriculture, and family planning. In this process of widening its activities it was not always clear, as the Bank's history points out, whether or in how far this reflected a broader view of the of inputs needed for growth, or alternatively, a broadening of the meaning of development itself (Mason and Asher 1973, p. 484).

8.6 Bank Lending for Structural Adjustment

In the course of the 1970s, the Bank became increasingly convinced of the crucial importance to the development process of correct macro- and microeconomic policies and of the risk that sound individual projects might fail to make their contribution to development in a setting of distorted interest rates and overvalued currencies. It had also found that the leverage for better macro-policies that it could exercise in the context of project loans was severely limited. The narrow scope of projects, the specialist approaches of the negotiators on both the Bank and the country sides, the differences in timetables applicable to individual projects on the one hand and the development of policy on broader aspects of the national economy on the other hand — all these factors made the conclusion inevitable that "individual projects in general are inefficient instruments for inducing policy change" (World Bank 1982, para. 306). The logical conclusion of these observations was to tilt Bank lending in the direction of policy loans as distinguished from project loans.

The opportunity to move in this direction presented itself with the darkening of the horizon for many developing countries that began with the second oil shock in 1979. During the 1970s, non-oil developing countries had managed to maintain respectable growth, in spite of the 1973 increase in the price of oil — in part, of course — because a large proportion of the increased income of the oil exporters was recycled to the oil-importing countries in the developing world. But after the second oil shock occurred in 1979-80, it became increasingly clear that this scenario would not play again. This worsening in the economic climate, soon reinforced by recession in the industrial world, high interest rates and declining commodity prices, enhanced the importance of an improvement of policies of the developing countries as a precondition for the maintenance or resumption of a satisfactory growth rate. As put by Bank

Senior Vice President Ernest Stern in a conference held in early 1982, "distortions in the policy and allocation framework that were undesirable in the 1960s [had] become unsustainable in the much more difficult international economic environment of the 1980s" (Stern 1983, p. 91).

The difficulties of adjustment experienced by many members did not only enhance the need for policy reform; they also meant that fewer projects were started. In these circumstances, priority shifted to finding financing to relieve the constraint on the use of existing capacity imposed by foreign exchange stringency. This gave a definite attractiveness to Bank loans that would be promptly available to finance general imports as against new project loans, for which the demand had declined. The impact of these financial developments was reinforced by the growing realisation, among development economists, of the primary contribution that good macroeconomic policies could make to growth.

Against this background the Bank introduced in early 1980 the concept of the Structural Adjustment Loan (SAL); (if IDA funds were used, the term was Structural Adjustment Credit — SAC). SAC programmes aimed at achieving certain structural objectives for the country's economy over the medium term (five to seven years), such as increasing agricultural output and non-traditional exports, reducing protection, or improving price incentives. Governments applying for such programmes outlined the broad measures to be taken for these purposes over time, as well as the specific policy actions they would take before or during the twelve- to eighteen-month period of an individual SAL operation.

From the start of the SAL programme, the Bank found only a limited receptivity for structural adjustment loans among its borrowing members, in particular the larger ones (Nelson 1986, p. 74). Thus, among the heavily indebted countries, Argentina, Brazil, Colombia, Mexico, Nigeria and Venezuela never negotiated a SAL with the Bank. The Bank's Annual Reports repeatedly complain about the unwillingness of many countries ("those where the need for structural adjustment is greatest") (World Bank AR 1981, p. 70) to adopt the necessary policies. By 1985, only 17 countries had qualified for one or more SALs, about the same number that had SALs, or were in the process of negotiating them, four years earlier. The Bank noted that "participation remains limited by the quality and credibility of the programmes with which governments propose to address their structural adjustment problems, despite support from the Bank through analytical and technical advice" (World Bank AR 1985, p. 52).

165

In view of the difficulties encountered in negotiating SALs, the Bank increasingly handled its adjustment lending "by supporting policy improvements on a more limited sectoral basis in the hope that they could be broadened gradually" (World Bank AR 1981, p. 70). Thus, a trade policy loan would deal with trade liberalisation, an agriculture policy loan with agricultural pricing, etc. Apart from the rapid disbursement feature, these loans had much in common with "project loans" of the 1960s and 1970s that also addressed sector-wide policy issues and were based on policy understandings concerning an entire sector. In the 1980s, the fact that the conditionality of sectoral adjustment loans was less comprehensive, and hence less intrusive, made such loans more widely acceptable than structural adjustment loans (Helleiner 1986, p. 50).

Sectoral adjustment loans had been negligible in FY 1980-82, but then increased sharply as structural adjustment lending declined (Table 8.3). The two forms of structural lending together had approached 25 per cent of Bank and IDA lending by 1987, and are expected to stay at about that level for a number of years ahead.

Table 8.3.   BANK AND IDA ADJUSTMENT LENDING

Fiscal years, $ million

	1980	1981	1982	1983	1984	1985	1986	1987
Structural adjustment loans (including programme loans)	360	787	1 241	1 395	1 302	163	816	665
Sectoral adjustment loans	65	137	0	641	1 318	1 475	2 284	3 453
Total	425	924	1 241	2 036	2 620	1 638	3 100	4 118
As per cent of total Bank and IDA lending	3.7	7.5	9.5	14.1	16.9	11.4	19.0	23.3

Source: World Bank.

Since the aim of structural lending (including sector lending) is to improve macroeconomic as well as microeconomic policies, such lending normally has a close link to arrangements that the borrowing country has with the Fund. Except in a limited number of cases where the country was judged to be implementing a satisfactory macroeconomic programme by itself, Bank adjustment loans have always been extended in the context of a financial arrangement with the Fund. This arrangement was expected to "provide the foundation for more detailed measures to improve incentives, eliminate distortions promote production and increase the efficiency of resource use" (Stern 1983, p. 90).

Since each SAL is normally made available in two tranches, and most sectoral loans are "tranched" as well, there is an opportunity for a mid-term review of the implementation of the programme, with the opportunity for discussions, and negotiations on better compliance, before the second tranche is released. However, since the basic approach of adjustment lending lies in a series of three or more loans over a stretch of years, the Bank's "conditionality" is exercised primarily by the expectation that the experience under one loan will affect negotiations for subsequent loans, and not by its tranching policy. In fact, tranching as an instrument of conditionality in SALs is only superficially similar to the Fund's tranche policy. In the Fund, conditions for the release of successive tranches usually are set quarterly, implying up to eleven check points after the initial drawing for a three-year EFF with quarterly performance criteria. In SALs, there is only a single such checkpoint. Fund conditions in standby arrangements are few in number (rarely exceeding six), and highly specific e.g. that domestic credit creation (precisely defined in terms of balance sheet items) shall not exceed a certain amount, or that reserves should increase by a specified minimum. Failure to meet these criteria interrupts drawings automatically, and drawings cannot be resumed unless the failure is waived by the Executive Board as inconsequential in magnitude, or the programme is renegotiated. In SALs and in some sector loans, the targets are far more numerous (often 15 to 20) and often defined in general terms ("adoption of a public investment programme satisfactory to the Bank"; "progress in carrying out an administrative reform programme", etc.). Conditionality so structured allows the Bank staff considerable discretion, first to judge whether individual performance criteria have been satisfactorily met, and then to weigh pluses and minuses to come to a decision on whether or not to release the second tranche. As noted, and perhaps not surprisingly, this decision was virtually always positive, sometimes after some further negotiation with respect to policy for the second period, even though performance was less than expected in many instances (see below).

How well has structural adjustment lending achieved the aims set out for it? There is no doubt that economic and financial policies in many developing countries have shifted toward greater emphasis on efficiency and adaptability in the use of resources. The changing perception of economic policies that induced the Bank to propose adjustment lending has spread through much of

167

its membership. It is obviously an unanswerable question to what extent this spread was attributable to a pervasive change in *Zeitgeist,* to the accompanying arrangements made by members with the Fund, or to the Bank's new lending technique. It is clear in any event that policy-based lending provided the basis for a more focused dialogue on macro- and microeconomic policies between the Bank and many of its members. This has served to enhance policy-makers' attention to the issues that are of central importance in current international conditions, and thus has helped to promote decision making on these issues (Nelson 1986, p. 76).

A recent review of SALs for ten countries by the Bank's independent Operations Evaluation Department concludes that the staff of the Bank had set its sights too high in the design of the early SALs. Only four of the ten countries (Côte d'Ivoire, Jamaica, Thailand, and Turkey) showed clear and substantial achievement of the reforms envisaged; in four others (Kenya, Pakistan, the Philippines and Senegal) the performance was partially satisfactory, and in two early SALs (Bolivia and Guyana), the operations were essentially failures. The report also notes with respect to major policy issues that most countries found it difficult to combine demand management and exchange rate policies to stimulate exports, or to achieve effective import liberalisation. But budgetary performance generally improved, as did the quality and composition of public-investment programmes (World Bank AR 1987, pp. 54-55).

The heavy emphasis put by the Bank on policy adjustment as the rationale for SALs should not lead one to minimise their financial aspects. A government might be convinced of the need for policy changes and might perhaps have introduced these changes without the carrot of Bank money; but it would hardly have gone through the (by no means negligible) formal steps required by a SAL if it were not for the financial benefits SALs offered. Indeed, structuring SALs in large round amounts that would make a significant financial difference was seen in the Bank as a means to interest a country's highest policy makers in concluding a SAL arrangement with the Bank (Berg and Batchelder 1985, *passim*).

Some writers from the side of the Bank have tended to play down the financial importance of the SAL, perhaps in deference to the limitations in the Articles on non-project lending or to dispel criticism that the Bank, by giving balance-of-payments financing, trespasses on the field of operation of the Fund. Stern makes a point of insisting that "the primary purpose of a SAL is not to fill a current account deficit but to support a medium-term programme of changes necessary to reorient the economy and to bring its current account deficit to a more sustainable level over a number of years" (1983, p. 103)[16]. That certainly is the correct view as to why the Bank is interested in SALs. But the balance-of-payments effect of SALs is much more than an incidental side-effect[17]. The quick-disbursing loans for imports were a very helpful response by the Bank to the difficult circumstances in which many members found (and find) themselves. When the utilisation of a country's existing capacity is kept down on account of a scarcity of imported inputs, a SAL serves the purpose of maintaining the country's growth rate in two ways: not only in the medium-term, via an improvement in the structure of its economy, but also in the crucial interim period, by providing the means to maintain an adequate level of imports.

8.7   Fund and Bank Lending Since the Debt Crisis

When the debt crisis broke in the summer of 1982 the IMF, and in particular its Managing Director, Jacques de Larosière, assumed a crucial role in the highly confused and potentially explosive situation. The Fund became the traffic policeman at a multiple intersection — negotiating with debtor countries on adjustment programmes without which no financial arrangements were possible; promising to lend its own resources on a large scale if agreement on programmes could be reached; working with the BIS and central banks on bridge financing pending the elaboration of a programme and their formal acceptance by the Fund; persuading governments to provide credit on a bilateral basis through export financing agencies or otherwise, and bringing heavy pressure to bear on the commercial banks to restructure loans falling due, to lend large sums in "new money" in proportion to their existing exposure, and to maintain interbank lines of credit to foreign branches of international banks located in indebted countries.

In this first phase of the management of the debt crisis, from late 1982 to late 1985, the Fund was the organiser of both the policy packages and the *quid pro quo* financial packages. In these latter packages, World Bank credit typically constituted only a rather small proportion, far larger amounts being lent by the Fund and the commercial banks. In the three calendar years 1983-85, the Fund lent more than $5\frac{1}{2}$ times as much to the six largest problem debtors as the Bank's adjustment loans to the same countries (Table 8.4). But by 1986-87, Fund lending had become much smaller than in the earlier period, and the Bank's adjustment lending much larger, so that the gross contributions of the two institutions in the form of direct balance-of-payments support to the same six countries became about equal. This also held to a large extent for individual countries, which underlines the linkage, mentioned earlier, between the existence of a Fund arrangement and the willingness of the Bank to proceed to substantial adjustment lending.

If allowance is made for a number of other capital flows between the two institutions and its members, a rather different picture emerges. The Bank continued project and other non-programme lending to these countries, even when they did not qualify for policy lending (the possibly "defensive" character of this lending is commented on in Section 8.9). Both the Bank and the Fund received large repayments from these members. Repayments of principal to the Bank amounted to $2.3 billion in 1982-84 and $3.7 billion in 1986-87; repurchases to the Fund were small in the earlier period (about $1.0 billion, with zero for Argentina, Brazil and Mexico), but they rose to $4.8 billion in 1986-87.

Table 8.4.   FUND LENDING AND WORLD BANK ADJUSTMENT LENDING TO CERTAIN LARGE DEBTORS

$ billion

	1983-85		1986-87	
	Fund	Bank	Fund	Bank
Argentina	2.7	—	1.8	1.5
Brazil	4.4	0.7	—	0.5
Chile	0.9	0.2	0.6	0.2
Mexico	2.7	0.3	1.6	1.8
Philippines	0.8	0.7	0.4	0.3
Yugoslavia	1.2	0.4	0.2	—
	12.7	2.3	4.6	4.3

Sources: Fund and Bank data. Fund figures in SDRs converted to US dollars at average annual $/SDR exchange rates.

The Baker initiative in late 1985 envisaged a more modest lending role for the Fund and larger lending by the World Bank. This materialised in the form of a succession of large sector loans, recognisable by their round amounts, to a number of these countries: two trade policy loans of $500 million each to Argentina, the same for Mexico, a trade policy loan of $452 million — the extra $2 million covered related technical assistance — to Nigeria, agricultural sector loans to Argentina ($350 million), Brazil ($500 million) and Mexico ($400 million), an "economic recovery" loan to the Philippines ($300 million), and so on. By 1987, all the heavily indebted countries, with the exception of Venezuela, had become adjustment borrowers from the Bank, with more than 60 per cent of the sectoral adjustment loans having gone to these countries.

8.8 Reasons for Fund and Bank Intervention in the Debt Crisis

For both institutions, the provision of large amounts of financial resources to the highly indebted countries appeared as a natural response to the evolving payments situation. The Fund's task includes giving balance-of-payments loans to its members, and these countries were facing serious balance-of-payments problems. The Bank provides development finance, and these countries were having obvious difficulties in attracting foreign capital for development. But this particular use of the resources of the two institutions has to be viewed not only in the framework of their own Articles of Agreement, but also in the context of parallel negotiations between the debtor countries and commercial creditors. Was it proper to insert lending by the international institutions into the process of negotiations between debtor countries and their creditors about commercial loans that had gone sour? It is obvious that this issue contains implications of moral hazard. Nevertheless, it would seem that the answer to this question should be in the affirmative, and that there were a number of systemic reasons to justify the activist response with which the institutions responded to the challenge put to them by the debt crisis (Krugman 1985, pp. 79-90).

First, international institutions are in the unique position that only they can contribute an essential ingredient to successful discussions between creditors and debtor: the seal of approval for a policy programme by the debtor country that enhances the likelihood that the creditors' claims will be serviced. In the normal course of business of the institutions, the seal of approval is implied in the willingness of the institution to grant credit. The standby arrangements concluded with the Fund traditionally performed this function, with the Fund's periodic announcements of successive drawings under such arrangements serving as indicators that the debtor country continued in compliance with the agreed conditions[18]. In some important cases, commercial banks have also accepted World Bank policy loans as supplementary or substitute assurances of the quality of borrowers' policies.

Second, while debtors and creditors have a common interest in reaching agreed solutions concerning debt service by the former and defensive lending by the latter rather than explicit default or an unresolved stand-off experience has shown that the parties may fail to reach agreement if left to themselves. International institutions can play a major mediating role by proposing a particular bargain in the light of their expertise, and they as well as national governments can twist the necessary arms to bring about "voluntary" agreement along the lines of the proposed bargain.

Third, the institutions and national governments carry a responsibility for the international monetary system and for domestic monetary systems in the major countries; both systems were seriously at risk in the first phase of the debt problem and the best place to defend them appeared to be on the defence perimeter, *viz.* by shoring up the banks' claims on developing countries. If successful (as it has proved to be so far), this operation would make it unnecessary to deal with the much larger problem of defending the financial integrity of many major banks across their entire balance sheets.

Fourth, the injection of new credit by the international institutions (and in some cases by governments) served to reduce the scope of the conflict of interest between the negotiating parties: official money reduced the combined effort that these parties would otherwise have been obliged to make — terms of immediate adjustment by the debtors and "new money" from the creditors — to reach a credible package for the period ahead[19].

8.9 Limits to the Influence of the International Institutions

As was indeed to be expected, the tremendous power the Fund exercised in 1982-84 over the flows of capital from various sources to the developing countries could not last. There were a number of reasons for this. After the Fund had "rescued", at least for the time being, the largest debtors (Mexico and Argentina in 1982, Brazil in early 1983) the banks' worry about a total collapse of the value of their claims on developing countries began to diminish and the banks no longer felt seriously threatened by the possibility that some smaller countries might fail to maintain the service of their foreign debt[20]. Secondly, the banks used the years since 1982 to strengthen their balance sheets, raise their capital positions and build up reserves against bad debts. As a result of these new safeguards, the banks felt themselves in a less exposed position even when, in the second phase of the debt crisis, the large debtors showed renewed signs of trouble; that is evident above all from the relaxed attitude displayed by the commercial banks at the flirtations of some debtor countries with default. After years of on-again, off-again minuets of negotiations, it is questionable whether banks and their debtors are still much in need of official intermediation and reconciliation efforts. Also, the banks have become more knowledgeable about the quality of debtors' adjustment programmes and their revealed ability to execute such programmes; in any event, they may no longer attach the same unquestioning importance to a seal of approval handed out by the Fund or the Bank.

This change in circumstances raises with particular weight the question of the acceptable degree of linkage between the arrangements that a country makes with the Fund and those that it makes with its commercial bank creditors. For many years the Fund's approach has been to avoid the activation of its own financial component of an arrangement negotiated with a member country until there was sufficient assurance that the country's balance-of-payments gap would be covered, taking into account the financing contributions on the part of all players that collaborated in a particular arrangement. Depending on the case, coverage might be provided, in addition to the Fund's contribution, by debt relief, World Bank loans, export credit guarantees, aid contributions and commercial bank loans. This approach was based on solid financial and negotiating grounds. On the financial side the Fund took the sensible view that it should not make its own resources available for a situation that showed a residual balance-of-payments gap, that is to say where the country's adjustment effort was insufficient in the light of the amount of financing that was assured. The fact that the Fund was willing to sponsor a particular financing package implied that the Fund considered the degree of adjustment incorporated in the negotiated arrangement as sufficient in the country's circumstances, or perhaps, as the maximum adjustment effort that could be asked from the country in these circumstances. But the Fund could not be confident that the degree of adjustment that it was prepared to accept for itself would indeed be sufficient until the financing package materialised and the Fund was certain of the amounts of financing that the other participants were prepared to make available.

From a negotiating point of view the Fund took the highly practical position that its leverage, both with the debtor country and with the various other creditors, was highest as long as it had not yet disbursed any money itself, and would weaken as successive instalments under any arrangement were released. By not agreeing to disbursement of its own resources until the entire financing package has been put in place, the Fund was able to play its leadership role in the debt crisis in the most effective way. Moreover, at least in the early stages of the debt crisis, the Fund's leverage worked. The implied threat that the entire package of adjustment and financing, including the contribution by the Fund, might fall apart, induced the commercial banks to bring together the "critical mass" of their own contribution within as little as six or eight weeks.

More recently, however, the Fund's negotiating approach has lost some of its effectiveness, as is evident from the fact that often much more time elapses between the conclusion of the Fund's negotiations with a member country and that country's agreement with its banking creditors. At the same time, the approach is increasingly exposing the Fund to criticism of unduly influencing the negotiations between a debtor country and the creditor banks. The criticism comes from both sides. The banks see the Fund's practice of determining the needed size of the total package, as well as its approximate allocation among the various creditors, as the imposition on them of "new money" targets. But the waiting attitude that the Fund adopts in the next phase can be regarded by the debtor country as putting it under pressure in its negotiation with the banks. The question thus deserves to be addressed whether this approach is still generally justified, or whether the Fund would do better in some cases to de-link its own lending to a member country from the status of that country's negotiations with commercial bank creditors.

To a large extent, these negotiations with the banks concern the timing of interest payments by the debtor in the context of the amount and timing of "new money" to be made available. Under this negotiating approach, the question of an "uncovered gap" — a situation that the Fund remains anxious to avoid — does not arise. Once the parties have reached agreement, the payments of interest are in part matched by "new money". Until that time, the interest payable is likely to build up as arrears, and the rest of the country's balance of payments remains fully financed. If the linkage is seen from this angle there is no longer a need for the Fund either to set "new money" targets for the banks or to make the entry into effect of its standby arrangement conditional on agreement between the banks and the country. It would, indeed, be particularly embarrassing for the Fund to withhold disbursements from a member country in situations in which the inability of the banks to reach agreement with the country was, in large part, due to protracted negotiations among the banks themselves.

Less linkage between Fund credit and the renegotiation of commercial bank credits would, in any event, be a healthy development. The debtor countries and the banks are jointly responsible for the loans made in the late 1970s and early 1980s. These loans may or may not have been sound at the time, when real interest rates were negative, and the proceeds may have been

174

used more or less well, all depending on the individual loans and the individual countries. As in any debtor/creditor relationship that has gone sour, it should be primarily up to the parties concerned to find their way out of the relationship into which they had entered. While international organisations and national governments have a role to play in these difficult negotiations between the two contending parties (as discussed in the preceding section), the Fund would want to avoid tilting the scales in favour of the banks and against the debtor countries. Market pressures against these countries to come to terms with the banks are, in any event, strong. The countries do not have the simple option of letting interest arrears accumulate and just waiting until those arrears force out compensating "new money"; as the stand-off between the country and the banks drags on, the country is likely to find that trade and other credits dry up or become more expensive.

The declining willingness of the commercial banks to respond to Fund and Bank initiatives for balanced adjustment-cum-financing solutions puts these institutions in an increasingly difficult position. If they make the extension of new credits conditional on parallel action by the commercial banks, they put themselves in the unenviable position of becoming the debt collectors against their developing member countries. But if they move too far ahead of the commercial banks in lending, they may arouse legitimate concern about the quality of their own loans.

The actions of the Fund and the Bank cannot be determined by the market's view of the creditworthiness of the countries to which they lend. But neither can these two institutions ignore their own judgments on the ability of debtor countries to overcome their payments problem. If the Fund or the Bank have the conviction that a country's agreed adjustment policies will vindicate their confidence, they can for some years lend to countries on which the market and the banks have their doubts; indeed, in those cases it is their duty to lend. But there are also limits to this approach. The World Bank can only be an effective and competitive intermediary between the world's capital markets and its clients if it maintains the AAA rating of its bonds; the need to preserve that credit rating sets limits to increases in the Bank's exposure to countries for which access to commercial credit remains closed. There is a similar constraint on the Fund, even though that institution has never engaged in market borrowing. The Fund, moreover, already has a serious problem of arrears on interest and principal of its credits, to an amount of some SDR 2 billion as of end-June 1988. This figure is still far from constituting a threat to the liquidity of SDR 30 billion claims by creditor members whose currencies the Fund has

175

drawn to finance its credits, but the realisation that the Fund does run a credit risk is beginning to have an impact on its willingness to enlarge its exposure. In this context, both institutions have to weigh the needs for credit of their other members against the needs of the highly-indebted countries. The Fund, moreover, cannot lose sight of the possibility that some day a world recession may bring a large increase in members' demands for its resources — a demand which, in the spirit of its Articles of Agreement, it should be in a position to meet.

One must note in this connection that the concept of "defensive lending" (lending to protect the service on existing claims) has entered into the considerations of international financial institutions. While the World Bank will not engage in policy lending to countries without an arrangement with the Fund, it does continue to make project loans to such countries; one consideration in this policy could well be the belief that debtor countries are less likely to fall behind on their payments to the Bank as long as the Bank can respond by closing the faucet of new disbursements. In the case of the Fund, the strong push made in 1987 for an Enhanced Structural Adjustment Facility (ESAF) reflected not only the evident need of the poorer countries for larger support than could be financed from the SAF, but also the hope of some that the allocation of large ESAF entitlements to certain countries might enable them to settle embarrassing arrears to the Fund. More recently, however, the Fund has taken a clear stand against the indirect use of ESAF money to reduce arrears. Instead, it looks for this purpose to financial support from friendly countries, with ESAF money to become available to countries that have been in arrears only after they have been in compliance for a certain period with a shadow programme and have met all new obligations falling due to the Fund.

All these developments point to the need for caution on the part of both institutions in the commitment of resources in connection with the continuing effects of the debt crisis. As has already been noted, the arguments that strongly favoured the institutions' activism in the past have lost some of their weight. At the same time, failure of the banks to carry a fair share of the financing burden creates a risk of putting pressure on the Fund and Bank to fill a larger proportion of the need for financing. But the question is not only one of the size of the contribution to be made by these institutions; that question can be handled by the adoption of certain conservative rules of thumb. The most difficult task is to recognise those cases in which the banks are right in not being prepared to expand their exposure — cases where the degree of adjustment that can effectively be achieved and maintained holds no promise of a return to creditworthiness. Experience shows that in such cases the institutions' major members will not necessarily hold them back from accepting too much risk. These members may prefer to risk "the Fund's money", or "the Bank's money" (which is their own money only in event of liquidation of the institution) rather than facing the alternatives: providing fresh money of their own or contemplating the financial and political implications of default. Surrounded by such pressures, the international institutions have only one compass to sail by, namely their own independent, objective judgment on the quality of a country's adjustment programme.

NOTES AND REFERENCES

1. See, on growth and adjustment respectively, the text of the Fund's second and fifth Purposes in its Articles of Agreement:

    ii) "to facilitate the expansion and balanced growth of international trade, and to contribute thereby to the promotion and maintenance of high levels of employment and real income and to the development of the productive resources of all members as primary objectives of economic policy."

    v) "... providing [members] with opportunity to correct maladjustments in their balance of payments without resorting to measures destructive of national or international prosperity."

2. Even export shortfall cases financed by the CFF not infrequently contained elements of policy inadequacy that were at least partially responsible for the observed payments difficulties. In what was probably an over-reaction to such cases, the Fund in 1983 brought the degree of conditionality that it applied to CFF drawings close to that of ordinary drawings [IMF(AR) 1984, p. 137].

3. Address by the Managing Director (Per Jacobsson) to the 1961 Fund Annual Meeting IMF Summary Proceedings [(SP) 1961, pp. 30-31].

4. Currency depreciation can also have a demand reducing effect as it lowers the real money stock, but this effect can readily be offset, to the extent desired, by monetary policy.

5. The SAF was established in 1986 on the basis of the repayments that began to be made in that year from ten-year loans that the Fund had granted to low-income countries in the period 1976-80, which had been financed from the profits of the sale of about one-sixth (25 million oz.) of the Fund's holdings of gold. These repayments are expected to total about

SDR 2.7 billion over the next few years. The resources of the SAF have recently been complemented by some SDR 6 billion made available by Fund members with higher incomes in response to an appeal by the Managing Director of the Fund, Michel Camdessus. These new resources, designed to assist the same low-income countries, are channeled through the Enhanced Structural Adjustment Facility (ESAF), whose objectives, procedures and financial conditions parallel those of the SAF.

6. The Fund uses a special terminology, based on its Articles, in which terms such as credit, reimbursement and interest are rendered as "purchases", "repurchases" and either "charges" for debit interest or "remuneration" for interest paid on creditor positions.

7. Nigeria concluded a stand-by arrangement with the Fund in 1987 but it has indicated that it does not intend to draw on it.

8. Since 1978 there has been some ambiguity in the measure of Fund credit to developing countries. The published figures on "use of Fund credit" do not include loans made in 1976-80 to low-income countries by the Trust Fund, an account administered by the Fund into which profits from the sale of part of the Fund's gold were channeled. The distinction between credits financed from the Fund's own or borrowed resources and credits from accounts administered by the Fund became blurred, however, when the reflows of Trust Fund loans were channeled into the Fund's own accounts and then relent as Fund credit under the SAF; and the distinction became even more blurred when the SAF was expanded into the ESAF, which is a facility of the Fund that draws part of its resources from the remaining SAF funds but most resources from a new administered account. From today's vantage point, Trust Fund loans, and SAF and ESAF credits can probably best be regarded as approximate counterparts to IDA credits in the World Bank Group. They were, or are, directed towards the same group of countries and carry the same minimal interest rate. To provide the proper focus on net Fund lending to developing countries in recent years, the figures quoted in this chapter for Fund credit include Trust Fund loans (now being repaid) and SAF credits. As of mid-1988, no ESAF loans had been made.

9. India cancelled its arrangement; Brazil failed to meet some of the conditions of its arrangement and apparently did not feel the need, in a year when it was in current account balance, to renegotiate with the Fund.

10. The reductions applied in recent years to the access limits under the policy on "enlarged access" (created in 1981) do not invalidate this observation concerning the long-run trend.

11. Article XVIII, Section (a) of the Fund's Articles of Agreement. The Fund's companion power to *reduce* world liquidity by the cancellation of SDRs has never been used and, because of the 85 per cent majority required, is probably unusable.

12. For a detailed discussion of this subject see Goode (1985, pp. 40-48).

13. Para. 7 of the Communiqué of the Interim Committee, dated 10th April 1986 (*IMF Survey* 21st April 1986, p. 116). The implied reference to the Link is conveyed in the statement that "the SDR ... should not be a means of transferring resources ...".

14. See Mason and Asher, (1973 pp. 180-183 and elsewhere). In the opinion of these authors, while the Bank's appraisals of creditworthiness were to be "more lenient than those of the private financial community, nothing in the Bank's charter encourages it to be bold"

(p. 180). It is interesting to note that there is no entry "Creditworthiness" in the subject index the Fund's 1945-65 History (Horsefield 1969, Vol. I).

15. The qualification "to developing countries" is important. Not only in the immediate post-war years, but through the 1960s, the Bank's clientele included industrial countries in Europe, as well as Australia, New Zealand, South Africa and Japan. More than 43 per cent of the Bank's lending in its first decade went to these countries (mostly as programme loans) and still 20 per cent in the second decade.

16. Similarly De Vries: "The essential feature of SALs is not their rapid disbursement ..." (1987 p. 57). Stanley Please makes the same point with even greater emphasis, and adding the defense that "the Bank considers the provision of emergency balance-of-payments assistance as entirely an IMF responsibility" (1984, p. 30). But Please takes a rather extreme position in general on the role of the Bank, seeing its place in the global institutional structure "primarily in terms of its non-financial role" (p. 9).

17. Cooper goes to the other extreme by regarding SALs as basically an excuse for large-scale programme lending (Cooper 1983, p. 576).

18. There is only a single instance where a country requested the Fund's explicit approval of its adjustment policies (in order to come to an agreement with its commercial bank creditors) without wanting to use the Fund's money: Colombia in 1985. The Fund was most hesitant to grant Colombia's request.

19. An emotional issue that has drawn much heat in this connection has been whether the use of official money in these circumstances should be seen as "bailing out the banks". Krugman (1985 p. 94) argues that it is, even if the Fund or the Bank charge commercial interest rates; for such rates do not protect official lenders against the risk of default. He argues, however, that bail-out or not, the action is justified because it buys a social good, the avoidance of default. In the same book Wood (p. 332) questions the assertion that these official loans convey an implied subsidy, citing the preferred creditor status that official institutions have traditionally been accorded in the event of debt rescheduling. The proof of this particular pudding is likely to come some considerable time after the eating, and, as noted below, it may well depend on the size of the helpings.

20. The references in this section to attitudes and positions of "the banks" ignore major differences among lending banks, such as the United States/Canadian banks as against those in Europe and Japan; in the United States, the money center vs. the regional banks, and also the stronger vs. weaker money center banks. It would lead us too far afield to analyse these distinctions, but it is in any event clear that differences in interests and financial strength among groups of banks sometimes accounted for the length of time it took "the banks" to arrive at a common position.

Chapter 9

THE DEBT CRISIS AND THE RESUMPTION OF GROWTH

9.1 Interactions Between Debt and Growth

There is wide agreement that there is a close connection between the resumption of satisfactory growth in the heavily indebted countries and the resolution of these countries' debt problems. The linkages run in both directions. If economies grow, a given amount of debt will become a declining proportion of GNP or exports and its service will thus become more bearable to the debtor countries and, at the same time, will appear more probable to be met in the eyes of the creditors. For both debtors and creditors, indebtedness that was excessive, judged by traditional ratios, can become reasonable as the debtor country grows into it. There is, moreover, a wide range of scenarios under which relatively modest increases in debt in the early years are fully compatible with the expectation of declining debt ratios over time. In short, therefore, growth can help to overcome the debt problem.

But, equally, finding solutions to the debt problem is essential to the promotion of growth. For the countries that have been strongly affected by the debt crisis, a high debt service holds back growth in a number of ways. Most directly, the payments to be made to creditors reduce the amounts of foreign exchange that are available to finance essential imports; in the short run, at least, this can keep down both the rate of current output and the installation of new capacity. Secondly, the expectation that for a long period in the future an important part of current output will have to be paid to foreign creditors may dampen the profit outlook, and hence the entrepreneurial spirit in the country. This will in particular be the case if the foreign capital on which the service has to be paid had been invested in projects of questionable economic yield, had been swallowed in increased private or governmental consumption, or had been re-exported as capital flight. Thirdly, and often related to the previous point, the need for the government to devote a sharply enlarged part of its revenue to debt service is likely to signal the risk that, if government domestic expenditure is inflexible downwards, the tax burden is likely to rise in one form or another, thus putting a further damper on enterprise.

And, finally, and perhaps most importantly, the absence of a resolution to the debt problem keeps interest rates in the debtor countries at exorbitant levels and thus depresses investment. The key consideration in this linkage is the fact that (as discussed in Chapter 6) the capital markets in the middle-income highly indebted countries are closely connected with the markets in the industrial countries. As a consequence, the impairment of a country's credit-worthiness means far more than the interruption of voluntary lending to it by the commercial banks in the main money centers. It means that claims on the indebted country's trade in secondary markets at implied rates of interest that compare unfavourably to interest rates on junk bonds. If a twenty-year claim at a nominal interest rate of, say, 8 per cent is quoted at 50 cents on the dollar, this implies an interest rate of nearly 16 per cent. If a country's obligations yield that much on foreign markets, arbitrage will keep interest rates for dollar claims in the internal market at a similar level; if rates were significantly lower, capital flight would be encouraged. Rates in local currency would, in addition, carry a premium reflecting the expected depreciation of that currency against the dollar. Such high interest rates will make only few investments profitable; low levels of investment/GDP ratios in all highly indebted countries confirm the working of this mechanism. Even though, in the short run, with consider-able excess capacity, low investment may not be the critical factor holding down growth, for the medium and longer run, the negative investment effects of a prolonged debt crisis will become an important factor retarding growth.

These mutual influences of debt and growth can produce a vicious circle scenario in which insufficient growth mires a country in an apparently endless debt struggle, and continuous debt problems keep growth forever below the critical value that would allow the country to break out of the circle.

In the early stages of the debt crisis this gloomy potential scenario was not generally recognised, not because the importance of growth was neglected but rather because the difficulty of overcoming the debt problem was underesti-mated. Since it was assumed that even the highly indebted countries would still be able to finance substantial current account deficits, the severe foreign exchange constraint on growth that actually materialised for these countries was not foreseen. The Fund's World Economic Outlook for 1983 assumed that a sustainable payments position of the non-oil developing countries could be achieved with a current account deficit of about 14 per cent of exports, as against the unusually high figure of 19.3 per cent in 1982; with the expected rates of real export growth and (modest) world inflation, this led the Fund staff to forecast a 1986 combined current account deficit for the non-oil LDCs of $93 billion, well in excess of the peak value reached in 1981 (IMF WEO 1983, Table 6, p. 205). The actual deficit of these countries in 1986 was $12 billion. The 15 heavily indebted countries, which had had a combined current account deficit of $50 billion in both 1981 and 1982, were forced into approximate current account balance in both 1984 and 1985.

The well-known "manageable scenario" that William Cline published in 1983 also presented the debt problem as a passing phenomenon. Basing his calculations on a growth rate in the heavily indebted countries (a somewhat different sample from that used by the Fund) increasing from 2.5 per cent in 1983 to 4.5 per cent in 1985 and 1986, OECD growth at 3 per cent, a decline in Libor, and an oil price of $29 per barrel, he found "a surprisingly favourable outcome" for the oil importing countries in his sample (Cline 1983, p. 55). Their debt/exports and debt service/exports ratios would decline by about one-third from 1982 to 1986. Cline draws even more sanguine conclusions from a statistical model of debt rescheduling, which is credited with providing "a more precise evaluation of the degree of improvement in the burden of developing country debt". This model shows only a limited number of cases in which the debt-servicing burden signals the likelihood of reschedulings, *viz.* in Brazil through 1985, Mexico and Argentina through 1984, Chile through 1984, and Ecuador through 1986. "Otherwise the projections (covering 19 countries in all) show few instances of serious debt-servicing difficulties, especially by 1985-86" (Cline 1983, pp. 69-70).

Before entering upon a discussion of the situations of groups of countries and the policy approaches countries can adopt to promote growth in the period ahead, it is necessary first to pay attention to the impact on growth arising from external factors relating to the world economy.

9.2 External Factors Affecting Growth

Some major external factors affect developing countries broadly speaking in the same direction, even if not in the same degree. These factors include the rate of growth and the containment of protectionism in the industrial world, both of which affect the demand for their exports, and the world interest rate, which determines the interest cost on variable-rate credits and on new fixed-rate credits. The direction of the impact of changes in other world variables may depend on the commodity composition of a country's trade or the currency composition of its indebtedness. A decline in primary product prices hurts most developing countries, but favours those that export predominantly industrial commodities. For countries whose debt is largely expressed in US dollars, but not for those whose debt is mainly expressed in other currencies, a decline in the value of the dollar will have a greater proportional effect on debt service than on export prices, which are related to demand and supply factors reflecting conditions in both the dollar and the non-dollar areas[1]. One other external factor, the price of oil, has of course a differential impact on countries' growth rates; a high petroleum price favours growth in the countries that are net exporters of oil and a low petroleum price in those that are oil importers.

From these relationships between external factors and LDC growth rates one can derive a number of policy canons for the industrial countries that would promote growth in the developing world in general and a resolution of the debt problem more in particular. These canons would include: maintain vigorous domestic growth; avoid protectionism; lower the real interest rate, in particular by better control over budget deficits; and dismantle agricultural policies that drive down the prices of primary products of major importance to developing countries, such as grains and sugar.

Realism forces one to acknowledge that, with respect to the macroeconomic items on this list, the industrial countries have only a limited degree of control. A higher growth rate and a lower real interest rate are of obvious domestic interest to the industrial countries themselves; they could also be very helpful to the achievement of an international objective that by all evidence concerns these countries even more than the debt problem, *viz.* greater exchange rate stability. Yet domestic immobilism on the part of some of the major actors — in particular the United States and Germany — has continued to stand in the way of progress toward this common policy objective. Against this evidence it would be naïve to hope that the "solution" of the debt problem, which so obviously depends on many other factors as well, would act as a more powerful incentive than exchange rate stability to pull the policy packages of the major industrial countries toward an international optimum, away from politically perceived national optima.

The situation is somewhat more hopeful with respect to the more microeconomic factors mentioned. On farm price support policies, there is a clear conflict of interest, in the Common Market and in the United States, between the small proportion of the population whose incomes benefit from these policies and the large majority that pays the price for it. Budgetary sanity on both sides of the Atlantic may in the end come to the assistance of enlightened economic foreign policies so that the worst aspects of farm policy can be overcome. With respect to protectionism more in general, one can observe that so far the line has tolerably been held, against strong economic pressure, to avoid the worst excesses. In this area everything should be done, by the pressure of interested industrial and developing countries, to make countries stick to the agreed rules of the game for international trade policy. Countries have taken on well-defined obligations under the GATT. These should be respected, even in the face of domestic protectionist pressures, and the more rigorously as the conditions of many developing countries (and again, not only or not mainly the heavily indebted ones) are recognised as being exceptionally difficult.

Even if, as concerns the external factors, one can muster only a qualified measure of optimism, it should be recalled that these factors do not by themselves determine the growth rates for individual countries. They determine the setting for such growth rates; but within this setting the choices made by a country among its own policy options can still make a large difference to the growth outcome. The important statistical differences in growth related to interest rate policy that were analysed in Chapter 3 may here be recalled.

9.3 Three Approaches to Growth

The sanguine view that the debt problem would prove manageable with reasonable growth in the industrial world, reasonable adjustment policies in the indebted countries, and good will all around to keep some capital flowing, began to weaken around 1984-85. The realisation, that unless attacked frontally, the debt problem could well continue to fester led to increasing attention to the conditions necessary for a resumption of growth.

In particular since the call by United States Secretary of the Treasury Baker for a "Programme for Sustained Growth" in his speech to the Fund-Bank Annual Meeting in Seoul on 8th October 1985, attention has been focused on solutions to the debt problem that were explicitly directed at growth in the developing countries and that envisaged mobilising capital flows for this purpose. Insufficient attention has, however, been given to the fact, that

185

"policies for growth" have meant different things or at least emphasis on different things to different observers. In the discussion of this subject in the last few years, three different approaches can be discerned: growth rates can be raised by greater efficiency; by additions from abroad to the supply of saving, and by reducing the constraint on imports.

i) Secretary Baker made it very clear what he considered the preconditions for growth, *viz.* the adoption of growth promoting policies in the developing countries. Specifically, he stated:

[Whether] there are reasonable prospects that growth will occur ... will depend upon the adoption of proper economic policies by the developing countries. Financing can only be prudently made available when and as effective policies to promote economic efficiency, competitiveness, and productivity — *the true foundations of growth* — are put in place. (Emphasis added.)

Thus, under the Baker approach, additional output (i.e. growth) can be coaxed out of the existing factors of production by means of market-oriented economic policies. If one could fully rely on this bootstrap operation, one might wonder why additional financing is required once this process has been put in motion. The implied answer would seem to be that better policies produce more growth over time only, and that additional capital from abroad can help to speed up growth in the meantime. Growth-oriented adjustment policies will carry their own reward over time; but the adoption of such policies is facilitated if an additional growth benefit can be counted on for the short run.

The two other approaches to growth, by contrast, put the first emphasis on the addition to growth that can be made by the availability of additional foreign exchange, but they differ on the question *how* foreign savings can enhance growth. One emphasizes the addition to the flow of savings, the other the addition to the supply of foreign exchange[2].

ii) The World Bank has been among the earliest and the most insistent advocates of efficiency in the use of the factors of production as the basis for growth. In its quantitative approach to the debt crisis, however, it focuses on the fact that high interest costs for foreign debt — attributable to past borrowing and the rise in interest rates — act as a drain on savings, thus reducing resources available for investment (Selowsky and van der Tak 1986). A low investment ratio means slow growth in the stock of capital and, hence, slow growth in output. To the extent that foreign savings compensate the drain on savings exercised by high interest payments, there is room for higher investment, which in due course will raise the growth rate of output. Higher output will, moreover, over time permit higher savings at home so as to reduce gradually the reliance on foreign savings, and ultimately to reverse it.

   iii)   The third approach concentrates its attention on the direct constraint on output exercised by the shortage of foreign exchange, rather than on the indirect effect via reduced investment. Since there is a close association between the level of output and the demand for imported inputs, shortage of foreign exchange may force the government to constrain output (using fiscal or monetary policy) below the level that would be possible on the basis of the existing stock of capital. In these circumstances, which are typical of the countries suffering from the debt crisis, an additional supply of foreign exchange (whether earned by higher exports or borrowed as new foreign credits) will mitigate the foreign exchange constraint and enable the government to allow the economy to run at a faster growth rate, while higher exports will stimulate the economy from the demand side. The correlations reported on in Table 3.4 confirmed the importance of this factor across countries over a twenty-year period. Initially, while the level of output is still mostly recovering from recession lows, not much of the additional output may be needed for new investment; most of it can go into higher consumption. However, as output continues to grow, more of it will have to be channeled into investment. The implicit assumption of this approach is that market forces in the economy, together with the government's fiscal policy, will bring about over time the required changes in the composition of output between investment and consumption as private investment and saving respond to profit opportunities. But one has to be aware of the possibility that in some countries an inadequate level of government infrastructure investment, brought about by extreme budgetary pressures, may hold down a growth rate that demand and other supply factors could have permitted.

9.4   Growth and the Balance of Payments

   This section analyses in some detail the relationship between the balance-of-payments constraint and the attainable growth rate. The analysis is directed to countries whose creditworthiness has not yet been restored and which can therefore not count on market access to foreign capital. It is, however, assumed that the country will be able to roll over any maturing debt and that it is not losing foreign exchange from capital flight (nor gaining reserves from the reversal of past capital flight). The possibility of debt relief is disregarded in this section; it will be taken up in the next chapter.

The balance-of-payments constraint is applied in the sense of the third approach set out in the preceding section; the second approach seems less relevant at a stage when shortage of foreign exchange forces many industries in the debt-afflicted countries to operate below capacity. Account is taken, however, of the possibility that countries can lower the import content of domestic absorption by a more competitive exchange rate.

As far as output is concerned, the focus is throughout on the annual growth rate, either in terms of gross national product or gross domestic product. Any specified growth rate for such a macro-variable implies, at the same time, a growth rate for the corresponding per capita variable, since population growth for the next few years is for all practical purposes determined by the existing demographic data. The focus on growth rates reflects the attention paid to these particular variables in the policy formulation of many of the heavily indebted countries. It is noteworthy that, quite apart from the figure chosen for a target growth rate, the concept of such a rate is less ambitious than that of an absolute target level for a particular variable. Almost all heavily indebted countries have encountered one or more years of negative economic growth, and many are still at per capita levels below the peaks reached around 1980 or 1981. To aim now for a certain rate of growth, rather than for recovery to a particular past level or, even more ambitiously, a return to the past trend — implies, in a sense, the implicit acceptance of the effects of the debt crisis that have already occurred, provided the future trend is sufficiently positive. Expressing the objective of policy as an annual growth rate also carries the implication that success of the policy can be measured one year at the time, and that under-performance in one year does not necessarily dog the record for subsequent years.

Our discussion chooses as a reference case a situation of balance in the current account. There are factual and analytical reasons for this choice. As a matter of fact, the combined current account of the 15 heavily indebted countries was almost exactly in balance in 1984 and again in 1985. In both 1981 and 1982 these countries had run a combined current account deficit of $50 billion. But then, finding it impossible to continue borrowing, they went through a severe adjustment process. This involved, for the group as a whole, a negative growth rate in 1982 and especially in 1983, and a decline in per capita consumption of nearly 2 per cent over the period 1980 to 1984. These adjustment efforts brought the group's combined current account into balance

188

in 1984 and 1985, as nine of these countries achieved balance or a surplus[3]. The improvement in 1984 no doubt benefited from the sharp rise in world trade in that year; but the current account for 1986 and 1987 stayed close to balance as well. In all four years, the combined growth rate of the 15 countries was positive, though still low: in the range of 2 to 3 per cent[4].

Taking current account balance as the starting point directs attention to the growth rate in exports as the crucial variable influencing the attainable growth rate for the economy. Higher output will require more imports, but as long as output growth does not exceed the growth rate of exports, it seems likely that the latter will produce enough foreign exchange to pay for the additional imports. Some World Bank estimates use a medium-term elasticity of the demand for imports in relation to income of unity, but this figure may be too low. A recent statistical study done at the World Bank (Pritchett 1987) found income elasticities for imports for the middle-income LDCs to cluster between 1.0 and 1.5, with a median value of about 1.25. This would imply that if income grows at the same rate as exports, imports will grow $1\frac{1}{4}$ times as fast as exports. But current account balance — the assumed starting point — implies exports exceeding imports by the amount of interest payments. For the countries with recent debt payment problems, such interest payments in recent years (1983-86) were about 23 per cent of exports of goods and services (IMF WEO 1986, p. 109). Hence, as a first approximation, a country starting from the position of current account balance, could *at a minimum* afford a medium-term rate of growth for its GDP approximately equal to the medium-term growth rate that it can achieve for its volume of exports.

The possible growth rate derived in this way is a first approximation because it is based on a statistical median value for the import elasticity of demand and because it does not allow for changes in the country's terms of trade nor for changes in world market interest rates (which would modify the amount of interest due on a given amount of debt). It is a minimum for two reasons. First, the country may have net access to long-term credit from governments (e.g. through export credits) and multilateral development banks, and to direct investment; these sources of funds would permit it to run a current account deficit even without access to net credit from commercial banks. Second, the growth rate as here derived makes no allowance for higher efficiency. In other words, the country may be able to add a "Baker component" of growth to the more traditional "foreign exchange component".

To make this approach applicable to an individual country, the assumptions in the model sketched would, of course, have to be replaced by "best guesses" of the relevant actual figures. But even in its general formulation the approach has considerable value for the understanding of what countries can and cannot do to accelerate growth.

The focus on export growth implies both the inevitable dependence of all countries on the external conditions in the world economy[5] and the scope for national efforts to do better than the demand-determined world average by the adoption of policies that serve to encourage exports and to reduce the reliance on imports. At the same time, this focus brings out clearly the limits on the GNP growth rate without policy changes. In particular, it would be hard to see how, starting again from an approximate current balance, a country could aim at a medium-term growth rate for its GDP that was substantially in excess of the growth rate of its export volume, corrected for changes in its terms of trade and in the interest rates it would have to pay, plus an allowance for official borrowing and direct investment. This growth-constraining role of the trend of exports would apply even if the country had ample access to additional bank credit, unless there were a clear prospect of the need for such credit declining in the future. Otherwise, the rising trend in the trade deficit resulting from a higher growth rate, and additional interest payments on account of increasing deficits financed by borrowing, could well put the country's foreign debt on an exponential growth path. For a country that was already heavily indebted, the implication of following a policy leading to a declining trade surplus together with an increasing interest burden would be to postpone forever its return to creditworthiness. All this would hold *a fortiori* for a country that had to take as its starting point a situation not of current account balance, but one of current account deficit.

This then raises the question as to what a potentially creditworthy country could do if it considered unacceptable the rate of GDP growth based on a plausible forecast of the import growth it could afford, starting from whatever was the initial current account position. In such a situation, further adjustment would be imperative to reduce the deficit. Such adjustment would have to be based on a combination of a target GDP growth rate somewhat below the expected export growth rate and new foreign borrowing to cover the (shrinking) current account deficit. The country's policy package would probably need to include real depreciation of its currency. This would, of course, have a once-and-for-all negative impact on real absorption, but it could put the country on a steeper growth curve thereafter. Other adjustment measures that the country might apply at the same time, such as those leading to a more efficient use of its resources, would not have the negative GDP impact of a real depreciation. Only with a set of policies in place that could reasonably be expected to bring about over time the needed degree of adjustment would it be prudent for a country to undertake additional borrowing, which should then be seen essentially as a bridging operation. If the horizon and the amount of this foreign borrowing are set within reasonable limits, the resulting temporary increase of the interest burden on the larger debt need not constitute a major deterrent. For any individual country, it should be possible to design a safe path of growth *cum* borrowing that would shrink the current account deficit to zero or a sustainable modest amount at a point not too far into the future[6].

Implicit in the approach here sketched is that for many countries a series of small reductions in their traditional debt ratios will not suffice to overcome the debt crisis. As the World Bank's 1987-88 volume on External Debt observes: "even had it not been so difficult to reduce debt ratios after 1982-83, it is uncertain that the return to ratio levels that attracted lending in the late 1970s would have stimulated a resumption of lending following a general loss of confidence, in the troubled conditions of the mid-1980s" [World Bank World Debt Tables 1987-88 (a), p. xii]. Thus, for many highly indebted countries the only available road to creditworthiness is likely to contain a long stretch of rather limited use of foreign capital, in other words, a current account in which a large trade surplus covers a substantial part of interest payments[7].

To observe, after six years of official concern with the debt problem, that this is the most likely path is not to imply that it is the most desirable path. Indeed, more attractive alternative scenarios can easily be constructed. A given amount of interest payments that was considered too high for creditworthiness in the mid-1980s — say 35 per cent of 1985 exports — could well become reasonably comfortable by the end of the century, assuming the volume of exports grew at about 5 per cent per annum, i.e. doubled in about fourteen years. Assuming, further, a 3 per cent increase in export prices (along with a similar rate of world inflation), the debtor would be able to borrow net each year an amount equal to 3 per cent of its outstanding debt (thus keeping its real debt constant) and still halve its debt service ratio by the year 2000. With the same assumptions about export growth and inflation, a higher annual ratio of borrowing could be justified — and thus a higher growth rate affordable — if the target year for reaching the "comfortable" level of debt service were moved further out to 2005, 2010 or 2015. A number of techniques have been suggested for achieving a resolution of the debt problem along those lines, i.e. with substantial new borrowing by countries already heavily indebted. These techniques include advance commitment by creditors to the concerted relending of part of the interest payments as "new money" and the partial capitalisation of interest payments. Another proposal would establish debt service at a fixed percentage of exports well below the current ratio of interest payments to exports; actual payments would rise over time as exports increased in volume and even more in value[8]. Under certain simplifying assumptions all these techniques could achieve more or less equivalent "optimal" solutions that would correct very gradually the excessive debt service ratios that provoked the debt crisis in the first place.

The fundamental weakness in these solutions of the debt problem does not lie in technical flaws — although most of them involve formidable technical problems — but rather in the single underlying assumption: *viz.* that creditors will make long-term unconditional commitments to lend to the very countries whose past policy inadequacies — including in particular insufficient attention to the measures required for a rapid growth of exports — were at least partially responsible for landing them in the debt crisis. Since there is no technique available to match such commitments with conditionality undertakings over an equally long period, creditors can have no assurance that these countries will for the next fifteen, twenty, twenty five years remain committed to policies that will turn the easy simulations of compound interest into a reality.

These inevitable limitations on agreements between private lenders and sovereign borrowers did not stand in the way of certain short-term arrangements that were protected by Fund conditionality, nor of long-term reschedulings of principal. For a few years, reform packages negotiated by the IMF gave private lenders sufficient confidence in debtors' policy attitudes for the near future to induce them to provide immediate relief by the least binding of the techniques referred to: the provision of a specified amount of "new money" for a limited period. Such "defensive lending" was clearly in the banks' interest, as against the risk that the debtor might be unable or unwilling to make the interest payments as they fell due: once it is clear to a bank that the choice for it is between an asset on its books called "interest arrears" as against a new "loan", the bank is obviously better off with the latter than the former[9]. But experience has shown the difficulty of negotiating "new money" packages when some of the banks that participated in the old loans preferred to take substantial losses in order to get out. In spite of these difficulties, and in part by the provision of escape hatches for minor participants in the form of "exit bonds", it has still proved possible, albeit with tremendous difficulties, to pull off a few more instances of that same approach (Mexico, Argentina, Brazil) since 1986. Given the banks' present attitudes, the chances seem slim that this technique will prove practical for a dozen or so countries over the next decade.

With respect to principal, at least the major banks were from the start reconciled to the proposition that debt repayment on any large scale would be impossible and would not necessarily be in the creditors' interest. Accordingly, the debt-stretching component of many of the negotiations could be achieved without excessive difficulties.

Neither the re-lending of part of the interest payment nor the agreements on stretching out the period of repayment of principal can be considered as debt relief. Indeed, the debt strategy has contained these two elements ever since 1982, with the only "relief" component in recent years being the low spreads on the renegotiated credits (such as the 13/16th of 1 per cent over Libor in the case of Mexico and Argentina), spreads that obviously did not reflect the banks' own perception of the quality of these credits[10]. We shall deal with questions of debt relief in the next chapter. But before doing so, we need to give some attention to a new facility in the Fund that is intended to enhance the likelihood that countries borrowing from the Fund will keep their adjustment programme on course in spite of unfavourable unexpected developments.

9.5 IMF Contingency Lending

Earlier in this chapter we discussed what a country might consider as the rate of GDP growth that it could afford for the medium term. But the best calculations for the medium term may be upset by short-run fluctuations in exports or in the two other variables mentioned in connection with exports: the terms of trade and world interest rates. Moreover, although these last six years have been extraordinarily difficult for the highly indebted countries, it is worthy of note that growth in the industrial world has consistently been in the positive range; since 1980-81, there has been no general recession in the industrial world. It would not be a matter for surprise if one did arrive on the scene before the countries struggling with the after-effects of the debt crisis had regained a position of creditworthiness. The need for the IMF to assist countries financially if one or more of these unfavourable events occurred should be fully recognised and provided for. A substantial increase in Fund quotas under the Ninth Review of Quotas, to be decided on in 1989, should provide the resources to meet the extra needs that might arise from such eventualities. But, in addition, and as a further encouragement for countries to enter into stabilization programmes and to accept the political cost that these programmes usually entail, these countries should have the Fund's assurance that they will be eligible for specific help if their programmes are buffeted by exogenous factors. As Secretary Baker stated in his speech at the Fund-Bank 1987 Annual Meeting, "the Fund should work to see that comprehensive, growth-oriented programmes are not blown off course by unforeseen developments beyond a country's control".

In response to this initiative, the Fund has put together provisions under which a member country that experiences unfavourable shocks of an exogenous nature in the course of an arrangement it has with the Fund can borrow additional resources to absorb part of these shocks. These provisions have been incorporated, together with a somewhat reduced version of the compensatory financing facility, in a joint Compensatory and Contingency Financing Facility (CCFF). The contingency component of this facility is designed to provide additional finance if, in the course of a programme year under any arrangement, deviations from the expected values of certain agreed major exogenous variables were to have, on balance, a substantial net negative impact on the country's balance of payments. Exogenous variables to be covered in the negotiation of an arrangement could include world market prices for major exports or imports, world interest rates, and demand conditions (growth rates) in a country's major foreign markets. In contrast to the CFF, where compensation is limited to export shortfalls that are judged to be not only exogenous ("largely beyond the control of the member") but also temporary, the contingency facility does not attempt to discriminate between reversible and non-reversible changes in a country's external variables; appraisal of that dimension of the problem is reserved for the discussion on the possible need to strengthen the programme that will precede any activation of the contingency facility and for the further policy discussions that will define the programme for the next year under the same arrangement, or for a follow-up programme under a new arrangement. The fact that the net adverse effect of contingencies will, in any event, not be fully compensated implies the necessity for the country to meet the contingency in part by further adjustment.

The CCFF programme as announced so far (*IMF Survey* 1988, p. 275) leaves many aspects of the contingency component of the facility for later decision, partly at the time when individual arrangements are concluded and partly when actual contingencies arise. Only certain upper limits have been decided so far: maximum access of 65 per cent of quota, or 70 per cent (or less)[11] of the amount of the arrangement, whichever is smaller, subject to a separate limit of 35 per cent of quota on the interest component. At the same time, the upper limit for compensatory drawings was (for most likely cases) reduced from 83 to 20, 40 or 65 per cent of quota depending on Fund judgments of the member's policies, and a combined limit for the contingency and compensatory components of the new facility was set at 105 per cent of quota.

It is too early to judge whether the new facility, whose technical complications are legion[12], will meet two critical tests: first, that it encourage countries in payments difficulties to come to the Fund at an early stage of their problems; and, second, that it will in fact assist countries to deal quickly and smoothly with such contingencies as may arise, in a manner that keeps their adjustment programmes intact without sacrificing their growth momentum.

NOTES AND REFERENCES

1. The fundamentals of how a change in the exchange rate between the dollar and the non-dollar areas affects prices of international commodities was first analysed in connection with the widespread devaluations that took place in September 1949 (De Vries 1950).

2. On a comparison between approaches *(ii)* and *(iii)*, see Bergsten *et al.* (1985 pp. 203-210), Appendix A "The Impact of Import Availability on Domestic Output".

3. Brazil, Côte d'Ivoire, Ecuador, Mexico, Nigeria, Peru, Philippines (1985 only), Venezuela (large surpluses) and Yugoslavia.

4. All figures cited in this paragraph are from IMF WEO April 1987. Figures for a grouping of 17 highly indebted countries compiled by the World Bank (which includes also Costa Rica and Jamaica) are only slightly different.

5. The constraint is not limited to developing countries, as became evident when France attempted, and failed, to go it alone on growth from 1981 to 1983.

6. Some of the formal World Bank modelling for enhanced growth based on the traditional Harrod-Domar model underplays the bridging character of the additional borrowing that may be needed to permit an acceptable growth rate. (Cf. Selowsky and van der Tak 1986; Development Committee 1986. The model underlying the latter publication is based on that in the former one.) If one assumes *(a)* that foreign saving is turned into income-producing domestic investment and *(b)* a high enough marginal propensity to save, standard growth models will always turn initial current account deficits into ultimate current account

195

surpluses. But in the depressed economic situation, combined with large government dissaving, that characterises many of the heavily indebted countries, it is questionable whether additional balance-of-payments room will produce much new investment, whether the results of that investment will be used to raise income, and whether higher income will by itself produce the needed larger savings. To provide light at the end of the tunnel, debtor country governments cannot simply rely on the ultimate working of the marginal propensity to save; they will need to introduce from the start policies and incentives that will raise the level of private and official savings during the transition period for which creditors can be persuaded to provide the bridging resources. In the verbal exposition of the papers referred to, the urgent need for policy improvements is realistically recognised and is spelled out in some considerable detail. But the formal models contribute certain unrealistic touches to the analysis, such as the implication that debtor countries could safely stretch the return to creditworthiness over a ten-year period, or that the growth rate of developing countries could be modeled independently of the growth rate of the industrial world, with a larger balance-of-payments gap in the event of slow OECD growth being made up by a larger stream of lending over the ten-year period.

7. An even more gloomy picture is found in the simulations performed by Selowsky and van der Tak. In every one of these, countries after a few years of new borrowing go through a number of years (from two to fifteen) of net debt repayment before they reach a ratio of interest payments to exports that the authors consider sufficiently low in historical terms to make it plausible that the countries would have returned to creditworthiness and hence to the ability to resume net borrowing on a voluntary basis.

8. For an excellent analysis of the issues of debt reform and a comparison of the implications of alternative techniques (cf. Krugman 1987, pp. 259-310).

9. The logic of defensive lending was first developed by Cline (1983, pp. 73-78). He demonstrates that "defensive" (or "involuntary") lending benefits the creditor provided the ratio of new lending to outstanding debt is smaller than the ratio between the probability of default after the new lending to the reduction in the probability of default brought about by that lending. Cline concludes that "over the range of most relevant situations likely to arise — except in cases of relatively clear insolvency — it will pay the banks to extend additional credit in order to secure the value of existing exposure" (p. 77).

10. For a clear distinction of the various "dimensions" of alternative debt initiatives (cf. Feldstein *et al.* 1987).

11. The percentage is to be specified at the time an arrangement is concluded. It "will generally not exceed 70 per cent of the amount of the arrangement".

12. A number of features of the contingency facility may limit its attractiveness to borrowing countries:

    a) The facility cannot be used for relatively small deviations because of specified threshold limits, and in the event of large deviations the need to agree with the Fund on major programme changes before the extra money is released may not appear very different from the need to renegotiate a stand-by arrangement in the absence of contingency provisions;

    b) The contingency facility is intended to be symmetrical. In the event of unexpected favourable deviations of the items covered, the member would be expected to set aside in its reserves part of this windfall, to forgo further drawings, or to repay previous contingency drawings. None of this would have been required if the member had not applied for the contingency feature;

c) While SAF and ESAF arrangements provide money at a minimal interest charge, any contingency money attached to such arrangements would be at close to market rates;

d) Insurance against export fluctuations would, in any event, be available to the member *ex post* through the compensatory facility, although the formula that would apply under that facility could yield quite different results.

Chapter 10

THE DEBT CRISIS AND BEYOND

10.1   From Debt Workout to Debt Relief

The analysis so far has concentrated on the process of debt workout: the process through which countries with debt problems could hope, over time, to master these problems by a combination of growth, adjustment and (relatively modest) capital inflows. This model — which would involve debt restructuring but not debt relief — would seem to fit many of the middle-income highly indebted countries, but it does not fit all of them, nor does it fit many of the low-income countries with large debts, in particular those in Africa.

It is therefore necessary to expand the discussion in Chapter 9 to deal with a further approach to the debt problem, namely debt relief. Debt relief is defined as agreement by the creditor to a reduction in the present value of debt service obligations; hence, mere rescheduling of debt is not considered debt relief. The question is discussed in steps. Section 10.2 considers proposals of a general nature for debt relief to middle-income countries, involving an official third party in addition to the debtors and the creditors. Bilateral approaches between countries of the same group and their commercial creditors are taken up in Sections 10.3 and 10.4. Section 10.5 then discusses debt relief for the low-income countries, with particular application to those in Sub-Saharan Africa.

10.2   Generalised Approaches to Debt Relief for Middle-income Countries

From the beginning of the debt crisis there have been voices insisting that the approach that was being followed to deal with the debt problem would not restore creditworthiness to the highly indebted countries and would, moreover, retard the expansion of world trade: the larger the interest payments that the debtors would have to make to the banks in the creditor countries, the less money would they have left to buy exports from the factories and farms in the same countries. Thus there originated a long series of proposals — from Kenen and Rohatyn in 1983 to Senator Bradley in 1986 and Robinson of Amexco in 1988. Most of these envisaged that some international agency, endowed with enough capital or guarantees by the industrial countries, would buy at a discount the claims on the middle-income highly indebted countries held by commercial banks and then lower the debt service that the debtor countries would have to pay on their liabilities, e.g. by bringing the interest rate to a level substantially below prevailing market rates and extending maturities[1]. It has always seemed highly unlikely that governments would find it politically or financially feasible to "bail out the banks", or even, if the banks absorbed the losses that had already taken place, to take over from them the risk of future losses. But there are more fundamental flaws in these proposals than that they will never fly, and these flaws have become more obvious as the discount on the banks' claims or these countries has tended to increase even in cases where policies appeared to improve.

The first flaw is that any generalised arrangement to relieve the banks of their claims on these countries would remove whatever incentive the banks, acting collectively, still have to raise the debtors' foreign exchange availability by "defensive lending". It is true that, in particular in the last few years, banks have shown themselves extremely hesitant to engage in defensive lending; yet, as I shall argue below, such lending may well be the only means available to the banks to improve the quality of their loans on the problem countries and to minimise the likely size of their losses.

Secondly, transferring the problem of negotiation with the debtor countries from the banks to an international governmental body would make it inevitable that the important distinctions among debtor countries would be subordinated to the principal task for which the new agency was created or with which an existing institution had been specifically charged, viz. "solving the debt problem". The possibilities that clearly exist in many of the major debtors for a debt work-out based on a combination of growth, adjustment and financing would be jeopardised by the application of what would in essence amount to a bankruptcy procedure[2].

While governments have never given any encouragement to proposals for the takeover of the banks' debt, a succession of such proposals could foster the belief, on the part of both the debtors and the banks, that there was some probability that some such proposal might in the end become a reality. An expectation to that effect, even if it was weakly held, could deflect creditors and debtors away from the joint pursuit of the best bilateral bargain and towards obtaining together the best deal from official funds. It was presumably for the purpose of deflating any illusions on this score held by the bilateral partners that the governments of the major economic powers (the G-7), in their 13th April 1988 communiqué, repeated their strong opposition to global debt-forgiveness proposals that transfer risks from the private sector to the international institutions or creditor governments (*IMF Survey* April 1988, p. 116).

10.3 Bilateral Debt Relief — Advantages and Costs

If debt relief by means of a direct contribution of public funds can be excluded as an option, attention needs to be focused on bilateral adjustments between debtors and creditors. Ideally these adjustments should represent a form of burden sharing for the failure of the loan contracts that the parties had entered into. In actual fact, such losses as creditor banks have so far accepted have not usually provided equivalent relief for the debtors; instead, a large part of the loss of the creditors, which is the potential gain of the debtors, ended up with third parties.

Thus, realised losses by the creditor banks are by no means the same thing as debt relief to the debtors. Moreover, how debt relief is brought about makes a large difference with respect to the benefits that the debtor country derives from it.

It is obvious that *ceteris paribus* any country would be better off achieving some measure of debt relief and that it would therefore benefit if its creditors would be prepared to grant what is called in current World Bank parlance "a reduction in existing debt service". Thus, if all indebted countries would receive a major reduction in their debt service through no action of their own, their economic outlook would be unambiguously improved. This could happen as a result of a radical decline in world interest rates (one not brought about by a world recession!). It could also, in theory, be brought about by a decision of the industrial countries to introduce any of the proposals to buy up LDC debt from the banks and then to reduce the nominal value or the interest rate on the debtors' liabilities that they had acquired.

201

But, as indicated above, debt relief of the *deus-ex-machina* variety is hardly what debtor countries can hope for. The debt relief option that they can pursue will inevitably have an impact on their standing in the credit markets, including the discount attaching to the market value for their liabilities. In that situation, other things will not be equal between a country that is all set on obtaining debt relief and another country that aims at keeping scrupulously to its debt service commitments.

Much has been made of the proposition that any form of *ex post* debt relief, especially if it is "market-based," involves a degree of moral hazard. If a country is more likely to receive debt relief, the less able it appears to service its debt, there can be an incentive to follow weak policies that will strengthen the statistical case for relief. The introduction of such moral hazard in international creditor-debtor relationships implies a weakening of the system, which could long outlast the current debt crisis. But it is doubtful whether moral hazard is the central issue. No government that approached its economic policy choices in a rational manner (whether its rationality was of the economic or the political variety) would opt for disorganised government finance, lax monetary policy, or an overvalued exchange rate for the purpose of building up its qualifications for debt relief. The domestic cost of such self-inflicted wounds would far outweigh what the country could extract from it creditors in terms of debt relief.

The pursuit of debt relief from creditor banks is not without its costs to the debtor. Suppose that country A managed to obtain an important interest rate concession, for example by unilateral interruptions in its debt service and by pointing to the market discounts on its liabilities as evidence of its "right" to debt relief; while country B announced its intention to meet its debt service as a matter of policy, decrying any market discount on its liabilities as a short-term aberration. A's current account would improve by the amount of debt relief while B's current account would remain unchanged. But what would happen on the capital side of the balance of payments? Presumably, A would have achieved the concession in part on the basis of its need, as evidenced by a persistent large discount for its liabilities in the secondary market. If A serviced its reduced debt once the relief had been granted, this discount might over time disappear. But the market view that A was a less than perfect debtor would not vanish overnight. The mere act of debt relief would not restore A's creditworthiness. Thus, for a period before and for a considerable period after the debt relief, A's access to voluntary credit would be non-existent. Country B, struggling to keep current, might not enjoy perfect creditworthiness either; its

202

obligations might be quoted at some discount too. But its reputation with the banks and with international lending agencies would surely be better than that of A. Accordingly, though it might not be much more successful in getting loans from commercial banks, its ability to borrow from multilateral development banks would not be subject to frequent interruptions such as those experienced by country A as that country's negotiations with the commercial banks or the Fund went through periodic crises.

We do not have exact replicas of "A" and "B" countries to compare statistically, but the evidence provided by Table 10.1 is nevertheless instructive. The Table compares net external borrowing, before and after the debt crisis, for countries that managed to avoid debt servicing problems and for those that did not. In order to focus on offsets between new borrowing and debt service, the figures on net capital inflows are expressed not only in billions of dollars but also as a ratio to the interest payments made. The table compares two periods, 1979-80 (just before the large surge in borrowing in 1981) and 1985-87, after the temporary phase of large concerted lending. Before the debt crisis, the two groups of countries shown (as well as the sub-group of what would become the 15 heavily indebted countries) borrowed net about twice the amount of their interest payments.

Table 10.1. NET EXTERNAL BORROWING (NXB) AND INTEREST PAYMENTS (IP)

Annual averages, $ billion

Countries	1979-80			1985-87		
	NXB	IP	Ratio	NXB	IP	Ratio
Without debt servicing problems	33	15	2.2	21	29	0.7
With debt servicing problems	56	30	1.9	16	53	0.3
(15 heavily indebted)	(42)	(21)	2.0	(8)	(42)	0.2

Source: IMF, *WEO* April 1987, Tables 38 and 42.

In the second half of the 1980s the interest payments of both groups of countries had nearly doubled. For the countries in payments difficulties, net external borrowing had declined very sharply, to the point where such borrowing would cover only some 30 per cent of interest payments (about 20 per cent for the 15 Baker countries). The countries that avoided the debt crisis have been much better able to keep up their capacity to borrow[3]; their capital inflow covers some 70 per cent of interest payments. This performance reflected no doubt in part the markets' rational appraisal of the quality of these countries' policies; but in the conditions of the mid-1980s, a record of recent debt restructurings would have cast a heavy shadow on even the best of policies. The figures show that if an average Baker country had the opportunity either to obtain 50 per cent debt relief in terms of interest payments or to switch ranks and get the average access to credit of a creditworthy LDC, it would come out about even in terms of balance-of-payments cash flow. In fact, of course, once any country entered into debt rescheduling in the 1980s, it did not have such an option. Indeed, most of the heavily indebted countries have had the worst of both worlds: they have paid full interest, partly out of borrowed money, and perhaps with some delays, but have had a much smaller access to foreign lending than the countries that stayed out of the debt crisis.

Not too much weight should perhaps be attached to the figures for the one Latin American country — Colombia — that managed to keep up the full service — interest and amortization — on its foreign debt; yet the figures for that country are striking. Colombia, it should be recalled, was able to maintain normal debt service because it had not embarked in the 1970s on the heavy spending policies of most other countries in Latin America and consequently had relatively little debt to commercial banks. In spite of this record, Colombia did not receive particularly favourable treatment from the commercial banks when it needed new credits. While other countries negotiated to reschedule amortization, Colombia found the resources to amortize by negotiating two $1 billion loans, one in 1985 and one in 1987, on terms that were marginally *less* favourable than the bank loans to countries such as Argentina and Mexico (higher spreads over Libor, shorter grace periods and maturities). But Colombia's total access to medium- and long-term debt from all sources (multilateral, bilateral, and commercial bank co-financing) shows a wide margin over that of the other Baker countries. Colombia was able to borrow abroad about $1.2 billion a year net in the period 1985-87, compared to an average of $735 million a year in 1978-81; two other Baker countries (Côte d'Ivoire and Ecuador) were able to borrow at about the same annual rate in the two periods, while each of the others received much less, in spite of jumbo loans to Mexico and Argentina in 1987. The amount borrowed by Colombia in 1985-87 more than covered its annual interest payments of about $1.0 billion; in other words, even though the country barely managed to skirt the debt crisis and had to go through difficult negotiations (which needed the support of the IMF and the World Bank) with the commercial banks, it ended up with a more favourable "net transfer" over the last three years than if it had been granted full remission of interest payments on its foreign debt.

While a deep discount on a country's foreign obligations may appear as a convenient argument in favour of debt relief, it is not without domestic costs to the debtor country. The discount translates, of course, to an effective interest rate far in excess of the nominal interest rate. Such an interest rate on one category of the country's liabilities will tend to spill over to all negotiable claims on that country, both those held abroad and those held within the country, and to claims expressed in domestic currency as well as those expressed in dollars. At the same time, the low supply of capital from abroad, as well as the low savings ratio that has characterised the most heavily indebted countries, will tend to raise interest rates from the inside. Through various connections including the possibility of residents' moving money in or out and the scope for arbitrage exercised by multinational corporations operating in the country — the internal and the external markets will (subject, of course, to important market imperfections) gravitate toward a single interest rate level that reflects all the forces bearing on the supply and demand of capital for this country (Dooley 1987). In foreign capital markets, questions about the country's creditworthiness will manifest themselves in a large discount in secondary markets. Within the country, real interest rates will be extremely high; figures in the order of 2 or $2\frac{1}{2}$ per cent a month can be found in many of the countries here discussed.

The scarcity of capital and the high interest rates will act as factors retarding growth, and these may in effect constitute the most telling costs of a country's lack of creditworthiness. The effect should not be expected to be proportional to the reduction in the rate of gross or net capital investment. If the ratio of investment to GDP was 24 per cent before the debt crisis, with a growth rate of 6 per cent per annum, one need not assume that an investment ratio of 18 per cent currently would force down the growth rate to $4\frac{1}{2}$ per cent[4]. There is room for substitution among the factors of production, the more so since the same countries that are now exposed to higher real interest rates have also experienced sharp declines in real wage rates. These two forces would no doubt produce some degree of substitution in the use of factors of production — when new capital goods are installed, when worn-out capital is replaced, when large scale uneconomic government investment is cut out, and even by means of a more intensive exploitation of existing machinery. Unfortunately, we know very little about the substitutability of factors of production in developing countries. We sorely lack an explanation of the growth of output in these countries along the lines developed by Denison (1977) for the industrial countries; only this grievous lacuna in existing research can explain the survival of the simplistic ICOR technique in spite of its obvious weaknesses (Denison 1967, Chapter 10; 1977; 1980, pp. 220-224).

10.4 Towards Creditor-Debtor Co-operation

In the early phase of the debt crisis, there was no question of the banks accepting any part of the cost of the misallocation of resources for which — in retrospect — they and the debtors had been jointly responsible.

While consenting to some new lending, the banks charged debtors a stiff rescheduling fee and raised the spread over Libor or over the prime rate to reflect some incipient doubts on the quality of rescheduled or new loans. But the new spreads — e.g. $1\frac{7}{8}$ per cent over Libor in the case of Mexico in 1982 and $2\frac{1}{4}$ per cent over Libor in the case of Brazil in 1983 — were not wide enough to cover a high degree of perceived risk.

These spreads were in line with a view of the debt problem as a temporary disturbance that all parties concerned would probably be able to ride out in a few years by means of a combination of adjustment and financing. In the same spirit, the banks could plausibly continue to value claims on the highly indebted countries at contractual values on their books. If the banks had to make concerted loans to enable debtors to pay interest in full (in other words, if the banks had to add to their existing loans part of the interest due on these loans), it was in their collective interest to do so rather than grant interest relief or see interest arrears developing. Individual, especially smaller, banks might have an advantage in acting as "free riders", collecting interest in full without participating in new lending; but at least initially these tendencies could be kept under control by pressure from the larger banks on the smaller ones. At the same time, the amount of new lending by all banks was moderated, and the pressures toward free-riding reduced, by the assumption of part of the financing burden by official lenders, in particular international financial institutions. In the framework of this approach, there was a good case for minimising the significance of any secondary market in banks' claims (Simonsen 1985, p. 111).

This non-equilibrium approach, which held up the value of LDC debt by collective action including the banks, debtor countries, creditor countries, and international organisations, was only viable if it could lead to an equilibrium situation over a moderately short time span. The approach required not only light at the end of tunnel, but a short tunnel as well. When it became apparent that the tunnel was a long one in the best of circumstances, the approach could no longer be maintained; it became necessary to give some degree of recognition to the realisation by individual banks of the reduced value of their claims on the highly indebted countries. This became the more compelling as these claims came to be regarded as the potential source of not one loss, but two losses: not only a debt service that might fall short of the debtor's contractual obligations, but also the implied obligation to participate in future concerted extensions of credit, which might also be of questionable quality.

This constellation of circumstances made the emergence of a recognised secondary market inevitable — a market, however imperfect, in which participating banks could sell to stop the losses incurred on existing sovereign claims and, at the same time, to protect themselves against pressure to share in future concerted lending to the same debtors.

Although initially mainly serving the interests of the minor banks, in the last year or two the largest United States, United Kingdom and Canadian consortium banks have joined in the recognition of the secondary market[5]. Their new attitude was demonstrated by decisions, starting with Citibank in May 1987, to set aside large reserves against these claims. The market saw this action by the banks as a confirmation of the doubts that they entertained concerning the value of their claims. This, together with a greater willingness on the part of the banks to dispose of some of their claims through the various options available for this purpose, depressed the prices quoted for bank claims on LDCs.

Once the discount on the banks' sovereign claims was widely acknowledged, United States Treasury Secretary Baker, the World Bank, the Fund, and others, sought to turn necessity into virtue by advocating a "market-determined menu approach" to the debt problem in which creditors would have a wide variety of options to use claims on debtor countries or sell them to others for use. Using the same culinary metaphor, Gerald Corrigan, President of the Federal Reserve Bank of New York, in an April 1988 address to the Institute for International Finance in Washington, suggested a broadening of the menu to a *smorgasbord*. As it is, banks can — depending on the debtor country — use portions of their claims (or sell them to others for this purpose): to make direct investments; to buy equity portfolios; to buy up privatised public sector enterprises; to obtain local currency, dollars, or bonds; to buy commodities for exports (so far limited to Peru); or to finance conservation projects (World Bank 1988, pp. 37-40).

Most of these ideas are not novel; they are a modern adaptation of the ingenuity applied in the 1930s to find some use for balances of the currencies of Germany and other European countries whose transfer had been blocked by the respective governments (League of Nations 1938). The resulting concern over unfair and arbitrary competition, as well as of monetary disorder, led to the incorporation into the Articles of Agreement of the IMF of "maintain[ing] orderly exchange arrangements" as one of the purposes of the IMF, [Article I, (iii)] as well as to the ban on multiple currency practices under Article VIII, Section 3. This background would seem to call for caution in the encouragement of similar arrangements in current circumstances.

The disposal by banks of claims at discount prices does not automatically involve debt relief for the debtor country. Typically, claims that have been acquired by buyers at a discount are converted by the Central Bank of the debtor country into local currency at the prevailing exchange rate against the dollar. Although in some instances the debtor country may apply a "conversion fee", or use an auction technique, to capture part of the discount, much of the benefit arising from the original discount accrues to the user of the claim, and to intermediaries.

Although the menu approach serves the interests of certain banks in improving their asset structures, its benefits to the debtor country are far less obvious. It will bring about some reduction in its outstanding debt, as the country gives up tradeables, or assets in its economy, to redeem a portion of the debt. The character of the debt service is changed, as the country owes a smaller amount of interest-bearing debt and a larger amount of investment claims, on which in due course dividends will have to be remitted as and when the investment yields profits (and subject to such time constraints on remittances as may have been imposed as condition for the conversion). On the balance sheet of the government of the debtor country, the change is merely a substitution of internal for external indebtedness, either directly, if the foreign investor is paid in government bonds (as is the practice of the Central Bank of Chile) or indirectly, as the government sells debt at home to obtain the domestic currency needed for this purpose[6]; if it issued the domestic currency without withdrawing the same amount by domestic borrowing, the effect of the swap would be inflationary — a consequence that debtor countries have for good reason been anxious to avoid.

On the economic side, making certain investment (or trade) transactions cheaper as a result of the discount may well promote some activities that would not otherwise have taken place on the same scale. But the case for implied foreign exchange subsidies, which are inherent in any form of multiple exchange rates, would seem particularly weak now that most of the heavily indebted countries have accepted large real depreciations for their currencies[7]. Politically, the complicated swap techniques may enable the debtor country to introduce certain policies, such as privatisation, liberalisation of investment from abroad, or *de facto* amnesty for nationals who repatriate capital, that would have been more difficult to do in a more direct fashion; but this would seem far from an obvious advantage in general. In view of the lack of clarity of the advantages to debtor countries, it is not surprising that the degree of enthusiasm shown for debt conversion techniques varies from strong support in some countries to grudging acceptance in others.

While the menu approach has been referred to as "market-based", it still contains many non-market elements. The buyer of a claim from a bank cannot trade this claim in a market for the currency of the debtor country; he can only obtain that currency from the central bank, provided he intends to use if for approved asset purchases, at a price in units of local currency per dollar set by the central bank (or sometimes determined in an auction process) by categories of investment, and subject to regulations on the remittance of profits and the invested capital. The difficulty of bringing together sellers and potential users of claims explains both the thinness of the market and the very substantial commissions made by middlemen. These market imperfections suggest that there should be room for other techniques. Such techniques should recognise the interests of debtor countries in reducing the discount on their indebtedness while, at the same time, channeling to them, rather than to the buyers of claims or to middlemen, the benefits from such discounts as sellers of claims are willing to accept to reduce their exposure.

Countries could achieve this market (no longer "market-based") solution by adopting a double policy of (a) strengthening as much as possible their balance of payments and (b) using any balance-of-payment surpluses to buy back their international debt as long as it trades at a discount from what the debtor country considers its fair value. This proposition needs some clarification in two respects. First, strengthening of the balance of payments is not intended to refer simply to the current account, and it is not meant to include welfare-reducing policies such as restraint on growth or severe import restrictions. Capital account policies could play a large role, including encouraging foreign investment, the return of flight capital, borrowing from MDBs, issuing bonds, as well as the exploration of emerging possibilities to borrow from the commercial banking system. Second, while some part of balance-of-payments surpluses may be needed to build up reserves to a safe level, beyond that level it is to the country's obvious advantage to use reserves, on which it typically earns a rate of interest close to Libor, to buy back its own debt, which may be trading at an effective interest rate that is twice as high. The debtor country can get the maximum benefit from a buy-back programme by determining from time to time the amount of money that it can use for the purpose, and inviting competitive offers of its outstanding debt at the lowest price.

This market approach to the debt problem would raise the importance of the prices quoted in the secondary markets, and that would be a constructive development in the perspective of debtors working their way out of the debt problem, once the excess holdings of smaller banks have been disposed of and a functioning market is established. While such a market would be influenced by many factors, the indications it gives could be helpful to borrowing countries in much the same way that a parallel exchange market can give valuable signals[8].

In a number of respects, the market model as here described was applied by Mexico in early 1988 to bring about some reduction in its bank debt. But a major difference was that Mexico did not offer cash for its outstanding claims, but new claims of a superior quality: their redemption in twenty years is collateralised by zero-coupon United States Treasury bonds that Mexico has bought and put in escrow, and the interest rate on the new claims is $1\frac{5}{8}$ per cent over Libor, as against 13/16 per cent on the old claims. These improvements were *not* sufficient to make the new claims trade at par, because the interest payments, which for a twenty-year bond are far more important than the redemption value, are not guaranteed; but they ensured a higher initial price for the new claims (about 75 per cent of par) than for the old ones (about 50 per cent).

The transaction makes eminent sense in its main ingredient: to buy back $100 of debt for $50, or, to put it differently, to use reserves on which a low interest rate is earned to buy back liabilities that carry a higher effective interest rate. Such a transaction should be expected to lower, marginally, the discount on the debtor country's liabilities[9].

What is not easy to understand is the use, in the actual conversion as conducted by Mexico, of additional money to upgrade the part of the debt represented by new claims. It is by no means clear what purpose is served by having some amount of Mexico's debt traded at a much reduced discount, thereby raising the discount on the bulk of the debt[10]. It is this general discount that determines Mexico's standing in the market and, through arbitrage, influences the interest rate in the domestic market. The conclusion to be drawn from this is that the best use for a debtor of available money would be a straight buy-back, without the application of any money to "credit enhancement". The same negative view would apply to the use of any of a country's access to credit (e.g. from the World Bank) for "credit enhancement". On the plausible assumption that any country's total access to World Bank credit is limited, a country would do better to use the resources to which it has access for straight buy-backs rather than for "credit enhancement".

The particular technique used by Mexico may have been inspired by restrictions against a straight buy-back in Mexico's loan agreements with the banks. Thus a solution was found under which existing claims were not bought back, but exchanged for other claims. But this "conversion" required waivers of the original loan contracts too. Moreover, the common interest that Mexico and the banks have in reducing the discount on Mexico's debt should make it worth the effort for both parties to agree on modifications of the loan agreements that would make the application of Mexican resources as effective as possible.

The question may be asked as to how much of a dent any highly indebted country can make in its outstanding debt by applying from time to time some excess reserves to buy-back auctions? The case of Mexico, where reserves had been swollen by large borrowing from the banks, a temporary current account surplus, and some reflux of flight capital, is almost certainly exceptional; and even here the quantitative impact of buy-backs cannot be very large. However, the question is essentially misconceived. The underlying assumption of a programme by any debtor country to repurchase debt whenever it can do so with advantage is that the country envisages itself as on the road to creditworthiness. That attitude, rather than the amounts applied, is the most important contribution that the country can make toward becoming creditworthy. Given that attitude as a determinant of policy — and given reasonably favourable external conditions, a point never to be overlooked — the country's road to viable debt ratios lies predominantly in raising its GNP and export levels, not in reducing the absolute amount of its debt.

Whether this favourable result will materialise will depend on three things: (i) the perseverance of the debtor country in the necessary adjustment policies, (ii) satisfactory world economic conditions, and (iii) supporting action by the banks themselves. Only at their peril can the banks ignore the last of

211

these three conditions and base their policies on a combination of hope that the first two conditions will be met and the building of reserves against the eventuality that this hope will prove false. A rational approach by the banks includes measures that they can take and which will both raise the probability of a satisfactory debt work-out (even though they cannot guarantee that outcome) and encourage the debtors in their pursuit of adjustment policies.

Some such measures have been taken by the banks, including stretching of maturities, lowering spreads and, with increasing reluctance as the debt crisis continued, lending of "new money". Some other measures probably involve more costs or more new risk for the banks than could be justified on the uncertain basis that they might reduce the risk to which the banks are already exposed. In this category would fall the proposals (discussed in Chapter 9) for automatic partial long-term refinancing of interest payments, as well as various proposals for interest caps or partial interest forgiveness[11].

There remains, then, one approach that is well within the range of normal bank practice and that does not involve disproportionate risks. That approach would be an expressed willingness by the banks to make annual "new money" loans (or to capitalise interest, at the bank's choice) up to, say, half the interest due, on condition that the debtor country continued to pursue a satisfactory adjustment programme. The banks might find it legally difficult to come to a binding judgment whether that condition was fulfilled; instead, they might prefer to derive this judgment from the country's relation with the Fund or the Bank. If pre-announced for a considerable span of years ahead, say five to seven years, this approach should dramatically raise the probability that the debt crisis would be on the way out for the countries that qualified for this assistance and showed every intention to continue to do so.

While none of the problem debtor countries have consistently earned trade surpluses that would cover their interest payments in full, there are many instances of countries able to cover half the interest from trade surpluses. (The non-problem debtors have more frequently not met this test for the simple reason that they did not need to, as their net access to foreign capital continued.) The advance announcement of a standard policy on the part of the banks of a willingness to lend half the interest due would remove the amount from the negotiating agenda; it would also remove the negative incentives of the present approach under which (after protracted negotiations) more money is in the end lent if performance has been less successful. One could note two further points about a conditional policy of lending half the interest: at current interest rates, it would keep the real (dollar) value of the banks' exposure about constant, and would of course reduce that exposure as a percentage of total bank assets; and it would protect the borrower against the immediate impact of half the risk of interest rate fluctuations[12].

There is no implication that adoption of a policy of the nature sketched would come easily to the banks. Among other things, the "free rider" problem would have to be faced, and that might involve some further "exits". Nor can it be assumed, even if the banks were willing to entertain such a policy, that all debtors would in the end recover creditworthiness so that the banks' provisions would have been unnecessary. For reasons that may be either political or economic (and the distinction may be neither clear nor important), some of the heavily indebted middle-income countries will likely prove unable to make the adjustments that will strengthen their payments position to the point at which they can meet even half the interest service of the existing debt. The banks will in the end stand to lose a large part of their claims on these countries. The price development in the secondary market will be giving signals to prepare the banks for this eventuality, and at some stage the inevitable will be recognised.

10.5 The Debt Problem of the Poorest Countries

The thrust of the preceding sections of this chapter was that the debt problem of many of the highly indebted middle-income countries may be open to resolution by a process of work-out based on sufficient policy readjustment by these countries, a collaborative attitude on the part of the commercial banks, and the maintenance of lending by national and international official creditors. There is no certainty about this outcome, and much will depend on the strength of external circumstances. But the scenario described carries sufficient probability to make it reasonable for all the major players to accept it as the basis for their policy planning.

By no stretch of the imagination could a comparable scenario be accepted for the poorest countries, most of which are found in Sub-Saharan Africa. This least developed part of the world has been in a state of stagnation and retrogression for a decade or longer[13]. Per capita incomes, which were among the lowest in the world, have been on a downward trend and earlier progress on health and education has been reversed. The role played in these tragic developments by inadequate economic and financial policies has been extensively documented in recent years (World Bank 1981), and the need for policy adjustment is now widely accepted by the governments in Africa. At the same time, external conditions have been harshly unfavourable. Four factors stand out as direct external causes of the deteriorating situation: drought and resulting food shortages over a large part of the continent in 1984 and 1985; a sharp deterioration in the terms of trade over the past decade; more than a doubling in interest payments on foreign debt as a percentage of exports over the same period; and a drying up of private capital flows since 1982. As a partial offset to these negative factors, net aid disbursements increased by about 7 per cent per annum in real terms.

The fact that many countries in Africa cannot, now or in the foreseeable future, service their foreign debt — mostly toward governments and to a smaller extent toward commercial banks and suppliers (see Table 10.2) — is widely acknowledged. In response to this situation, creditor governments have taken a variety of actions. Many have forgiven ODA credits to the poorest countries, as recommended by UNCTAD Resolution 165 adopted in 1978. Donor countries' contributions to ESAF and earlier initiatives have enlarged the supply of the concessional resources available to low-income countries. More recent proposals for debt relief are referred to below. But what the creditor countries have not done is to adapt their procedures to the fact that much of Africa's remaining debt simply cannot be serviced on existing (and some of it perhaps on any) terms.

First, debt owed to governments and accumulated interest continue to be rescheduled year after year under the auspices of the Paris Club, provided the country has a stand-by arrangement with the Fund. Rescheduling does not mean debt cancellation or reduction of the debt. Moreover, since the Paris Club does not determine the interest rates on the rescheduled debt, bilateral negotiations between debtor and creditor countries are needed for this purpose. In these negotiations, into which other outstanding issues between the parties concerned may also be discussed, the creditor country normally insists on a rate of interest for all except ODA credits that reflects rates prevailing in its market. In an attempt at debt relief introduced in 1987, the period of rescheduling has been extended from ten to twenty years, and the grace period from five to ten years for the poorest countries; but this changes nothing for the first five years, and the maintenance of the existing procedure with respect to interest rates continues the fiction that these countries can take on new credits at market interest rates to discharge liabilities as they fall due.

The procedures followed by the Paris Club, including the conclusion of bilateral implementing agreements, serve the accounting, budgetary and legal constraints of the creditor countries, and this is a relevant consideration to the debtor countries as well, since they continue to depend on new aid flows and new export-credit guarantees from these same creditor countries. Both parties may therefore be satisfied to keep up the annual charade of debt rescheduling, as long as it is understood that no operational significance is to be attached to the ever-increasing figures for the size of the debt to which this process leads for many countries.

Table 10.2.   DEBT OF SUB-SAHARAN AFRICA ON 31ST DECEMBER 1986

$ billion

Government and government-guaranteed medium-term debt	90.4
"Preferred creditors"	22.7
IMF	7.0
IDA-IBRD	13.3
AfDB	2.4
Foreign governments	41.2
Private creditors	26.5
Commercial banks	22.9
Suppliers	3.6
Other (unguaranteed and short-term)	11.6
Total	102.0

Source: UN Report, *op. cit.,* p. 21. A tabulation by the Fund puts total debt for end-1986 at $122.4 billion and for end-1987 at $137.8 billion. About half the difference in the 1986 figure is due to the inclusion in the Fund's figures of some $12 billion for arrears. Both the UN and the Fund tabulation include Nigeria (*IMF Survey,* June 1988, Supplement on Sub-Saharan African Debt).

But this is a questionable view of the whole process on a number of counts. First, the maintenance on the books of a contractual debt service well beyond what can ever realistically be expected to be performed can be expected to sap the interest of the debtor country in improving its payments position. The debt service overhang is the equivalent of a 100 per cent marginal tax owed by the country to foreign governments.

Second — more technically — the continuing stream of bilateral negotiations, which tend to carry over from one annual Paris Club exercise to the next, while not particularly burdensome to the creditors with their large professional staffs, represents a serious waste of scarce time of senior officials of the debtor countries — time that could far better be spent on managing the country's business[14].

Third, the Paris Club insistence on a Fund programme as a precondition for rescheduling, while sensible in the case of middle-income debtors, makes little sense for most African debtors. The point here is not that these countries are not in need of Fund programmes, either of the standby variety or a structural programme under the EFF, the SAF or the ESAF; surely, the near-desperate financial condition of many African countries makes the technical and financial assistance that a Fund programme can contribute a virtual necessity. But with or without such a programme, these countries cannot service their debt for many years to come. In the presence of extreme over-indebtedness, debt rescheduling is no longer a favour of the creditor to the debtor, to which conditions can realistically be attached; instead it has become a procedural ritual, necessary to avoid the even less attractive alternative of arrears or default.

In recognition of the fact that the debtor's difficulties are not temporary, a long-term approach to the African debt problem is necessary. Such an approach is also possible without the risks of encouraging policy laxity that militates against it for the middle-income countries. We observed in Section 9.4 that in the absence of arrangements for conditionality over a long period it would be unreasonable to expect commercial bank creditors to enter into long-term commitments that would backload debt service into the distant future. In the case of the African countries, however, the presence of creditor imposed conditionality is unlikely to be a passing condition. Not only are these countries likely to need Fund and Bank programmes for many years to come; they will be dependent for decades to come on foreign aid from donor countries. Donors — essentially the same countries as the Paris Club creditors — could far more sensibly insist on policy conditions as a *quid pro quo* for continued bilateral aid, where the donors make a substantive contribution to the country, than for debt relief, where their only choice is between accepting rescheduling or accepting arrears. Moreover, donors can justifiably take the position that conditions on broad macro-policies are immediately relevant to the effectiveness of foreign aid while they bear very little relation to debt rescheduling.

In the light of these considerations particular attention deserves to be paid to a proposal for a long-term solution of the debt problems of African countries put forward by the African Development Bank (1987) and S.G. Warburg Co. Ltd. The proposal starts out from the proposition that while the payments on their debt to which debtor countries are formally committed are wholly unrealistic, countries can and do pay certain annual amounts that are not

216

insubstantial. If the obligation to pay were set — in negotiation between creditors and debtors — at an annual rate that had proved to be realistic on the basis of past experience, the debt service so agreed could reasonably be expected to be met. These sums would be used to pay a modest interest rate on the debt, after setting aside an amount each year that would suffice, if invested at compound interest, to redeem the principal of the debt after twenty years[15].

Even though the distinction between payment of interest and principal is (as we saw in the case of the Mexican debt-conversion proposal) essentially immaterial to the creditor, the concept of full repayment of principal over a not excessively long horizon serves to underline the debtor's commitment to the service of the debt within the limits of his ability to do so. The political value of maintenance of interest payments at some arbitrary low rate would seem less compelling, in particular if these payments ultimately have to be financed by higher aid. There are many other, more detailed, aspects to the AfDB/ Warburg proposal, including the assumption that, in accordance with established practice, the debt owed to international agencies would not be rescheduled, but that the institutions would instead aim at maintaining their exposure in the debtor countries.

It is interesting to observe that the AfDB proposal succeeds in overcoming the drawbacks inherent in the current approach. By stipulating fixed annual payments, it removes the disincentive of the equivalent of a high marginal tax rate[16]. By settling for a single agreement for a long period, it eliminates the time consuming Paris Club *cum* bilaterals machinery. And by proposing the linkage of bilateral aid to policy conditionality (normally to be administered by Fund and Bank) it attaches the constructive idea of conditionality to the concept of enhancing the effectiveness of foreign aid.

This fundamental approach to a solution of the debt problem for Africa cannot stand by itself. It needs to supported, as the UN Report convincingly argues, by increased flows of multilateral and bilateral aid, as well as by provisions for contingency financing, as discussed in Chapter 9.

10.6 Concluding Observations

In the past, too, many countries have suffered the costly after-effects of excessive foreign indebtedness. In one way or another, these debt problems of the past were resolved. Some highly indebted countries maintained debt

217

service in full, or resumed it after interruption and regained creditworthiness in that way. Some negotiated concessions from their creditors. Some defaulted, in whole or in part, in name or *de facto*: they too, ultimately, came to be considered again as attractive clients for capital exports.

There can be little doubt but that the debt crisis of the 1980s will pass into history in much the same way. What seems certain is that nowadays no country will, for long, perform debt service beyond the limits of what it considers compatible with its best chances for growth in the long run.

But the choices countries face are often far from clear — and the same applies to the choices creditors have to make. Many complex considerations enter into the calculations that debtor countries, creditor banks and creditor governments have to make. The evidence of recent years suggests strongly that actors in each of these three groups need time and experience to arrive at correct appraisals as to where their best interests lie. That is why the process of decision making and negotiation has already taken an inordinate number of years. The glaring inefficiency of this process has entailed large costs to the indebted countries — unnecessary costs that are superimposed on the unavoidable costs of adjustment. Public policy requires that every effort be made to speed up the process and bring it to an early and satisfactory solution.

This chapter has presented a number of suggestions towards resolving the debt crisis for the two main groupings of debtor countries. These suggestions are not blueprints of preferred solutions: instead, they aim at laying out the analytical guidelines within which any solutions will have to be found. The sooner they are found, the better.

Annex to Chapter 10

DEBT BUY-BACK *vs.* DEBT CONVERSION

On the plausible assumption that the holders of a country's total foreign debt put a notional value on this debt equal to the country's present assets (especially reserves) plus the discounted value of net future balance-of-payments streams, the average market price per unit of debt will not be affected by the use of some part of these assets to buy back debt at the prevailing market price (Dooley 1988, pp. 215-229). At most, the price would be affected by the fact that the interest saving on the operation raises future net balance-of-payments streams somewhat; unless the buy-back were very large, the impact on the market price would be too small to be observable in a thin market with a wide spread between bid and ask quotations.

Disregarding this minor effect on the average price of the debt, it is easily shown that the reduction in the nominal value of debt that can be brought about is equal to the amount of reserves applied to this purpose divided by the market price; it is independent of whether the available resources are used in a straight buy-back or in an exchange for "credit enhanced" new bonds.

If a country uses R in reserves in a straight buy-back for debt quoted at a price, as a ratio of face value, of p, the amount of debt reduction is R/p. E.g. with debt quoted at 50 cents on the dollar, an outlay of $2 billion reduces the nominal value of the debt by $4 billion.

Now consider the alternative under which the government offers to swap an announced amount y of old debt for $\times$ in new debt, the amount of $\times$ to be determined in an auction. The government also makes R available for "credit enhancement", e.g. by purchasing assets as collateral for redemption, or some amount of interest insurance, or any other fixed cost measure to benefit the holders of new debt. Participants in the auction will consider the value of the new debt as equal to the old debt they tender, plus the value of the sweetener. Hence their offer will be determined by:

$$px + R = py, \text{ or}$$
$$y - x = R/p$$

The reduction in debt, y - x, is again equal to R/p.

Obviously, the new debt, having been sweetened by R, will trade at a price above p. If the market-valuation of the total debt is unchanged, the price of the old debt must fall below p as a result of the conversion operation.

NOTES AND REFERENCES

1. Note that the extension of maturities, as agreed in some of the bank debt restructurings, does not imply debt relief unless the rate of interest is also reduced to a concessional level; but if interest rates are below market levels, the extension of time adds another dimension to the concessionality: even though at the market interest rate, a thirty-year loan has the same present value as a ten-year loan, a thirty-year loan at a concessional rate has a much larger "grant content" than a ten-year loan at the same rate.

2. As calculated by Feldstein *et al.* (1987, pp. 67-68), these proposals to lower interest rates and extend maturities to the debtors would imply the acceptance of very large capital losses on the claims — losses that would not be necessary if allowance were made for the likely improvements over time in the ability of the debtor countries to service their debt on the basis of increasing exports.

3. The figures for 1985-87 no doubt understate the capacity to borrow of this group. South Korea, e.g., voluntarily moved into net repayment of its debt during this period.

4. One can come to an even gloomier result by comparing figures for net investment ratios, obtained by deducting say 10 per cent of GDP for depreciation. On that assumption, net investment would be cut in half (from 12 per cent to 6 per cent) and assuming the same capital-output ratio, growth would be down from 6 per cent p.a. to 3 per cent p.a.

5. Provisioning against Third World loans by continental European banks started well before that time.

6. The exception would be when the foreign creditor accepts for its claim real assets which the government is prepared to privatise. In this case the government does not need to borrow at home, but forgoes the reduction in its borrowing requirement that it would have received from privatising official assets to domestic buyers.

7. This is in contrast to the European countries referred to above, which had kept up artificially the official gold value of their currencies and thus felt a strong need to make their exports of goods and services more competitive by allowing the market value of their currencies abroad to become depreciated. But Peru, the one country that engaged in debt-for-export swaps, also stands out by clinging to a highly overvalued currency.

8. Recent experience with quotations in secondary markets suggests that price movements in these markets are less informative concerning countries' policies, and hence probably less valuable as warning signals, than was suggested by Swoboda a few years ago (1985, p. 170): "Fluctuations in the price of existing bank loans (or other securities) serve to induce prudent behavior on the part of borrowers. Banks have been complaining that they cannot exercise conditionality on sovereign borrowers. Although an individual bank cannot do so, the markets can. A fall in the price of claims on a particular country immediately raises the cost of new borrowing. This is a powerful inducement.to the country to service its debt regularly and promptly. It is also an incentive to adopt policies that have a favourable impact on its borrowing costs and to offer credible precommitments on such policies. Furthermore, a country could buy back its own debt if it proved advantageous and thus could send signals of its capacity to maintain creditworthiness".

9. In itself, the use of part of a country's assets to buy back liabilities at the market rate should not change the market valuation of the remaining debt. But the interest saving on the operation raises the resources available to the country to service the debt, and should thus improve its market value. For a modest amount of buy-back, the effect would, however, be too small to be observable in a thin market with a wide spread between bid and ask quotations. For a more detailed discussion, see Annex to this chapter.

10. This will happen even if the new debt has no seniority over the old debt. It simply reflects the fact that the new claims will be entitled to a larger proportion of Mexico's current and prospective assets than the old claims which they replace, thus leaving less of these assets available for the service of the old claims.

11. One such proposal (which envisaged parallel interest reductions by all creditors — governments, international institutions, and banks) was put forward in 1987 by Alfred Herrhausen of the Deutsche Bank and is listed among the Debt Relief Proposals tabulated by the World Bank (1988 World Debt Tables, Vol. I). It appears to have been quietly withdrawn, however, in response to negative reactions from other banks.

12. Unlike an interest rate cap, the debtor country would be enabled to borrow (half) the cost of interest rate increases, and would thus ultimately pay for them — as it would under the IMF contingency facility coverage of interest rate increases.

13. The source for the information on Africa in this section is a recent excellent United Nations report (1988). Most of the statistical data on Sub-Saharan Africa in this report exclude Nigeria, which is set apart by its size and its large oil exports. The policy conclusions in this section apply to some of the heavily indebted low-income countries on other continents as well.

14. This is not the only, and perhaps not the worst, misuse of the time of African debtor countries' officials imposed by donor countries. More serious is the proliferation of donors' pet projects and the related burden of bilateral negotiation of conditions.

15. The proposal to reduce interest rates on rescheduled African debt owed to governments

made by Chancellor of the Exchequer Nigel Lawson in his 9th April 1987 statement to the IMF Interim Committee, and that of President François Mitterrand to forgive one-third of the principal of that debt represent alternative approaches to the same problem, but they were not presented as alternatives to the Paris Club procedure.

16. The proposal includes a suggestion that the payments could be raised or lowered in the light of performance (p. 7), but this idea would presumably be implemented in a manner to ensure that "the debtor country would have a real incentive to pursue the economic policies agreed with the IMF and the World Bank" (p. 10).

BIBLIOGRAPHY

ADAMS, D.W.
"Are the Arguments for Cheap Agricultural Credit Sound?", in D.W. Adams *et al.*, *Undermining Rural Development with Cheap Credit*, (Special studies in social, political and economic development series), Boulder, Colorado, Westview, 1984.

ADLER, J.H.
"Development Theory and the Bank's Developing Strategy — A Review", IMF/World Bank, *Finance and Development*, December 1977.

AFRICAN DEVELOPMENT BANK
Proposal for Refinancing African Debt, Abidjan, 1987.

AGHEVLI, Bijan B. and Jorge MARQUEZ-RUARTE
A Case of Successful Adjustment: Korea's Experience During 1980-84, Washington, D.C., IMF Occasional Paper No. 39, 1985.

AGARWALA, R.
Price Distortions and Growth in Developing Countries, Washington, D.C., World Bank Staff Working Paper No. 575, 1983.

BALASSA, Bela, G.M. BUENO, P.P. KUCZYNSKI and M.H. SIMONSEN
Toward Renewed Economic Growth in Latin America, Washington, D.C., Institute for International Economics, 1987.

BENOIT, J.P.
"Artificially Low Interest Rates Versus Realistic or Market Interest Rates", in Denis Kessler and Pierre Antoine Ullmo, eds., *Savings and Development, Proceedings of a Colloquium held in Paris 28th-30th May 1984,* Paris, Economica, 1985.

BERG, E. and A. BATCHELDER
Structural Adjustment Lending: A Critical View, World Bank, mimeo, 1985.

BERGSTEN, Fred C., T. HORST and T.H. MORAN
American Multinationals and American Interests, Washington, D.C., Brookings Institution, 1978.

BERGSTEN, Fred C., William CLINE and John WILLIAMSON
Bank Lending to Developing Countries, Washington, D.C., Institute for International Economics, 1985.

BLAIR, H.W.
"Agricultural Credit, Political Economy, and Patronage", in D.W. Adams *et al.*, *Undermining Rural Development with Cheap Credit*, (Special studies in social, political and economic development series), Boulder, Colorado, Westview, 1984.

CASSEN, R. and ASSOCIATES
Does Aid Work, Oxford, Oxford University Press, 1986.

CHELLIA, R.J.
"Growth Oriented Adjustment Programs: Fiscal Policy Issues", in V. Corbo, M. Goldstein and M. Khan, *Growth Oriented Adjustment Programs,* Washington, D.C., IMF and World Bank, 1987.

CLINE, William R.
International Debt and the Stability of the World Economy, Washington, D.C., Institute for International Economics, 1983.

Systemic Risk and Policy Response, Washington, D.C., Institute for International Economics, 1984.

CONESA, E.R.
Fuga de Capitales en America Latina, 1970-86, Washington, D.C., Inter-American Development Bank, 1987.

COOPER, Richard N.
"Conclusions and Policy Implications", in John Williamson, ed., *IMF Conditionality,* Washington, D.C. Institute for International Economics, 1983.

COOPER, Richard N. and Jeffrey D. SACHS
"Borrowing Abroad: the Debtor's Perspective", in Gordon W. Smith and John T. Cuddington, eds., *International Debt and the Developing Countries* (a World Bank Symposium), Washington, D.C., World Bank, 1985.

CORBO, Vittorio
"Reforms with Macroeconomic Adjustment in Chile During 1974-84", *World Development,* Vol. 13, No. 8, August 1985.

CORBO, V., M. GOLDSTEIN and M. KHAN
Growth-Oriented Adjustment Programs, Washington, D.C., IMF and World Bank, 1987.

CUDDINGTON, John T.
Capital Flight: Estimates, Issues and Explanations, Princeton, N.J., Princeton University (Princeton Studies in International Finance No. 58), 1986.

CUMBY, R. and R. LEVICH
"On the Definition and Magnitude of Recent Capital Flight", in Donald R. Lessard and John Williamson, *Capital Flight and the World Debt,* Washington, D.C., Institute for International Economics, 1987.

DELL, Sidney
On Being Grandmotherly: The Evolution of IMF Conditionality, Princeton, N.J., Princeton Univesity (Princeton University Essays in International Finance No. 144), October 1981.

DENISON, E.F.

Why Growth Rates Differ: Postwar Experience in Nine Western Countries, Washington, D.C., Brookings Institution, 1967.

"The Contribution of Capital to the Postwar Growth of Industrial Countries", in Joint Economic Committee *Studies,* Washington, D.C., Brookings General Series Reprint No. 324, 1977.

"The Contribution of Capital to Economic Growth", *American Economic Review,* May 1980.

DEPPLER, Michael and Martin WILLIAMSON

"Capital Flight: Concepts, Measurement, and Issues", in *Staff Studies for the World Economic Outlook,* Washington, D.C., IMF, 1987.

DE VRIES, B.A.

"Immediate Effects of Devaluation on Prices of Raw Materials", *IMF Staff Papers,* September 1950.

Remaking the World Bank, Washington, D.C., World Bank, 1987.

DIAZ-ALEJANDRO, Carlos P.

"Good-bye Financial Repression, Hello Financial Crash", Yale University Economic Growth Centre, Discussion Paper No. 441, May 1983.

DILLON, B.K. and L. DURAN-DOWNING

Officially Supported Export Credits, Washington, D.C., IMF, 1988.

DINSMOOR, James D. Jr.

Brazil, National Responses to the Debt Crisis, Washington, D.C., Inter-American Development Bank, 1987.

DOOLEY, Michael P.

"Market Valuation of External Debt", IMF/World Bank *Finance and Development,* March 1987.

"Buy-Backs and Market Valuation of External Debt", *IMF Staff Papers,* June 1988.

DOOLEY, Michael P., Jeffrey FRANKEL and Donald MATHIESON

"International Capital Mobility: What Do Saving-Investment Correlations Tell Us?", *IMF Staff Papers,* September 1987.

DUNNING, John H.

International Production and the Multinational Enterprise, London, Allen and Unwin, 1981.

ELLIS, Howard E.

Exchange Control in Central Europe, Cambridge, 1941.

ENDERS, Thomas O. and Richard P. MATTIONE

Latin America -- The Crisis of Debt and Growth, Washington, D.C., Brookings Institution, 1984.

FEDER, G.

"On Exports and Economic Growth", *Journal of Development Economics,* February/April 1983.

FELDSTEIN, M. and C. HORIOKA
"Domestic Savings and International Capital Flows", *Economic Journal*, June 1980.

FELDSTEIN, M. *et al.*
Restoring Growth in the Debt-Laden Third World, New York, Report No. 33 to the Trilateral Commission, 1987.

FEINBERG, Richard E. *et al.*
Between Two Worlds: The World Bank's Next Decade, Washington, D.C. Overseas Development Council, 1986.

FISHLOW, A.
"The Debt Crisis: A Longer Perspective", *Journal of Development Planning*, No. 16, 1985.

"Capital Requirements of Developing Countries in the Next Decade", *Journal of Development Planning*, No. 17, 1987.

FRY, Maxwell A.
"Interest Rates in Asia", a study prepared for the Asian Department of the IMF, unpublished, 1981.

GERMIDIS, D. and R. MEGHIR
The Role of Financial Intermediation in the Mobilisation of Household Savings in Developing Countries, Paris, OECD Development Centre, forthcoming.

GOLDSBROUGH, David and Iqbal ZAIDI
"Transmission of Economic Influences from Industrial to Developing Countries", in *Staff Studies for the World Economic Outlook*, Washington, D.C., IMF, 1986.

GOLDSMITH, R.W.
Financial Structure and Development, New Haven, Yale University Press, 1969.

The Financial Development of Japan, 1968-77, New Haven, Yale University Press, 1983.

GONZALEZ-VEGA, C.
"Credit Rationing Behavior of Agricultural Lenders: The Iron Law of Interest-Rate Restrictions", in D.W. Adams *et al.*, *Undermining Rural Development with Cheap Credit*, (Special studies in social, political and economic development series), Boulder, Colorado, Westview, 1984.

GOODE, Richard
Government Finance in Developing Countries, Washington, D.C., Brookings Institution, 1984.

Economic Assistance to Developing Countries through the IMF, Washington, D.C., Brookings Institution, 1985.

GROUP OF THIRTY
Foreign Direct Investment, 1973-1987, New York, 1984.

GUITIAN, Manuel
Fund Conditionality -- Evolution of Principles and Practices, Washington, D.C., IMF Pamphlet No. 38, 1981.

GUTOWSKI, Armin and Manfred HOLTHUS
"Limits to International Indebtedness", in Gutowski *et al.*, eds., *Indebtedness and Growth in Developing Countries*, Hamburg, Verlag Weltarchiv, 1986.

226

GUTOWSKI, Armin *et al.*, eds.
Indebtedness and Growth in Developing Countries, Hamburg, Verlag Weltarchiv, 1986.

HANSON, James A. and Craig R. NEAL
Interest Rate Policies in Selected Developing Countries, 1970-82, Washington, D.C., World Bank, 1986.

HARBERGER, A.C.
"Comentarios" in Banco Central de Chile, *Alternativas de Politicas Financieras en Economias Pequenas y Abiertas al Exterior,* Santiago de Chile, 1981.

"Lessons for Debtor Country Managers and Policymakers" in Gordon W. Smith and John T. Cuddington, eds., *International Debt and the Developing Countries,* A World Bank Symposium, Washington, D.C., 1985.

HELLEINER, G.A.
"Policy-Based Program Lending: A Look at the Bank's New Role", in Richard E. Feinberg *et al., Between Two Worlds: The World Bank's Next Decade,* Washington, D.C. Overseas Development Council, 1986.

HELLER, Peter S.
"Impact of Inflation on Fiscal Policy in Developing Countries", *IMF Staff Papers,* December 1980.

HIRSCHMAN, Albert O.
The Strategy of Economic Development, New Haven, Yale University Press, 1958.

HOLTHUS, M. and K. STANZEL
"The Credit Standing of Developing Countries", in A. Gutowski *et al.,* eds., *Indebtedness and Growth in Developing Countries, 1970-82,* Hamburg, Verlag Weltarchiv, 1986.

HOMMES, R.
"Case Study on Colombia", in Donald R. Lessard and John Williamson, *Capital Flight and Third World Debt, Washington, D.C.,* Institute for International Economics, 1987.

HORSEFIELD, J. Keith
The International Monetary Fund, 1945-1965, Washington, D.C., IMF, 1969.

IBRD see World Bank.

ILO
The Cost of Social Security, 1976-78, Geneva, 1981.

The Cost of Social Security, 1978-80, Geneva, 1985.

IMF
International Financial Statistics, Supplement on Trade Statistics, 1982, Washington, D.C.

International Capital Markets, Developments and Prospects, 1984, Occasional Paper No. 31, Washington, D.C.

Foreign Private Investment in Developing Countries, Occasional Paper No. 33, Washington, D.C., 1985.

Final Report of the Working Party on the Statistical Discrepancy in World Current Account Balances, Washington, D.C., 1987.

Annual Report, 1984, 1985, 1986, Washington, D.C.

IMF Survey, 1984, 1986, 1988, Washington, D.C.

Summary Proceedings Annual Meeting, 1961, 1985, 1986, 1987, Washington, D.C.

Staff Studies for the World Economic Outlook, 1986, 1987, Washington, D.C.

World Economic Outlook, 1983, 1984, 1986, 1987, Washington, D.C.

INTER-AMERICAN DEVELOPMENT BANK

Economic and Social Progress in Latin America, 1982, Washington, D.C.

IZE, Alain and Guillermo ORTIZ

"Fiscal Rigidities, Public Debt, and Capital Flight", *IMF Staff Papers,* June 1987.

KAFKA, A.

"Economic Effects of Capital Imports", in John Adler, ed., *Capital Movements and Economic Development,* New York, 1967.

KENEN, P.B.

Financing, Adjustment, and the IMF, Washington, D.C., Brookings Institution, 1986.

KESSLER, Denis and Dominique STRAUSS-KAHN

"Existe-t-il un lien entre l'épargne intérieure et l'afflux de capitaux extérieurs?", *Revue Tiers Monde,* April/June 1984.

KEYNES, J.M.

A Tract on Monetary Reform, London, Macmillan, 1923.

The General Theory of Employment, Interest and Money, London, Macmillan, 1936.

KHAN, Mohsin S. and Nadeem UL HAQUE

"Foreign Borrowing and Capital Flight", *IMF Staff Papers,* December 1985.

KHAN, Mohsin S. and Malcolm D. KNIGHT

Fund Supported Adjustment Programs and Economic Growth, Washington, D.C., IMF Occasional Paper No. 41, 1985.

KHATKHATE, D.R.

"Assessing the Impact of Interest Rates in Less Developed Countries", IMF, Washington, D.C., mimeo., 1985.

KILLICK, T.

The IMF and Stabilisation, Aldershot, Gower, 1984.

KIM, Mahn Je

"Korea's Adjustment Policies and Their Implications for Other Countries", in V. Corbo, M. Goldstein and M. Khan, *Growth-Oriented Adjustment Programs,* Washington, D.C., IMF and World Bank, 1987.

KINDLEBERGER, C.P.

"Capital Flight — A Historical Perspective", in Donald R. Lessard and John Williamson, *Capital Flight and Third World Debt,* Washington, D.C., Institute for International Economics, 1987.

KOPITS, George

Structural Reform, Stabilization, and Growth in Turkey, Washington, D.C., IMF Occasional Paper No. 52, 1987.

KOPITS, George and Padma GOTUR
"The Influence of Social Security on Household Savings: A Cross-Country Investigation", *IMF Staff Papers,* March 1980.

KOSKELA, Erkki and Matti VIREN
"Social Security and Household Saving in an International Cross Section", *American Economic Review,* March 1983.

KRUEGER, Anne O.
"Aid in the Development Process", *The World Bank Research Observer,* January 1986.

KRUGMAN, Paul
"International Debt Strategies in an Uncertain World", in Gordon W. Smith and John T. Cuddington, eds., *International Debt and the Developing Countries,* A World Bank Symposium, Washington, D.C., 1985.

"Prospects for International Debt Reform", in UNCTAD, *International Monetary and Financial Issues for the Developing Countries,* New York, 1987.

LANDAU, Luis
Differences in Savings Ratios Among Latin American Countries, Cambridge, 1969.

LANYI, Anthony and Rusdu SARACOGLU
Interest Rate Policies in Developing Countries, Washington, D.C., IMF Occasional Paper No. 22.

LEAGUE OF NATIONS
Report on Exchange Control, Geneva, 1938.

Report of the Delegation of Economic Depressions, Part I, The Transition from War to Peace Economy, Geneva, 1943.

LESSARD, Donald R. and John WILLIAMSON
Financial Intermediation Beyond the Debt Crisis, Washington, D.C., Institute for International Economics, 1985.

Capital Flight and Third World Debt, Washington, D.C., Institute for International Economics, 1987.

LEVY, Fred C.
Chile: An Economy in Transition, Washington, D.C., World Bank, 1979.

LEWIS, W.A.
"Economic Development with Unlimited Supplies of Labour", *The Manchester School,* Vol. 22, May 1954.

LITTLE, Ian M.D.
Economic Development, New York, Basic Books, 1982.

LITTLE, I.M.D. and J-M. CLIFFORD
"International Aid", in *The Need for Capital,* London, George Allen and Unwin, 1965.

LITTLE, Ian M.D., Tibor SCITOVSKY and Maurice SCOTT
Industry and Trade in Some Developing Countries, London, Oxford University Press for OECD Development Centre, Paris, 1970.

LONG, Millard
    Review of Financial Sector Work, Washington, D.C., World Bank, 1983,

MACHLUP, Fritz
    International Payments, Debts and Gold -- Collected Essays, New York, New York University Press, 1976.

MANCERA, Miguel
    Economic Adjustment and Structural Change in Mexico, Washington, D.C., Institute for International Economics, 1987.

MASON, E.S. and Robert ASHER
    The World Bank Since Bretton Woods, Washington, D.C., Brookings Institution, 1973.

MAXCY, George
    The Multinational Automobile Industry, London, St. Martin, 1981.

McKINNON, R.I.
    Money and Capital in Economic Development, Washington, D.C., Brookings Institution, 1973.

    "Savings Propensities and the Korean Monetary Reform in Retrospect", in McKinnon, ed., *Money and Finance in Economic Growth and Development,* Stanford, 1974.

    "Financial Liberalization in Retrospect: Interest Rate Policies in LDC's", Stanford, 1986.

MICHALOPOULOS, C.
    "World Bank Programs for Adjustment and Growth", in V. Corbo, M. Goldstein and M. Khan, *Growth-Oriented Adjustment Programs,* Washington, D.C., IMF and World Bank, 1987.

MODIGLIANI, Franco
    "The Life Cycle Hypothesis on Saving and Intercountry Differences in the Savings Ratio", in W.A. Eltis, *Induction, Growth and Trade: Essays in Honour of Sir Roy Harrod,* Oxford, 1970.

MORAZETZ, David
    Twenty-Five Years of Economic Development, 1950 to 1975, Baltimore and London, World Bank, 1977.

MORGAN GUARANTY
    International Capital Markets, New York, June/July 1987.

MOSLEY, Paul
    "Aid, Savings and Growth Revisited", *Oxford Bulletin of Economics and Statistics,* May, 1980.

MUNNELL, A.H.
    "The Impact of Social Security on Personal Savings", *National Tax Journal,* December 1974.

MYERS, Robert J., ed.
    The Political Morality of the International Monetary Fund, New York, Carnegie Ethics and International Affairs, 1987.

NELSON, Joan M.

"The Diplomacy of Policy-Based Lending", in Richard E. Feinberg *et al.*, *Between Two Worlds: The World Bank's Next Decade,* Washington, D.C., Overseas Development Council, 1986.

OECD

The Growth of Output 1960-1980, Retrospect, Prospect and Problems of Policy, Paris, 1970.

Twenty-Five Years of Development Cooperation, A Review, Paris, 1985.

OMAN, Charles

New Forms of International Investment in Developing Countries, Paris, OECD Development Centre, 1984.

ORTIZ, Guillermo

"Economic Expansion, Crisis, and Adjustment in Mexico (1977-83)", in Michael B. Connolly and John McDermott, *The Economics of the Caribbean Basin,* New York, Praeger, 1985.

PANI, P.K.

"Cultivators' Demand for Credit: A Cross-Section Analysis", *International Economic Review,* May 1966.

PAPANEK, Gustav F.

"The Effect of Aid and Other Resource Transfers on Savings and Growth in Less Developed Countries", *Economic Journal,* September 1972.

"Aid, Growth and Equity in Southern Asia", in J.R. Parkinson, ed., *Poverty and Aid,* Oxford, St. Martin, 1983.

PLEASE, Stanley

The Hobbled Giant: Essays on the World Bank, Boulder, Colorado, Westview, 1984.

POLAK, J.J.

"Balance of Payments Problems of Countries Reconstructing with the Help of Foreign Loans", *Quarterly Journal of Economics,* February 1943.

"Monetary Analysis of Income Formation and Payments Problems", *IMF Staff Papers,* November 1957.

"The Impasse Concerning the Role of the SDR" in W. Eizinga *et al.*, eds., *The Quest for National and Global Stability -- Essays in Honour of H.J. Witteveen,* Dordrecht, 1988.

PREBISCH, Raul

The Economic Development of Latin America and its Principal Problems, New York, Lake Success, 1950.

PRITCHETT, Lant

Import Demand Elasticities: Estimates and Determinants, Washington, D.C., World Bank Division Working Paper No. 1987-4.

RAKSHIT, M.

"Income, Saving and Capital Formation in India", *Economic and Political Weekly,* 1982.

REISEN, Helmut

"Export Orientation, Public Debt and Fiscal Rigidities: The Different Performance in Brazil, Korea and Mexico", *Journal of International Economic Integration,* (Seoul), 1988.

REISEN, Helmut and Axel VAN TROTSENBURG
   Developing Country Debt: The Budgetary and Transfer Problem, Paris, OECD Development Centre, 1988.

Revue des Deux Mondes
   1st April 1937.

ROBICHEK, E. Walter
   "Some Reflections About Public Debt Management", in Banco Central de Chile, *Alternativas de Politicas Financieras en Economias Pequenas y Abiertas al Exterior,* Santiago de Chile, 1981.

ROBINSON, Sherman
   "Sources of Growth in Less Developed Countries", *Quarterly Journal of Economics,* August 1971.

RODRIGUEZ, Miguel A.
   "Consequences of Capital Flight for Latin American Debtor Countries", in Donald R. Lessard and John Williamson, *Capital Flight and Third World Debt,* Washington, D.C., Institute for International Economics, 1987.

ROSSI, Nicola
   "Government Spending, the Real Interest Rate, and the Behavior of Liquidity — Constrained Consumers in Developing Countries," *IMF Staff Papers,* March 1988, pp. 104-140.

SACHS, Jeffrey D.
   "External Debt and Macroeconomic Performance in Latin America and East Asia", in *Brookings Papers on Economic Activity,* Vol. 2, 1985.

SCHATTNER, Susanne
   "Mineral Economics — Indebtedness without Growth", in Armin Gutowski *et al.,* eds., *Indebtedness and Growth in Developing Countries, 1970-82,* Hamburg, Verlag Weltarchiv, 1986.

SELOWSKY, Marcello and Herman G. van der TAK
   "The Debt Problem and Growth", *World Development,* Vol. 14, No. 9, September 1986.

SIMONSEN, Mario Henrique
   "The Developing Country Debt Problem", in Gordon W. Smith and John T. Cuddington, eds., *International Debt and the Developing Countries,* A World Bank Symposium, Washington, D.C., 1985.

SJAASTAD, Larry A.
   "The International Debt Quagmire; To Whom Do We Owe It?", *The World Economy,* September 1983.

SMITH, Gordon W. and John T. CUDDINGTON, eds.
   International Debt and the Developing Countries, A World Bank Symposium, Washington, D.C., 1985.

STERN, Ernest
   "World Bank Financing of Structural Adjustment", in John Williamson, ed., *IMF Conditionality,* Washington, D.C., Institute for International Economics, 1983.

SUMMERS, Lawrence H.

"The Nonadjustment of Nominal Interest Rates: A Study of the Fisher Effect", in James Tobin, ed., *Macro-economics, Prices, and Quantities: Essays in memory of Arthur O. Okun,* Brookings Institution, Washington, D.C., 1982.

SWOBODA, Alexander K.

"Debt and the Efficiency and Stability of the International Financial System", in Gordon W. Smith and John T. Cuddington, eds., *International Debt and the Developing Countries,* A World Bank Symposium, Washington, D.C., 1985.

TANZI, Vito

"Inflation, Real Tax Revenue, and the Case for Inflationary Finance: Theory with an Application to Argentina", *IMF Staff Papers,* September 1978.

TANZI, Vito and Mario I. BLEJER

"Public Debt and Fiscal Policy in Developing Countries", in Arrow and Boskin, eds., *The Economics of Public Debt,* forthcoming.

TANZI, Vito, Mario I. BLEJER and Mario O. TEIJEIRO

"Inflation and the Measurement of Fiscal Deficits", *IMF Staff Papers,* December 1987.

UNITED NATIONS

Financing Africa's Recovery, report and recommendations of the Advisory Group on Financial Flows for Africa, New York, 1988.

VAITSOS, Constantine V.

Inter-Country Income Distribution and Transnational Enterprises, Oxford, Oxford University Press, 1974.

VAN WIJNBERGEN, S.

"Interest Rate Management in LDCs", *Journal of Monetary Economics,* 1983.

WAI, U Tun

"Interest Rates Outside the Organized Money Markets of Underdeveloped Countries", *IMF Staff Papers,* November 1957.

WALLICH, Christine

Savings Mobilization Through Social Security, The Experience of Chile During 1916-77, Washington, D.C., World Bank Staff Working Paper No. 553, 1983.

WELLONS, Philip, Dimitri GERMIDIS and Bianca GLAVANIS

Banks and Specialised Financial Intermediaries in Development, Paris, OECD Development Centre, 1986.

WIDER (World Institute for Development Economics Research)

Mobilising International Surpluses for World Development, A WIDER Plan for a Japanese Initiative, Helsinki, 1987.

WIESNER, Eduardo D.

Memoria del Departemento Nacional de Planeacion, 1978-80, Bogota, n.d.

WILLIAMSON, John, ed.

IMF Conditionality, Washington, D.C., Institute for International Economics, 1983.

WILLIAMSON, John
  "Comment" on Jeffrey D. Sachs, "External Debt and Macroeconomic Performance in Latin America and East Asia", in *Brookings Papers on Economic Activity*, Vol. 2, 1985.
WOOD, D. Joseph
  "Issues, Institutions and Reforms", in Smith and Cuddington, 1985.
WORLD BANK
  Accelerated Development in Africa: An Agenda for Action, Washington, D.C., 1981.
  Eighth Annual Review of Project Performance Audit Reports, Washington, D.C., 1982.
  A Strategy for Restoration of Growth in Middle-Income Countries that Face Debt-Servicing Difficulties (Development Committee pamphlet No. 10), Washington, D.C., 1986.
  Market-Based Menu Approach, mimeo., Washington, D.C., 1988.
  Annual Report 1948, 1981, 1985, 1987, Washington, D.C.
  World Development Report, 1982, 1985, 1986, 1987, 1988, Washington, D.C.
  World Debt Tables, 1986-87, 1987-88, Washington, D.C.
YOTOPOULOS, P. and S. FLOR
  The Role of Financial Intermediation in the Mobilisation and Allocation of Household Savings in the Philippines: Interlinks Between Organised and Informal Circuits, Paris, OECD Development Centre Working Paper, 1988.

WHERE TO OBTAIN OECD PUBLICATIONS
OÙ OBTENIR LES PUBLICATIONS DE L'OCDE

ARGENTINA - ARGENTINE
Carlos Hirsch S.R.L.,
Florida 165, 4º Piso,
(Galeria Guemes) 1333 Buenos Aires
Tel. 33.1787.2391 y 30.7122

AUSTRALIA - AUSTRALIE
D.A. Book (Aust.) Pty. Ltd.
11-13 Station Street (P.O. Box 163)
Mitcham, Vic. 3132   Tel. (03) 873 4411

AUSTRIA - AUTRICHE
OECD Publications and Information Centre,
4 Simrockstrasse,
5300 Bonn (Germany)   Tel. (0228) 21.60.45
Gerold & Co., Graben 31, Wien 1 Tel. 52.22.35

BELGIUM - BELGIQUE
Jean de Lannoy,
Avenue du Roi 202
B-1060 Bruxelles   Tel. (02) 538.51.69

CANADA
Renouf Publishing Company Ltd/
Éditions Renouf Ltée,
1294 Algoma Road, Ottawa, Ont. K1B 3W8
Tel: (613) 741-4333
Toll Free/Sans Frais:
Ontario, Quebec, Maritimes:
1-800-267-1805
Western Canada, Newfoundland:
1-800-267-1826
Stores/Magasins:
61 rue Sparks St., Ottawa, Ont. K1P 5A6
Tel: (613) 238-8985
211 rue Yonge St., Toronto, Ont. M5B 1M4
Tel: (416) 363-3171
Federal Publications Inc.,
301-303 King St. W.,
Toronto, Ont. M5V 1J5   Tel. (416)581-1552
Les Éditions la Liberté inc.,
3020 Chemin Sainte-Foy,
Sainte-Foy, P.Q. GIX 3V6, Tel. (418)658-3763

DENMARK - DANEMARK
Munksgaard Export and Subscription Service
35, Nørre Søgade, DK-1370 København K
Tel. +45.1.12.85.70

FINLAND - FINLANDE
Akateeminen Kirjakauppa,
Keskuskatu 1, 00100 Helsinki 10 Tel. 0.12141

FRANCE
OCDE/OECD
Mail Orders/Commandes par correspondance :
2, rue André-Pascal,
75775 Paris Cedex 16   Tel. (1) 45.24.82.00
Bookshop/Librairie : 33, rue Octave-Feuillet
75016 Paris
Tel. (1) 45.24.81.67 et/ou (1) 45.24.81.81
Librairie de l'Université,
12a, rue Nazareth,
13602 Aix-en-Provence   Tel. 42.26.18.08

GERMANY - ALLEMAGNE
OECD Publications and Information Centre,
4 Simrockstrasse,
5300 Bonn   Tel. (0228) 21.60.45

GREECE - GRÈCE
Librairie Kauffmann,
28, rue du Stade, 105 64 Athens Tel. 322.21.60

HONG KONG
Government Information Services,
Publications (Sales) Office,
Information Services Department
No. 1, Battery Path, Central

ICELAND - ISLANDE
Snæbjörn Jónsson & Co., h.f.,
Hafnarstræti 4 & 9,
P.O.B. 1131 – Reykjavik
Tel. 13133/14281/11936

INDIA - INDE
Oxford Book and Stationery Co.,
Scindia House, New Delhi 110001
Tel. 331.5896/5308
17 Park St., Calcutta 700016   Tel. 240832

INDONESIA - INDONÉSIE
Pdii-Lipi, P.O. Box 3065/JKT.Jakarta
Tel. 583467

IRELAND - IRLANDE
TDC Publishers - Library Suppliers,
12 North Frederick Street, Dublin 1
Tel. 744835-749677

ITALY - ITALIE
Libreria Commissionaria Sansoni,
Via Benedetto Fortini 120/10,
50125 Firenze   Tel. 055/645415
Via Bartolini 29, 20155 Milano   Tel. 365083
La diffusione delle pubblicazioni OCSE viene
assicurata dalle principali librerie ed anche da :
Editrice e Libreria Herder,
Piazza Montecitorio 120, 00186 Roma
Tel. 6794628
Libreria Hœpli,
Via Hœpli 5, 20121 Milano   Tel. 865446
Libreria Scientifica
Dott. Lucio de Biasio "Aeiou"
Via Meravigli 16, 20123 Milano   Tel. 807679

JAPAN - JAPON
OECD Publications and Information Centre,
Landic Akasaka Bldg., 2-3-4 Akasaka,
Minato-ku, Tokyo 107   Tel. 586.2016

KOREA - CORÉE
Kyobo Book Centre Co. Ltd.
P.O.Box: Kwang Hwa Moon 1658,
Seoul   Tel. (REP) 730.78.91

LEBANON - LIBAN
Documenta Scientifica/Redico,
Edison Building, Bliss St.,
P.O.B. 5641, Beirut   Tel. 354429-344425

MALAYSIA/SINGAPORE -
MALAISIE/SINGAPOUR
University of Malaya Co-operative Bookshop
Ltd.,
7 Lrg 51A/227A, Petaling Jaya
Malaysia   Tel. 7565000/7565425
Information Publications Pte Ltd
Pei-Fu Industrial Building,
24 New Industrial Road No. 02-06
Singapore 1953   Tel. 2831786, 2831798

NETHERLANDS - PAYS-BAS
SDU Uitgeverij
Christoffel Plantijnstraat 2
Postbus 20014
2500 EA's-Gravenhage   Tel. 070-789911
Voor bestellingen: Tel. 070-789880

NEW ZEALAND - NOUVELLE-ZÉLANDE
Government Printing Office Bookshops:
Auckland: Retail Bookshop, 25 Rutland Stseet,
Mail Orders, 85 Beach Road
Private Bag C.P.O.
Hamilton: Retail: Ward Street,
Mail Orders, P.O. Box 857
Wellington: Retail, Mulgrave Street, (Head
Office)
Cubacade World Trade Centre,
Mail Orders, Private Bag
Christchurch: Retail, 159 Hereford Street,
Mail Orders, Private Bag
Dunedin: Retail, Princes Street,
Mail Orders, P.O. Box 1104

NORWAY - NORVÈGE
Narvesen Info Center – NIC,
Bertrand Narvesens vei 2,
P.O.B. 6125 Etterstad, 0602 Oslo 6
Tel. (02) 67.83.10, (02) 68.40.20

PAKISTAN
Mirza Book Agency
65 Shahrah Quaid-E-Azam, Lahore 3 Tel. 66839

PHILIPPINES
I.J. Sagun Enterprises, Inc.
P.O. Box 4322 CPO Manila
Tel. 695-1946, 922-9495

PORTUGAL
Livraria Portugal, Rua do Carmo 70-74,
1117 Lisboa Codex   Tel. 360582/3

SINGAPORE/MALAYSIA -
SINGAPOUR/MALAISIE
See "Malaysia/Singapor". Voir
« Malaisie/Singapour »

SPAIN - ESPAGNE
Mundi-Prensa Libros, S.A.,
Castelló 37, Apartado 1223, Madrid-28001
Tel. 431.33.99
Libreria Bosch, Ronda Universidad 11,
Barcelona 7   Tel. 317.53.08/317.53.58

SWEDEN - SUÈDE
AB CE Fritzes Kungl. Hovbokhandel,
Box 16356, S 103 27 STH,
Regeringsgatan 12,
DS Stockholm   Tel. (08) 23.89.00
Subscription Agency/Abonnements:
Wennergren-Williams AB,
Box 30004, S104 25 Stockholm Tel. (08)54.12.00

SWITZERLAND - SUISSE
OECD Publications and Information Centre,
4 Simrockstrasse,
5300 Bonn (Germany)   Tel. (0228) 21.60.45
Librairie Payot,
6 rue Grenus, 1211 Genève 11
Tel. (022) 31.89.50
Maditec S.A.
Ch. des Palettes 4
1020 – Renens/Lausanne   Tel. (021) 35.08.65
United Nations Bookshop/Librairie des Nations-
Unies
Palais des Nations, 1211 – Geneva 10
Tel. 022-34-60-11 (ext. 48 72)

TAIWAN - FORMOSE
Good Faith Worldwide Int'l Co., Ltd.
9th floor, No. 118, Sec.2, Chung Hsiao E. Road
Taipei   Tel. 391.7396/391.7397

THAILAND - THAILANDE
Suksit Siam Co., Ltd., 1715 Rama IV Rd.,
Samyam Bangkok 5   Tel. 2511630
INDEX Book Promotion & Service Ltd.
59/6 Soi Lang Suan, Ploenchit Road
Patjumawwan, Bangkok 10500
Tel. 250-1919, 252-1066

TURKEY - TURQUIE
Kültur Yayinlari Is-Türk Ltd. Sti.
Atatürk Bulvari No: 191/Kat. 21
Kavaklidere/Ankara   Tel. 25.07.60
Dolmabahce Cad. No: 29
Besiktas/Istanbul   Tel. 160.71.88

UNITED KINGDOM - ROYAUME-UNI
H.M. Stationery Office,
Postal orders only: (01)211-5656
P.O.B. 276, London SW8 5DT
Telephone orders: (01) 622.3316, or
Personal callers:
49 High Holborn, London WC1V 6HB
Branches at: Belfast, Birmingham,
Bristol, Edinburgh, Manchester

UNITED STATES - ÉTATS-UNIS
OECD Publications and Information Centre,
2001 L Street, N.W., Suite 700,
Washington, D.C. 20036 - 4095
Tel. (202) 785.6323

VENEZUELA
Libreria del Este,
Avda F. Miranda 52, Aptdo. 60337,
Edificio Galipan, Caracas 106
Tel. 951.17.05/951.23.07/951.12.97

YUGOSLAVIA - YOUGOSLAVIE
Jugoslovenska Knjiga, Knez Mihajlova 2,
P.O.B. 36, Beograd   Tel. 621.992

Orders and inquiries from countries where
Distributors have not yet been appointed should be
sent to:
OECD, Publications Service, 2, rue André-Pascal,
75775 PARIS CEDEX 16.

Les commandes provenant de pays où l'OCDE n'a
pas encore désigné de distributeur doivent être
adressées à :
OCDE, Service des Publications. 2, rue André-
Pascal, 75775 PARIS CEDEX 16.

72233-12-1988

OECD PUBLICATIONS, 2, rue André-Pascal, 75775 PARIS CEDEX 16 - No. 44641 1988
PRINTED IN FRANCE
(41 89 01 1) ISBN 92-64-13187-6